Creativity in the Age of AI
Toolkits for the Modern Mind

Jerry Wind

with

Mukul Pandya and Deborah Yao

CREATIVITY
in the
AGE OF AI
Toolkits for the Modern Mind

Jerry Wind

with

Mukul Pandya and Deborah Yao

DE GRUYTER

ISBN 978-3-11-169810-6
e-ISBN (PDF) 978-3-11-169881-6
e-ISBN (EPUB) 978-3-11-169944-8

Library of Congress Control Number: 2025945712

Bibliographic information published by the Deutsche Nationalbibliothek
The Deutsche Nationalbibliothek lists this publication in the Deutsche Nationalbibliografie; detailed bibliographic data are available on the internet at http://dnb.dnb.de.

© 2025 Walter de Gruyter GmbH, Berlin/Boston, Genthiner Straße 13, 10785 Berlin
Cover image: Muhammad Akram ~99~ through 99designs; and Barbara Gizzi, Berlin
Typesetting: York Publishing Solutions Pvt. Ltd.

Questions about General Product Safety Regulation:
productsafety@degruyterbrill.com

Advance Praise for *Creativity in the Age of AI*

"Jerry Wind's new book *Creativity in the Age of AI* turns our conventional ideas about creativity inside-out. His is a Socratic approach, insisting that we pivot from asking 'the how of things' to questioning 'the why of things.' Questioning is at the heart of creativity and its absence forecloses the imagination. Wind's book helps us unmask the roadblocks to creativity and calls on all of us to think on a bigger playing field where awe, wonder, imagination, empathy, and transcendence become the sine qua non of the creative act in the age of AI. Wind takes us into a new mindset where vulnerability is less about bouncing back and more about being vulnerable to exploring the unknown unknowns, where vulnerability becomes the agency to trigger the creativity in all of us. The book is a precious gift and will help each of us learn how to flourish on an animated planet."

— **Jeremy Rifkin,** author of *Planet Aqua: Rethinking our Home in the Universe, The 3rd Industrial Revolution* and over 20 other bestselling books

"In an era where AI's role in human endeavors is rapidly expanding, *Creativity in the Age of AI* is a timely and essential guide. This book brilliantly bridges the gap between the art of human creativity and the science of artificial intelligence, demonstrating how these two forces, rather than being at odds, can synergize to unlock unprecedented potential. The authors provide a clear, actionable framework for anyone looking to not only understand, but to actively harness AI as a powerful co-pilot in their creative journey. This isn't just another book about AI; it's a practical blueprint for the future of innovation."

— **Shelly Palmer,** CEO, The Palmer Group

"AI represents a unique development for all of us. This book encourages us all to embrace AI in a creative and thoughtful way. It lays out how to go about this, thus making the book both practical and inspiring."

— **Colin Crook,** former CTO for Citicorp

"*Creativity in the Age of AI* shows how technology can be a tool for artists and creative thinkers to break out of rigid mindsets to make space for the essential work of creation. Wind and his colleagues offer an approach that is both practical and inspiring, showing how AI can amplify imagination rather than replace it."

— **Dr. David Serkin Ludwig**, Dean of Music and Chair of Composition, The Juilliard School

"I've known Jerry for years, and his ability to spot timely themes and simplify them with clarity stands out every time. *Creativity in the Age of AI* is no exception. It presents AI as a creative superpower, offering practical ways to harness this moment where human potential meets technological advancement. A timely and essential guide to the future of intelligent creativity."

— **Deepa Nagraj**, Senior Vice President & Head-ESG, Sparkle Innovation Ecosystem and Communications

"*Creativity in the Age of AI* is a vital and timely guide for navigating the rapidly evolving landscape of AI and innovation. By seamlessly blending scientific insight with practical, actionable frameworks, it demonstrates how AI can amplify—rather than replace—

human creativity. This book empowers professionals across industries to unlock data-driven innovation, scale their creative impact, and shape a future where technology enhances our capacity to create value and meaning. A must-read for forward-thinking leaders in the digital era."

> — **Margherita Pagani**, Professor of Human Centric AI and Digital Marketing and Director, SKEMA Center for Artificial Intelligence

"Leading Continental Grain Company through decades of market transformation has taught me that sustainable success demands creative thinking. *Creativity in the Age of AI* brilliantly captures what forward-thinking organizations need today. The book's premise that 'AI' does not replace human creativity but amplifies it, resonates deeply with our approach. We understand that the future belongs to companies that harness AI as a creative partner, not a replacement for human ingenuity."

> — **Paul J. Fribourg**, *Chairman and Chief Executive Officer,* Continental Grain Company

"This book is an essential read. Creativity is at the center of economic value creation. And AI can amplify this process. But this is not automatic. The book discusses twelve ways where creativity and AI go together. This emphasis on 'how to make a higher level creativity happen' is a major plus. And, on top of this, there are numerous helpful examples that further guide the readers. Congratulations to Jerry Wind and his two collaborators for putting together this superb book!"

> — **Peter Lorange**, Honorary President, IMD

"Jerry Wind's coauthored book, *Creativity in the Age of AI*, made me think that business schools must be totally redesigned in the age of AI. I would recommend to the designers of a new MBA program that all the incoming students read this book. It will prepare them for the main themes and skills they will need to flourish in the New Global Economy. If *Creativity in the Age of AI* doesn't excite them, they are better off seeking a different domain of knowledge. College admission offices will increasingly choose students in the same way that companies choose employees: Are they creative? And are they skilled in AI?"

> — **Philip Kotler**, Distinguished Professor of International Marketing, Kellogg School of Management, Northwestern University (emeritus)

"AI promises unlimited creativity. But Wind, Pandya, and Yao deliver the crucial insight that true innovation depends on more than technology's power. It requires the courage to confront deep-rooted human and organizational obstacles.

This isn't just another AI guide. It spotlights the irreplaceable human qualities of persistence, ethical judgment, and strategic vision, and makes the point that these traits are essential for directing AI as a powerful tool for innovation and meaningful change. Without them, we risk creative outsourcing or bland uniformity.

The future belongs to those who harness AI to magnify human talent, ingenuity and hard work. This book masterfully shows how to build your toolkit to do just that."

> — **Sabrina Fung**, Group Managing Director of Fung Retailing Group

"We have benefitted greatly from Jerry's marketing expertise on the board of the Philadelphia Museum of Art for many years. As a longtime trustee, Jerry has helped us rethink our approach to marketing and attract new audiences. This book will play an important role in helping us navigate the new AI enhanced world. I continue to be enormously grateful to Jerry for his ongoing support."

— **Sasha Suda, George D.** Widener Director and CEO and Office of the Director and CEO of The Philadelphia Museum of Art

"*Creativity in the Age of AI* offers a timely and refreshingly human-centered approach to artificial intelligence. Rather than dwelling on the potential of AI to replace human creativity, this book brilliantly demonstrates how AI can enhance and accelerate our own creative capabilities. With its hands-on approach, Wind and colleagues provide both inspiration and practical tools for harnessing AI as a partner in creative discovery. This is essential reading for anyone who believes—as I do—that technology should serve human flourishing rather than human obsolescence."

— **Stefano Puntoni,** Co-director, Wharton Human-AI Research, Sebastian S. Kresge Professor of Marketing, The Wharton School, University of Pennsylvania

"If your work depends on fresh thinking—but you don't have time to wait for inspiration—*Creativity in the Age of AI* offers a practical way forward. It delivers twelve strategies to help you generate, shape, and apply ideas with clarity and intent in our AI-transformed world. Rather than fearing AI's advance or expecting it to do your thinking, this practical guide gives you the know-how to create a powerful alliance between human creativity and artificial intelligence—whether you're leading a team, building a brand, or revitalizing your own creative practice. This isn't just a book of ideas; it's a catalyst for creative momentum when you need it most."

— **Stephen D. Rappaport,** Consulting LLC

"People come to art museums to encounter creativity and push against the boundaries of conventional thinking. I recommend *Creativity in the Age of AI* to museum staff, thought leaders, educators, and artists alike to amplify creativity and reimagine cultural storytelling. The book demystifies AI, encourages experimentation, and envisions a future in which humanistic ideas and the tools of AI work hand in hand to create positive impact. In our fast-changing digital age, in which engaging stories and innovative experiences are key, this book is an inspiring guide to using AI as a partner.

— **William R. Valerio, PhD,** The Patricia Van Burgh Allison Director & CEO, Woodmere

"*Creativity in the Age of AI* is more than a book about technology, it is a call to action for how we lead in this new era. As someone who believes in conscious leadership and in designing workplaces that reflect the needs of the collective, I see this book as a roadmap for ensuring that AI amplifies human potential rather than diminishes it. It shows us how to harness AI as a collaborator while keeping imagination, authenticity, and humanity at the center. A timely and essential read for leaders who want to innovate with purpose and create a future where creativity and technology move forward together."

— **Shelley Zalis,** Founder and CEO of The Female Quotient

Content Navigator

Dedication

This book is dedicated to the courageous people who challenge the status quo and launch creative initiatives that change the way we live, work and play.

With deep gratitude and love to Jerry's inspiring wife, Barbara Eberlein, and to the love and support of our family.

To Mukul's two angels—Hema and Tara.

And to Deborah's family and friends who have been wonderful cheerleaders of this effort.

Acknowledgments

This book would not have been possible without the insights, collaboration, and creative energy of many remarkable individuals and communities.

First, I extend my deepest gratitude to the many Wharton MBA students who championed my Creativity Course, to the Wharton Fellows who participated in our "Next Big Thing" programs, and to the consulting clients and colleagues I've worked with for many years. It was their curiosity, imagination, and willingness to challenge the status quo, that continuously shaped my thinking. Creativity is not a solo act but a collaborative process nurtured by diverse perspectives and driven by courageous exploration.

Second, I am especially thankful to the generous and thoughtful reviewers who offered their time, wisdom, and constructive feedback throughout this journey: Lee Wind, John Wind, Barbara Eberlein, Caroline Dilsheimer, David Bell, Stefano Puntoni, and Stephen Rapaport. Their comments helped sharpen the ideas, clarify the message and elevate the overall impact of this book.

Finally, I offer heartfelt thanks to the talented team who brought this book to life. To my co-authors, Mukul Pandya and Deb Yao: thank you for your insight, commitment and deep belief in the value of this work. To our editor, Jaya Dalal: your guidance and clarity were invaluable. I am also deeply grateful to Mary Cummings for her diligence and editorial contributions. To my executive assistant Rachel Oliver for her dedication and continuous help. To designer Lara Taber, who collaborated with me—and with a variety of generative AI platforms—to craft the visuals that accompany each chapter: thank you for your creativity and care. A special thanks as well to 99designs, whose vibrant community submitted more than 100 cover concepts, and to the entire production team at De Gruyter, whose professionalism and support helped bring this book into the world.

To all readers—innovators, educators, artists, entrepreneurs, students, and all who seek to challenge the status quo and enhance their creativity—this book is for you. May it encourage you to actively experiment with the many approaches outlined in these pages, to enrich and expand your own creative process in addressing your personal and professional challenges.

In our turbulent world, it is our uniquely human creativity—supported by proven approaches to enhance it and now turbocharged by AI—that will determine what kind of future we create together and for the benefit of all.

Contents

Foreword

Creativity and AI—both separately and together—have already changed the paradigm of our lives. At key inflection points across history, both innovation and technology conspire together to jolt ahead business and lifestyle—to literally change the way we all work, live, and play. We live at such an inflection point.

Today, all business leaders and all leaders should take control of these paradigm-shifting forces of change—and this masterful book shows you how to do so. Jerry Wind, Mukul Pandya, and Deborah Yao have given us a battlefield manual to put AI to work and drive forward the kind of creativity and change we can, at this writing, only imagine.

Over 70 years ago, management consulting legend Peter F. Drucker wrote, "Business has only two functions: marketing and innovation. These produce revenues. All other functions are costs." And the simple brilliance of Drucker's adage remains as true today as in 1954—and the book you now hold or have on-screen presents a breakthrough framework and checklist to attack and bolster these two core challenges facing all businesses today: *marketing* and *innovation*.

Longtime Wharton professor and multi-book author Jerry Wind is recognized today as one of history's preeminent marketing experts—one reason the Lauder Professor Emeritus and Professor of Marketing at the Wharton School was, in 2017, inducted into the Marketing Hall of Fame. He knows marketing.

But now, Professor Wind—along with Mukul Pandya and Deborah Yao—puts his mark on business' second grand imperative: *innovation*. Today, there are powerful books on Creativity, such as *Steal Like an Artist*, *The Creative Habit*, and *The War of Art*, ... and on AI, such as *The Coming Wave*, *Genesis*, and *Artificial Intelligence: A Modern Approach*. But you are about to read the first book to connect the dots and build the bridge between *both* creativity and AI—and to show you how best to quickly and effectively walk across this bridge to pursue benefits that will surely change our businesses and our lives.

Below, Professor Wind and the authors cite McKinsey research showing that companies in the top quartile for innovation achieve 2.4× higher revenue growth—but that 70% of today's executives report that their teams struggle with creative problem-solving. And so, the second part of Drucker's adage—*innovation*—will not only be at the center of all business and leadership challenges over the coming decades—it will continue to be exponentialized.

In the face of these kinds of exponentialized creative problem-solving challenges, this book exploits the age-old adage that success leaves clues. It argues well that AI will not replace human creativity—but rather will amplify it exponentially. And it is replete with examples, lessons, borrowed principles, and case studies from breakthrough companies such as Netflix, Amazon, Airbnb, Google, Tesla, and others.

The book focuses on 12 sets of approaches to enhance creativity—each turbo-charged by AI. It empowers readers of all ages, professions, and countries to experiment with various approaches and to apply them to both their professional and personal challenges—creating their own personalized and dynamic portfolio of AI-fueled approaches to fully enhance creativity.

Finally, like its authors, this book is not just a sturdy academic treatise. It is a ground-breaking pragmatic workbook and a clarion call to learn, absorb, empower, and to lead AI rather than the reverse. It's the new primer on how to put AI to work for you.

This book's final section is entitled: "Your Creative Legacy Starts Now." And so, it must. Facing the kinds of mega-change described in these pages, our basic choices are to ignore it, be swept along by its currents or—far, far better—to find and empower your own creative superpowers. This book, then, is a call to lead change and to walk the great arterial bridge from AI all the way across to creativity, innovation, and breakthrough.

From these pages, "Your Creative Legacy Starts Now!" Go create. Go lead. Go change the world.

David Morey
Chairman and CEO, DMG Global;
best-selling author;
advisor to 22 winning global presidential campaigns,
five Nobel Peace Prize winners,
and a who's who of Fortune 500 CEOs and companies

Introduction

Picture this: Your company is losing market share to a nimble startup that see-mingly came out of nowhere. Your team is stuck in the same brainstorming loops, producing variations of familiar ideas. Meanwhile, your competitor is leveraging AI to innovate at unprecedented speed. What's their edge? Creative thinking enhan-ced by AI.

Or imagine a visionary architect sketching a sustainable city, blending nature with urban life, and with AI assistance, innovative architectural concepts emerge in hours instead of months—living buildings that breathe, streets that generate energy, and communities designed for harmony with the environment. A scientist, driven by curiosity and powered by AI analysis, spots patterns in complex data that others overlooked, leading to a breakthrough in disease treatment. A musician experiments fearlessly, using AI to fuse sounds from different cultures and eras, birthing an entirely new genre that captivates millions.

This isn't science fiction, it's happening right now. And it's the power you'll unlock by reading this book, which we have written for people of all professions and ages around the world. This perspective is based on our conviction that while not everyone can match the creative genius of Leonardo da Vinci or Thomas Edison, each of us can nurture and develop our own creativity if we build a toolkit of creativity approaches and enhance it with the use of AI. By the end of this book, you will know how to build your own creativity toolkit and start using it to enrich your own personal and professional life and that of others around you.

The Creative Imperative in Business

In today's rapidly evolving marketplace, creativity is more than simply a "nice-to-have"; it's a matter of survival. McKinsey research shows that companies in the top quartile for innovation achieve 2.4x higher revenue growth.[1] Meanwhile, 70% of executives report that their teams struggle with creative problem-solving.[2] The gap between creative leaders and followers is widening dramatically.

Consider the evidence:

- Organizations using systematic creativity approaches report 25% to 40% faster innovation cycles[3]
- Teams trained in morphological analysis generate 3x more viable solutions[4]
- Companies applying trend analysis techniques identify market opportunities 18 months ahead of competitors[5]
- Businesses that integrate AI-enhanced creativity see productivity gains[6]

Yet most professionals have never been taught how to be systematically creative—until now.

For Business Leaders and Professionals: Your Competitive Edge

Whether you're a CEO navigating industry disruption, a product manager seeking breakthrough innovations, a consultant solving complex client challenges, or an entrepreneur building the next big thing, this book provides battle-tested approaches used by companies like Google, Tesla, Netflix, and Airbnb, with 12 creativity approaches that have been proven in boardrooms, innovation labs, and startup accelerators worldwide.

Professional Impact You'll Achieve:

- Lead more innovative teams that consistently outperform competitors
- Identify market opportunities others miss through systematic trend analysis
- Reduce time-to-solution for complex business challenges
- Build a culture of innovation that attracts top talent
- Leverage AI tools to speed and amplify your ideation and analysis capabilities
- Transform meetings from time-wasters into breakthrough sessions

This book is designed for you regardless of your age, profession, creative background, or level of experience with technology. We believe anyone can be creative if they use the right approaches, and we offer a range of approaches that can be enhanced and accelerated by AI. This will boost your creativity and the creative output of your organization in addressing personal and professional challenges.

> " This book is designed for you regardless of your age, profession, creative background or level of experience with technology. "

The AI Advantage: Your Creative Superpower

Today, we stand on the cusp of an unprecedented explosion in creativity in the age of AI. AI models such as ChatGPT and others act as intelligent collaborative tools that can serve as launchpads for further innovation. They can write, create images, compose music, craft videos, code, brainstorm, research, analyze, and more—capabilities that can supercharge a broad swath of industries. Now, there are AI agents that go beyond AI chatbots to complete multi-step tasks for you autonomously.

But here's the crucial insight: AI doesn't replace human creativity—it amplifies it exponentially. Learn to use ChatGPT for rapid prototyping, Claude for strategic analysis, or emerging AI tools for market research, competitive intelligence, and scenario planning. Transform hours of brainstorming into minutes of AI-enhanced ideation.

The professionals and organizations mastering AI-human creative partnerships are pulling ahead at lightning speed. The question is: Will you be among them?

Proven Results from Real Organizations

The approaches shared in this book have been adopted by organizations that created industry-altering solutions:

- **Netflix** used trend analysis (Approach #7) to pivot from DVD rental to streaming, revolutionizing entertainment.
- **Tesla** challenged mental models (Approach #1) to redefine the automotive industry and force every competitor to go electric.
- **Amazon's** customer obsession (Approach #7) and experimental culture (Approach #8), exemplifies transformation processes that generated hundreds of billions in value.
- **Airbnb** applied morphological analysis (Approach #3) to disrupt the hospitality industry worth $600 billion.
- **Google** built a culture of curiosity (Approach #9) that spawned breakthrough products from Search to Android to AI.

These examples are the result of the systematic creative thinking that you'll master from this book.

Historical Context: Why Creativity Matters More Than Ever

Creativity, as we understand it today, has relatively recent origins. MIT Technology Review's examination of Samuel Franklin's *The Cult of Creativity* reveals that our modern understanding emerged primarily after World War II in America.[7] Creativity became a response to society's growing conformity and bureaucratization, providing what Franklin describes as "a way to unleash individualism within order, and revive the spirit of the lone inventor within the maze of the modern corporation."

This historical perspective shows why creativity has become a fundamental value in contemporary society. Silicon Valley particularly exemplifies this trend, valuing creativity precisely because it combines novelty with utility—two elements highly prized in technology markets. As AI increasingly participates in creative processes, understanding this context becomes more relevant. Our definitions and practices of creativity continue to evolve alongside technological and social changes.

Break Free from Institutional Constraints

At this point, you might protest that you're not the creative type: most of us aren't Beethovens or Picassos. But you don't have to be a prodigy to benefit from being dramatically more creative in everything you do, from solving everyday problems to developing breakthrough strategies.

Ironically, the institutions meant to encourage creative thinking are the same ones stifling its emergence. Schools focus on rote memorization and standardized tests, often neglecting creative thinking development. Students are rewarded for conformity and regurgitating information rather than original thought and problem-solving skills. Organizations inadvertently suppress creativity through rigid hierarchies, bureaucratic processes, and resistance to change.

These societal shackles leave us trapped in old mental models that influence how we interpret information, solve problems, and make decisions. These models create blind spots and restrict our thinking to conventional pathways that block innovative solutions.

But here's the exciting news: Challenging these mental models is the first step to unlocking extraordinary creativity. By changing your mind, you can change your future.

Your Roadmap to Creative Mastery

Creativity in the Age of AI: Toolkits for the Modern Mind will teach you the skills you need to thrive in a future where AI enhances cognitive efficiency. The approaches are based on a popular Wharton MBA elective taught by the lead author, Yoram 'Jerry' Wind: 12 sets of approaches that have been scientifically proven to unlock creativity, with exercises to help you think not just outside the box, but way beyond it.

The book's structure guides you through this transformation:

Foundation Section (Chapters 1–4): Master the conceptual and empirical foundations.
Chapter 1 introduces creativity, providing insights into the creative process, what creativity is, and, perhaps importantly, what it isn't.
Chapter 2 explores psychological paradigms and neuroscience insights as the foundation for creativity.
Chapter 3 examines the intersection of artificial intelligence and creative processes, providing practical guidance on leveraging AI tools effectively.
Chapter 4 discusses ways to overcome obstacles to creativity and innovation, helping you break through common barriers that limit creative thinking.

12 Powerful Approaches to Enhance Creativity (Chapters 5–16): Each chapter provides battle-tested approaches enhanced by AI:
Chapter 5: Challenge Your Mental Models—Break free from "that's how we've always done it" thinking. Learn Tesla's approach to disrupting established industries and discover AI prompts that expose hidden assumptions limiting your team's potential.
Chapter 6: Create New Paradigms—Establish revolutionary thinking patterns. See how Spotify transformed music consumption and how you can create industry-disrupting innovations.

Chapter 7: Use Morphological Analysis—Systematically break down complex problems and solutions into components and recombine them for breakthrough solutions. Master the technique that helped Airbnb reimagine hospitality.

Chapter 8: Employ Analogies and Benchmarking—Generate novel ideas by connecting seemingly unrelated fields. Learn how IDEO used Formula One pit stops to revolutionize operating room design.

Chapter 9: Engage in Interdisciplinary Collaboration—Harness the power of diverse perspectives and open innovation. Discover how NASA solved complex problems by engaging global communities.

Chapter 10: Adopt Rules and Tools—Implement structured methods like SCAMPER, SWOT, and Blue Ocean strategies enhanced by AI analysis for maximum creative output.

Chapter 11: Extract Insights from Trends—Identify market opportunities before competitors through systematic analysis across consumer behavior, technology, business, and cultural trends.

Chapter 12: Embrace Experimentation and Iteration—Transform assumptions into data-driven insights through refinement cycles and experimentation that reduce risk and accelerate innovation.

Chapter 13: Foster Curiosity and Imagination—Develop the mindful inquisitiveness that leads to breakthrough discoveries and revolutionary ideas.

Chapter 14: Leverage Emerging Technologies—Master cutting-edge AI tools and emerging scientific and technological advances to expand creative horizons and enable future-oriented thinking.

Chapter 15: Customize Your Own Toolkit—Create a personalized dynamic arsenal of creativity approaches tailored to your specific goals and industry challenges.

Chapter 16: Cultivate Courage and Persistence—Develop the mental fortitude and courage to face uncertainty, embrace failure as learning, and persist through obstacles that stop others.

Conclusion: Ignite Your Creative Future—Transform insights into action with a personal and organizational strategy for continuous creative growth and competitive advantage.

What You'll Learn

You will gain a scientifically proven path to unlocking your creative potential and learn how to leverage cutting-edge AI tools to amplify your natural abilities. The book will help you:

- **Gain unshakeable confidence** in your creative abilities through understanding the neuroscience behind breakthrough thinking.
- **Master 12 sets of powerful creativity approaches** proven by companies generating billions in value.

- **10x your ideation speed** using AI-enhanced brainstorming and analysis techniques.
- **Build a customized dynamic creativity toolkit** tailored to your unique challenges and industry.
- **Overcome common obstacles** that derail creative implementation in organizations.
- **Draw inspiration from innovators**, including Nobel prize winners, disruptive entrepreneurs, and industry revolutionaries.

The book is designed to be intensely practical, with exercises and challenges that encourage you to apply what you learn to real problems. You can dive deeper through an accompanying Coursera course featuring 60 video interviews with creativity experts across art, science, technology, and business.[8]

As you grow creatively and your circumstances evolve, you'll find that some approaches become more relevant while others recede. This is your dynamic toolkit for continuous creative advantage.

> **"** You can dive deeper through an accompanying Coursera course featuring 60 video interviews with creativity experts across art, science, technology, and business. **"**

Your Creative Edge Starts Now

Every day you delay developing these capabilities is a day your competition gains ground. The tools, frameworks, and AI techniques in this book are already being used by forward-thinking leaders across industries. The question isn't whether you need enhanced creativity; it's whether you'll develop it before your competitors do.

The gap between creative leaders and creative followers is widening rapidly. AI is accelerating this divide, rewarding those who can think creatively about leveraging these powerful tools while leaving others behind. The future belongs to creative problem-solvers who can harness AI to amplify human ingenuity. Your journey to joining their ranks begins with turning the page.

Creativity in the Age of AI: Toolkits for the Modern Mind will equip you with tools to tap into and amplify your creativity in an era of superintelligent machines. Your creative transformation starts now.

Are you ready to unleash your creative power?

Notes

1   McKinsey & Company, "The Eight Essentials of Innovation," *McKinsey Quarterly*, 2015. https://www.mckinsey.com/capabilities/strategy-and-corporate-finance/our-insights/the-eight-essentials-of-innovation

2   Adobe, "State of Create: 2022 Global Benchmark Study on Creativity," Adobe, 2022. https://www.adobe.com/creativecloud/business/reports/state-of-create.html

3   Innovation Excellence, "Systematic Innovation Approaches Deliver Results," *Innovation Excellence Research Report*, 2023.

4   Design Management Institute, "Design-Driven Companies Outperform S&P by 228%," *Design Management Review*, 2022.

5   Corporate Innovation Survey, "Trend Analysis and Competitive Advantage," *Harvard Business Review*, 2023.

6   Accenture Research, "Human + Machine: Reimagining Work in the Age of AI," *Accenture*, 2024.

7   *MIT Technology Review*, "How Creativity Became the Reigning Value of Our Time," April 18, 2025, accessed May 12, 2025. https://www.technologyreview.com/2025/04/18/1114478/cult-of-creativity-samuel-franklin-book-technology-ai/

8   The concluding chapter includes the list of the creatives who appear in Jerry Wind's Coursera course, *Creativity in Business and Other Disciplines*, https://www.coursera.org/learn/creativity-in-business/

Part 1

CHAPTER 3
How AI Can
Give You
Creative
Superpowers

CHAPTER 4
Overcoming
Obstacles to
Creativity and
Innovation

CHAPTER 1
Creativity
Decoded

CHAPTER 2
What's
Neuroscience
Got to Do
with It?

Foundations

Part 1

Foundations

We stand at a fascinating intersection of human potential and technological advancement, where our innate creative abilities meet powerful new tools that can amplify, enhance, and challenge how we think and create.

Part 1 lays the groundwork through four foundational chapters that will transform how you understand creativity in today's world. We'll decode creativity—what it truly means and how it manifests in human endeavors. We'll explore the neuroscience behind creative thinking and how our brains work when generating novel ideas, and we'll see how AI can serve as a powerful ally in your creative journey, giving you capabilities that might not have seemed possible before. Finally, we'll confront obstacles between you and your creative potential.

These chapters are a practical foundation for everything else that follows. Each insight builds upon the former, preparing you to fully engage with the 12 sets of approaches to unlocking creativity presented in Part 2. However, we recognize that you may be familiar with these foundational topics and wish to skip them and go directly to the 12 sets of approaches in Part 2.

Whether you're a business leader seeking new ways to tap into innovation, an artist keen to push your creative boundaries, a student exploring, as yet, territory unknown, or someone who wants to think more creatively in daily life, these foundations will equip you with the understanding you need.

The creativity landscape has fundamentally changed. AI doesn't replace human creativity; it transforms and turbocharges it. Understanding this new relationship is essential if you want to thrive in what might be the most creative period in human history.

Are you ready to decode creativity, understand your brain's creative potential, harness AI as your creative partner, and overcome any barriers holding you back? Our next section will discuss these in greater detail.

Creativity Decoded

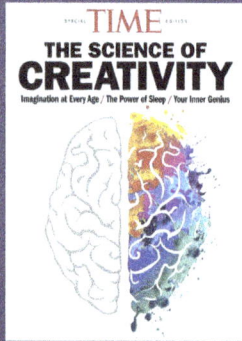

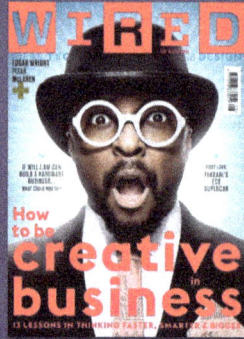

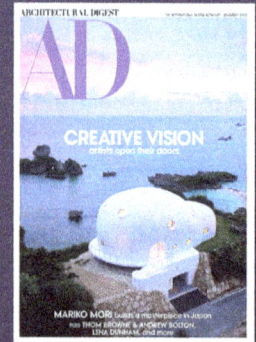

Chapter 1
Creativity Decoded

Everything you can imagine is real.
—Pablo Picasso

Picasso's assertion that 'everything you can imagine is real' reminds us that creativity begins with imagination, but as we'll explore, translating imagination into reality requires novelty and practical value.

Creativity is a fundamental aspect of human experience, valued across cultures and throughout history for its role in driving innovation, artistry, and progress. It manifests in various forms, from scientific breakthroughs to compelling works of art, shaping how we understand and interact with the world.

Everyone needs creativity. From the world leader aiming to wipe out poverty in their country; the business executive seeking to revive a flagging line of products; the musician looking for inspiration for a new song; the lab scientist searching for a new approach to drug discovery; the small business owner striving to stay ahead of big box retailers; and many others in between.

> **Everyone needs creativity.**

Creativity is often enhanced by specific tools and approaches that help artists, thinkers, scientists, and innovators break limitations. For example, Vincent van Gogh used a perspective frame to refine his compositions, allowing him to master depth and proportion in his paintings. In art and literature, Surrealists sought to unite the rational with dreams and the power of the unconscious mind. Architect Frank Gehry used paper models and crumpled sketches to conceive his fluid architectural designs before translating them into buildings. Brian Eno pioneered the 'Oblique Strategies' cards in music, a set of prompts designed to push musicians out of creative blocks. These diverse tools and techniques demonstrate how structured methods can paradoxically free the mind, leading to groundbreaking creative achievements.

Today, creativity is evolving in unprecedented ways. As our understanding of the creative process deepens, we discover new pathways for unlocking human ingenuity and imagination. The tools and approaches at our disposal have increased dramatically, giving us fresh perspectives and methodologies to expand creative boundaries. Contemporary artists blend traditional techniques with new media, scientists cross disciplinary boundaries, and businesses reimagine conventional models. This democratization of creative tools means that not only can the naturally gifted enhance their capabilities, but those who don't consider themselves creative can also find ways to innovate personally and professionally.

Yet, as we embrace these new possibilities, fundamental questions arise: How can we best nurture and develop our creative abilities? How do we balance structure and spontaneity in the creative process? What environments best support creative thinking? And how can we utilize the gamut of AI tools that have become available to us, rapidly evolving and becoming dynamically adaptive? The answers will shape how we approach innovation and define what it means to be creative in today's world.

A Dynamic Definition of Creativity

What exactly is creativity? The term evokes something abstract, yet its results are tangible. You may not know how creativity is sparked in Gehry's brain. Still, you can see the results: The Walt Disney Concert Hall in Los Angeles, the Guggenheim Museum in Bilbao, Spain, and the Fondation Louis Vuitton in Paris are some of his most famous architectural designs. Gehry's breakthrough is to challenge the traditional concept of a museum building as confined to four walls, devising a dramatically different structure that is fluid and curvilinear.

Most conventional definitions of creativity are confined to psychological processes—thinking outside the box. But the reality is much more dynamic. Teresa Amabile, an influential academic in this field and a professor of business administration at Harvard Business School, developed the 'componential theory' of creativity. It is recognized as one of the significant theories of creativity for individuals and organizations.

In a 2012 paper,[1] Amabile defined creativity as "the production of a novel and appropriate response, product, or solution to an open-ended task." But novelty alone does not invoke creativity. For example, she argued that the nonsensical mutterings of a mentally impaired person may be unusual, but few would see them as creative. The creative output, therefore, must be appropriate to the task or problem at hand and evaluated. The task also must be open-ended, not fixed with a single, obvious solution.

We can argue that both novelty and usefulness are necessary for acts of creativity. "Creativity has to have value to be successful. You can develop many ideas, but if you are not adding value to the stakeholders, they are not (truly) creative ideas."[2]

> " Both novelty and usefulness are necessary for acts of creativity. "

In her paper, Amabile broke down the components of creativity into four parts:[3] three are within an individual or organization, and one is external.

1. **Domain-relevant skills**: Your knowledge, expertise, technical skills, intelligence, and talent are the raw materials for the creative process to help you assess the creative result.

2. **Creativity-relevant processes**: Cognitive and personality processes are conducive to novel thinking and encourage independence, risk-taking, and taking new perspectives, coupled with disciplined work styles, skills in

generating ideas, and a tolerance for ambiguity. This last characteristic is one of the best predictors of creativity.

Under this category are sub-processes that include analyzing and articulating the problem, preparing for the solution, gathering information and sharpening the required skills, generating ideas and testing the solution, and communicating the solution to others.

3. **Intrinsic task motivation or passion:** People are most creative when they feel motivated primarily by the interest, enjoyment, satisfaction, and challenge of the work itself. Amabile would later include outside factors such as reaping rewards for the endeavor.

4. **Social environment:** This is the only outside factor affecting creativity and pertains to the work or social situation. Some environments are conducive to creativity, some are not. Rigid belief systems can create a social environment where creativity struggles to flourish. This happens when powerful groups reject different or so-called contradictory perspectives and foster a climate of conformity or censorship in which people become reluctant to challenge established thinking or propose innovative solutions. These environments exist across political spectrums, organizations, and communities—the fear of speaking up directly undermines creativity, which requires challenging the status quo (Approach 1) and implementing changes with courage (Approach 12). Research also shows that specific work environments can stifle creativity. When new ideas are harshly criticized, there are internal politics to navigate, reluctance to change the status quo, low tolerance for risk from top management, and excessive time pressure.

    On the flip side, what encourages creativity is to have meaningful work that is intrinsically motivating, supervisors who support new ideas, and top management that clearly articulates their vision for innovation, recognizes and develops mechanisms for creative work, and shares ideas across the organization. In a social context, history shows that the most innovative breakthroughs come from environments that welcome diverse viewpoints and protect those who question orthodoxy.

While creativity and innovation are often used interchangeably, they represent distinct creative process aspects. Creativity generates novel and valuable ideas, while innovation successfully implements those ideas in an organizational context. Creativity operates primarily in the conceptual domain, while innovation encompasses the practical realization of creative ideas through processes, products, or business models. This book focuses on creativity as the foundational capability that drives innovation, the spark that ignites transformative change.

Creativity is at its peak when these four factors operate optimally: The intrinsically motivated person with high domain expertise and skilled in creative thinking works in a highly supportive creative environment.

Leaders would do well to design their organizations in a way that enhances creativity, which includes developing a culture that values innovation, putting in place a structure and processes that encourage experimentation, setting up a rewards and compensation framework to encourage appropriate risk-taking, and hiring visionary managers who empower their teams.[4]

A great example of a corporate culture that encourages creativity and innovation is the culture and values created by Brad Jackson, the CEO of Slalom Consulting. The Slalom culture is characterized by a strong emphasis on core values, employee ownership, and a collaborative, growth-oriented environment. They prioritize authenticity, connection, and a focus on outcomes, encouraging employees to be passionate and driven.

Key aspects of Slalom's culture highlights: *Core values* that include "Do what is right, always," "Drive connection and teamwork," and "Inspire passion and adventure." *Growth, innovation and willingness to learn,* encouraging employees to "Stay humble and curious" and "Fuel growth and innovation," *Authenticity* encouraging employees to be their authentic selves and celebrate individual differences. And *human focus,* emphasizing understanding clients' "why" and partnering with them to deliver customized solutions.

But a determined employee can still overcome a hostile work environment if properly motivated. The Apollo 11 moon landing in 1969 might not have happened if it hadn't been for an engineer named John C. Houbolt, who persisted despite his unconventional idea being widely mocked internally.[5] He creatively proposed launching a rocket into lunar orbit, after which a smaller lander would be dispersed to the moon's surface.

Most engineers pursued a more conventional idea of building a massive rocket that could land directly on the moon, however precariously, and return home. But Houbolt was so convinced he was right that he broke protocol by writing to NASA's top executives.[6] It worked, and Apollo 11 made history.

While organizations shape creative environments, individuals can create a space that fosters creativity. Start by challenging your assumptions, even in small ways. Build a diverse network of people across fields and backgrounds who will encourage you to challenge your thinking and make regular time for reflection and idea generation away from distractions. Develop routines that protect new ideas despite external pressures, and consider sharing your ideas with trusted peers who can provide constructive feedback. In Houbolt's example cited above, sometimes you need the courage to persist with unconventional ideas despite resistance. Your creative environment begins with deliberate choices about whom you connect with, how you structure your time, and your willingness to explore beyond your comfort zone.

The Multifaceted Nature of Creativity

Consider the collaborative creative process used in filmmaking to see the components of creativity in action. The groundbreaking film *Parasite* directed by

Bong Joon Ho was the first non-English film to win an Academy Award for Best Picture and the Palme d'Or at the Cannes Film Festival, earning over $250 million on a budget of $11 million. The film exemplifies creativity through its original storyline, innovative cinematography, meticulously designed sets, and powerful social commentary.

The creation of *Parasite* drew upon multiple creative domains, with each contributor providing domain-specific expertise. But the film's revolutionary impact came from how these elements were synthesized into a cohesive whole that redefined cinematic storytelling about class struggle.

This collaborative process exemplifies Amabile's four components of creativity:

- **Domain-relevant skills**: Each department brought specialized knowledge and technical expertise, namely, the director's vision, the screenwriters' narrative craft, the cinematographer's visual language, the production designer's spatial concepts, the actors' emotional interpretations, and the editor's rhythmic sensibilities.
- **Creativity-relevant processes**: The team employed unconventional approaches, such as the distinctive architectural contrasts between the wealthy and low-income families' homes, and the film's genre-bending narrative that shifts between comedy, thriller, and social drama.
- **Intrinsic task motivation**: Director Bong and his team were deeply motivated by their desire to create an original work that commented on social inequality—a subject personally meaningful to the creators.
- **Social environment**: The production fostered an atmosphere where cross-disciplinary collaboration was encouraged, allowing innovative ideas to flourish regardless of their source.

Similar creative dynamics can be found in other fields. In science, the Human Genome Project united biologists, computer scientists, mathematicians, and ethicists in a massive collaborative effort to map human DNA. In business, design thinking brings together diverse teams to solve complex problems through empathy, ideation, and prototyping. Even seemingly solo creative acts like writing novels or composing music often involve editors, producers, and collaborators who help refine and elevate the work.

Other schools of thought around understanding creativity include neuroscience (see Chapter 2); creative cognition theory; theory of creativity (individual and environmental factors); emotional intelligence; empowerment theory; self-determination theory; generative theory; and explicit-implicit interaction theory.

Table 1.1 provides a synopsis of some of these theories in a marketing context from the paper, "Unlocking Marketing Creativity Using Artificial Intelligence," which was published in the *Journal of Interactive Marketing* in 2024, written by professors Margherita Pagani from the Skema Business School in Paris and Jerry Wind.

Table 1.1: Theories Informing Creativity in Marketing

Theory	Authors and Year	Dimension	Relevance to Marketing Creativity
Creative cognition theory	Balietti and Riedl (2021)	Cognitive	Provides insights into cognitive processes in problem-solving and idea generation for marketing challenges.
Theory of creativity	Im, Montoya, and Workman (2013); Vitrano, Altarriba, and Leblebici-Basar (2021)	Individual and environmental	Examines how personal traits and external factors shape creativity in marketing, aiding in understanding the creative process.
Emotional intelligence	Khalili (2016)	Emotional	Helps in understanding the role of emotions in marketing creativity, enhancing customer engagement, and response.
Empowerment theory	Cheng et al. (2019)	Leadership and empowerment	Connects leadership and empowerment to innovative marketing strategies, fostering creativity in marketing solutions.
Self-determination theory	Fischer, Malycha, and Schafmann (2019)	Intrinsic motivation	Emphasizes the role of intrinsic motivation in driving creative marketing ideas, advocating for fostering internal motivation.
Generative theory	Peteranetz et al. (2017)	Generative processes	Explores how creative ideas are generated and developed in marketing, guiding the creation of impactful marketing campaigns.
Explicit–implicit interaction theory	Helie and Sun (2009); Altarriba and Avery (2021)	Cognitive interaction	Examines cognitive engagement in creative problem-solving, informing the cognitive dynamics involved in innovative marketing strategies.

To explore creativity more deeply, consider the biographies written by Walter Isaacson, an American journalist, former CEO of the Aspen Institute, and the former editor of TIME. His books have encapsulated the life stories of many innovative thinkers, including Leonardo da Vinci, Benjamin Franklin, Albert Einstein, Steve Jobs, Elon Musk, and the Innovators, a group of hackers, geniuses, and geeks who created the digital revolution.

Other helpful books offering contemporary perspectives include *Creativity, Inc.*, by Ed Catmull; *The Creative Act: A Way of Being*, by Rick Rubin; *Big Magic: Creative Living Beyond Fear* by Elizabeth Gilbert; *Imagine: How Creativity Works* by Jonah Lehrer; *The Artist's Way* by Julia Cameron; and *The Power of Impossible Thinking*, by Yoram 'Jerry' Wind and Colin Crook, and more recently, Dan Hunter, *Learning and Teaching Creativity.*[7]

Creativity at Any Age

Readers of a certain age may wonder whether creativity is a young person's game, if their most creative years may be behind them. Certain cognitive abilities decline with age, but knowledge

" **Creativity can increase at any age.** "

and expertise, the other determinants of creativity, increase as one ages,[8] according to a paper co-authored by Martin Seligman, the founder of positive psychology and director of the Positive Psychology Center at the University of Pennsylvania.

These two factors "play a major, necessary role in creativity," Seligman and his co-authors wrote. More specifically, their research found that the following skills and knowledge increase or remain stable with age:[9]

- Domain-specific knowledge and expertise
- General knowledge
- Pattern recognition, intuition, and heuristics
- Diversity of experience
- Interest and motivation
- Grit and self-efficacy
- Effective collaboration

When combined, these traits aid creativity. The authors said it's rare to see a creative genius from someone with a singular, exceptional, often inborn talent; instead, it "may occur when someone is 'merely' very good in all of them."[10]

Take golf champion Tiger Woods, who is "not the best in putting, driving, or the short approach," they wrote. Rather, he is known for his exceptional all-around game, combining distance, iron play, short game, and putting. This combined proficiency made him one of golf's greatest players. Since success is rooted in a combination of "very good" skills, our review suggests that it is indeed possible that creativity can increase even as we age, a surprising hypothesis rarely discussed in the literature.

A poem by ChatGPT on creativity at any age

Creativity is not a gift for the few,
But something all of us can do.
It's not confined to brush or pen,
It lives in the hearts and hands of when.

It builds in boardrooms, kitchens, and streets,
In labs, on farms, and in trading fleets.
A teacher's plan, a dancer's move—
Each act is a chance to think and prove.

It sparks in young and old alike,
In quiet minds or those that spike.
No flag, no job, no age or name
Can dim the bold, creative flame.

It's grown with practice, play, and trust—
Asking more than saying is a must.
Combine the strange, embrace the mess,
Make room for doubt, and say yes less.

So let no label hold you back—
A nation, role, or seasoned track.
The gift to shape, to dream, to see—
It is part of your humanity.

Expecting the 'Eureka' Moment

Here's another counterintuitive fact: Creative breakthroughs rarely come from sudden epiphanies or so-called "divine inspiration." Instead, they often emerge after incubation, during which ideas percolate in the subconscious mind.

> **"** Creative breakthroughs rarely come from sudden epiphanies but after a period of incubation. **"**

In his 1926 book,[11] "The Art of the Thought", psychologist Graham Wallas, cofounder of the London School of Economics, identified four stages of the creative process: preparation, incubation, illumination, and verification. Creativity encompasses a journey through these stages, with moments of insight emerging from subconscious processing.

His four stages are the following:

- **Preparation**: During which an individual consciously identifies a problem or challenge and gathers relevant information and knowledge about it.
- **Incubation**: The individual steps away from the problem and allows their subconscious mind to work on it. The ideas are allowed to develop and connect without conscious effort.
- **Illumination**: The 'Aha!' moment, when the creative idea or solution emerges into conscious awareness. It is often sudden and unexpected.
- **Verification**: The individual consciously evaluates and refines the idea to ensure its feasibility and effectiveness. They may make adjustments or modifications to the original idea.

These four stages exemplify the idea that creativity is as much a product of perspiration as is inspiration. Breakthroughs often stem from persistent efforts and systematic problem-solving rather than spontaneous flashes of genius. One famous example is Thomas Edison, whose invention of the first commercial light bulb in the late 19th century resulted from many iterations and failures.

Edison tested thousands of materials to find the right alloy to make the filament for a light bulb.[12] Most combinations of metals he tried did not initially work because the light they generated was too dim or they burned up too rapidly. But he didn't give up. Edison believed he didn't fail; he found thousands of ways that his idea didn't work.[13] By reframing what failure and success meant, Edison could persist until he found the right alloy, bringing electric light to the masses.

Modern research has expanded on Wallas' model, identifying additional nuances in the creative process. Mihaly Csikszentmihalyi, known for his work on 'flow' states, observed that creativity flourishes when fully immersed in challenging but not overwhelming tasks that demand our complete attention.[14] Neuroscientists have also discovered that creative insights often occur when the brain's default mode network is active, typically during periods of rest or low-focus activities like walking, showering, or daydreaming.[15] Both are different phases of the creative cycle.

Edison's experience makes clear that creativity is far from a linear process. Understanding the multifaceted nature of creativity is the first step toward unlocking one's creative potential. By recognizing creativity as a dynamic interplay of individual attributes, environmental factors, and cognitive processes, we can better understand how to nurture and develop our creative abilities.

Mental models shape our perception of reality, often limiting what we believe is possible. By questioning and disrupting these models, we free our minds from subconscious constraints, allowing us to see connections, opportunities, and solutions that were previously invisible. This liberation from habitual thinking patterns is frequently the spark that ignites breakthrough creativity.

The approaches and exercises in this book will help you develop and strengthen your creative muscles, leading to your innovations and breakthroughs.

Individual and Team Creativity

While history celebrates individual geniuses, modern innovation increasingly emerges from collaborative efforts. As Walter Isaacson reveals in *The Innovators*, even technological visionaries like Bill Gates, Steve Jobs, and Steve Wozniak achieved breakthroughs by combining their unique talents with others'. These collaborations create cognitive diversity that sparks creativity through the collision of different perspectives, expertise, and thinking styles. Today's most innovative organizations deliberately design teams that blend disciplines, backgrounds, and viewpoints, recognizing that creativity flourishes at these intersections. Even as we nurture our creative potential, we must develop the skills to collaborate effectively, knowing that our ideas gain strength when refined through diverse perspectives.

The creative tension between individual brilliance and collective innovation has produced some of humanity's most outstanding achievements. The Renaissance workshops of Florence combined the vision of master artists with the technical skills of numerous apprentices. The Manhattan Project unified the theoretical genius of scientists like Robert Oppenheimer with the practical engineering expertise of thousands of technicians. Even great novelists' seemingly solitary creative work typically involves extensive collaboration with editors, readers, and literary influences.

This dynamic interplay between individual and collective creativity manifests in various ways across disciplines:

- In scientific research, breakthroughs increasingly come from interdisciplinary teams that combine diverse perspectives and methodologies.
- In business, innovation labs foster collaboration between engineering, design, marketing, and user experience specialists.
- In the arts, traditional boundaries between creator and audience are blurring, with interactive installations and participatory performances co-creating experiences.

As interdisciplinary teams become the norm in most scientific and medical fields, identifying the individual star becomes tougher. This is a real challenge to the judges of awards such as the Franklin Institute laureates as they search for "true visionaries, pushing the boundaries of innovation to find solutions to some of the world's most pressing challenges—and their achievements are transformative."[16]

Today's most innovative organizations recognize this reality, designing spaces and processes that support individual thinking time and collaborative co-creation. They understand that creativity flourishes when we balance the depth of individual expertise with the breadth of collective wisdom. Yet, for most of us, the insight is clear. While each should do their best to enhance their creativity, being able to collaborate with others is key and should not be ignored.

In Summary

1. Creativity is about making an impact.

You have brilliant ideas inside you, but real creativity happens when those ideas matter. It's not enough to be novel; you must deliver something valuable to the people around you. Think bold but think practical. Combine your imagination with intention, and you'll create something unforgettable.

What impact do you want your ideas to make, and who will benefit most from your creative vision?

2. Four forces fuel your creative potential. Are you using all of them?
To unlock your full creative power, you need more than just talent. You need to master your craft (domain expertise), learn how to think in new ways (creative thinking), stay internally driven (intrinsic motivation), and surround yourself with the right people and conditions (a supportive environment). When these four align, your creativity explodes into success.

Which of these four forces is underdeveloped in your work, and how might strengthening it transform your creative output?

3. Don't wait for inspiration. Create your own spark.
Creativity doesn't come in flashes of inspiration. Breakthroughs follow a process. First, you prepare, then you allow ideas to simmer, and when insight strikes, you shape it into reality.

What daily ritual could you establish to fuel your creative process rather than waiting for inspiration?

In Summary (contd.)

> **4. Your vision can change the world if you invite others in.**
> Great ideas start with one person, you, but they flourish even further when you join forces with others. Marry your unique vision with diverse voices and perspectives. Innovation happens when individual brilliance meets collective power.
>
> *Who could you bring into your creative process that thinks differently from you?*

Now that you understand creativity as a skill that can be systematically developed and enhanced, the remainder of this book, including the 12 sets of targeted approaches that show you how to include AI, will equip you to unlock your creative potential.

But first, let's dig a little deeper into the root of creativity by examining the science behind it.

Notes

[1] T. M. Amabile. Componential Theory of Creativity. Harvard Business School Working Paper 12-096, 2012. https://www.hbs.edu/ris/Publication%20Files/12-096.pdf

[2] Knowledge@Wharton. "Can Creativity Be Taught?" *Knowledge@Wharton*, August 27, 2014, accessed February 26, 2025. https://knowledge.wharton.upenn.edu/article/can-creativity-be-taught/

[3] There are many other formulations of the component's determinants of creativity that break down the 4 Amabile components into subsets. Consider for example the following formulation offered by ChatGPT in response to the prompt "what are the key determinants of creativity?"

1. Cognitive Factors
   • Divergent Thinking—The ability to generate multiple ideas or solutions to a problem.
   • Convergent Thinking—The ability to refine and select the best idea among many.
   • Cognitive Flexibility—The ability to shift perspectives and adapt to new ideas.
   • Analogical Thinking—Drawing connections between seemingly unrelated concepts.
   • Working Memory—The ability to retain and manipulate information in real time.
   • Pattern Recognition—Identifying underlying structures or trends in data.

2. Personality Traits
   • Openness to Experience—A willingness to explore novel ideas and experiences.
   • Curiosity—A strong desire to acquire knowledge and understand the unknown.
   • Risk-Taking—Willingness to experiment and embrace failure.
   • Intrinsic Motivation—Creating for personal fulfillment rather than external rewards.
   • Tolerance for Ambiguity—Comfort with uncertainty and incomplete information.
   • Perseverance—The ability to persist despite obstacles or failures.

3. Emotional and Psychological States
   • Positive Mood—Enhances cognitive flexibility and idea generation.
   • Mindfulness—Heightened awareness can improve insight-based creativity.
   • Daydreaming—Spontaneous thought processes can lead to novel ideas.
   • Flow State—Deep immersion in a task, where creativity flourishes effortlessly.

4. Environmental and Social Influences
   • Cultural Exposure—Experiencing diverse traditions and ideas fosters creativity.
   • Collaborative Networks—Engaging with others leads to cross-pollination of ideas.
   • Freedom and Autonomy—An environment that encourages exploration enhances creativity.
   • Resource Availability—Access to materials, knowledge, and tools fuels innovation.
   • Challenging Constraints—Limitations can push individuals to think outside the box.

5. Knowledge and Expertise
   • Domain Knowledge—A deep understanding of a field enables meaningful innovation.
   • Interdisciplinary Learning—Combining insights from different fields fosters breakthrough ideas.
   • Deliberate Practice—Repetitive learning and refinement of skills support creative mastery.

6. Technology and Tools
   • AI and Digital Tools—Expanding creative possibilities in art, music, and design.
   • Augmented Reality/Virtual Reality—Providing immersive environments for ideation.
   • New Media & Platforms—Allowing creators to express themselves in unprecedented ways.

[4] Nitin Rakesh and Jerry Wind. *Transformation in Times of Crisis: Eight Principles for Creating Opportunities and Value in the Post-Pandemic World* (Chennai, India: Notion Press, 2020).

5 Scott Neuman. "Meet John Houboult: He Figured Out How to Go to the Moon, But Few Were Listening." NPR, July 18, 2019. https://www.npr.org/2019/07/18/739934923/meet-john-houbolt-he-figured-out-how-to-go-to-the-moon-but-few-were-listening

6 Ibid.

7 E. Catmull and A. Wallace. *Creativity, Inc.: Overcoming the Unseen Forces that Stand in the Way of True Inspiration* (Random House, 2014); R. Rubin. *The Creative Act: A Way of Being* (Penguin Press, 2023); E. Gilbert. *Big Magic: Creative Living beyond Fear* (Riverhead Books, 2015); J. Lehrer. *Imagine: How Creativity Works* (Houghton Mifflin Harcourt, 2012); J. Cameron. *The Artist's Way: A Spiritual Path to Higher Creativity* (10th anniversary ed.) (TarcherPerigee, 2002) (Original work published 1992); Y. J. Wind and C. Crook. *The Power of Impossible Thinking: Transform the Business of Your Life and the Life of Your Business* (Wharton School Publishing, 2004); D. Hunter. *Learning and Teaching Creativity* (Edward Elgar Publishing, 2002).

8 Martin Seligman, Marie Forgeard, and Scott Barry Kaufman. "Creativity and Aging: What We Can Make With What We Have Left." 2016. https://scottbarrykaufman.com/wp-content/uploads/2016/05/Seligman-Forgeard-Kaufman-2016.pdf

9 Ibid.

10 Ibid.

11 Graham Wallas. "The Art of the Thought." Harcourt, Brace and Company, 1926. Internet Archive. https://archive.org/details/theartofthought

12 The Franklin Institute, "Edison's Lightbulb," accessed June 8, 2024. https://fi.edu/en/science-and-education/collection/edisons-lightbulb

13 Frank Lewis Dyer, Thomas Commerford Martin. *Edison, His Life and Inventions* (New York: Harpers, 1929). https://www.gutenberg.org/files/820/820-h/820-h.htm

14 "Creative Potential: The Power of Flow in Creativity," *CreativeC*, accessed March 13, 2025. https://www.creativec.com.au/blog/creative-potential-the-power-of-flow-in-creativity

15 Wei Luo et al., "Rest to Promote Learning: A Brain Default Mode Network Perspective," *Frontiers in Psychology*, eds. Eleanor Dommett and Anne-Laure Le Cunff, PMCID: PMC11047624, PMID: 38667145, accessed March 13, 2025. https://pmc.ncbi.nlm.nih.gov/articles/PMC11047624/

16 The Franklin Institute, Instagram post, February 6, 2025. https://www.instagram.com/franklininstitute/p/DFvoiLypVZr/

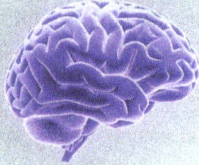

Chapter 2
What's Neuroscience Got to Do with It?

The brain is the most fascinating object in the universe.
—Nobel Laureate and neurologist Stanley B. Prusiner

Like all subjective concepts tied to the arts, creativity defies precise explanation. Most people relegate it to the mysterious inclination of the talented few born to create objects of admiration or innovation. However, there is a scientific basis for creativity, which is found in the workings of the human brain. This might be of comfort to you if you think you are not naturally creative. Its scientific underpinnings mean creativity can be replicated and nurtured if we engage in practices that stimulate the brain's creative networks.

Studies in neuroscience have identified specific brain networks linked to creative thinking:

- **Default Mode Network:** It is engaged during mind-wandering and spontaneous thought and facilitates the generation of novel ideas.
- **Executive Control Network:** It is involved in planning, decision-making, and evaluating and refining ideas to ensure they are practical and relevant.
- **Salience Network:** It detects important stimuli and mediates the transition between the first two, balancing idea generation with critical assessment.

The interplay among these networks underpins the creative process, demonstrating that creativity arises from complex brain functions rather than being an inexplicable gift. Scientists have studied the link between neuroscience and creativity since the mid-twentieth century. However, technological advances in the twenty-first century have enabled us to have a greater understanding.

> **"** Creativity arises from complex brain functions rather than being an inexplicable gift. **"**

The Psychological Foundations of Creativity

While neuroscience helps us understand the physical basis of creativity in the brain, psychological research has revealed crucial insights into how creative thinking emerges and can be developed. Several key psychological frameworks help explain the creative process:

1. **Divergent and convergent thinking**
    Creative thinking involves divergent thinking (generating many possible solutions) and convergent thinking (evaluating and selecting the best solution). Research shows that individuals who can effectively switch between the two tend to be more creative.

2. **Cognitive flexibility**
   The ability to break free from established thinking patterns and adapt to new situations is crucial for creativity. This includes:
   - Breaking mental sets and overcoming functional fixedness
   - Making novel connections between seemingly unrelated concepts
   - Maintaining openness to new experiences and perspectives.
3. **Intrinsic motivation**
   Studies have consistently shown that intrinsic motivation—driven by personal interest and enjoyment rather than external rewards—leads to higher levels of creativity. This aligns with Amabile's componential theory discussed in Chapter 1.
4. **Psychological safety**
   The willingness to take creative risks is closely tied to feeling psychologically safe. In environments where failure is seen as a learning opportunity rather than a threat, individuals are more likely to explore creative solutions.
5. **Tolerance for ambiguity**
   This is one of the major predictors of creativity because it allows individuals to remain open to uncertainty, contradictions, and complexity, navigating unknowns and adjusting perspectives, risk taking, problem-solving in novel contexts, suspending judgement—all elements often inherent in the creative process.

The Spark that Ignited Research into Creativity

In 1950, J.P. Guilford, president of the American Psychological Association, articulated his vision for studying creativity in a speech before his fellow psychologists. His impassioned talk kick-started the field of creativity research. For half a century after, researchers added incrementally to its understanding, focusing on creative people's personality traits and the creative process's cognitive aspects.[1]

But it all changed in the twenty-first century. Advances in neuroimaging led to an explosion of research in which psychologists and neuroscientists discovered new details about creativity and embarked on a mission to find ways to develop this skill.[2] For neuroscientists, the way to encapsulate the essence of creativity was to look at what's happening inside the brain rather than focusing on the artistic output.

They found two brain regions that often collaborate in creativity: the Executive Control Network and the Default Mode Network. Recall that the former is responsible for goal-directed thinking and problem-solving, and the latter is active during rest, daydreaming, and mind-wandering, facilitating the free flow of thoughts.

The two work together to generate, evaluate, and refine creative ideas, ensuring they are original and practical. The Salience Network monitors internal and external stimuli to identify the most pertinent, facilitating transitions between the first two. It enables a balance between generating novel ideas and critically assessing them.

Neuroscientist Adam Green, founder of the Society for the Neuroscience of Creativity, found evidence that the brain's frontopolar cortex, in the frontal lobes, is linked to creative thinking. Moreover, a research paper he co-authored showed that stimulating this area enabled participants to make semantically distant analogies.[3] They became more creative. While the results were promising, no single brain region is responsible for creativity. It also differs by individual.

Carsten De Dreu's dual pathway model offers insight into how creativity emerges in the brain. This model identifies two complementary routes to creative outcomes: cognitive flexibility (the ability to switch between different ideas and perspectives) and cognitive persistence (the thorough exploration of a specific category or approach). Flexibility allows you to generate diverse ideas across multiple fields, and persistence allows you to develop ideas thoroughly within a single field. AI systems can strengthen both approaches. They support flexibility by exploring different conceptual areas quickly and persistence by conducting detailed analysis within specific domains.

Human cognitive strengths combined with AI capabilities create significant opportunities for creative collaboration. You bring the intuition and contextual understanding: AI brings the computational power and pattern recognition. Together, you can explore broader possibilities while also examining specific areas in greater depth.

Human + AI Creativity

Many of today's AI systems take a page from the human brain, mimicking its architecture through artificial neural networks (ANNs) that learn from vast datasets to generate creative content. Both ANNs and the human brain comprise networks of units—called neurons in the brain and nodes in ANNs—to process and transmit information. However, their structures and functions fundamentally differ in complexity, flexibility, and operation.

The human brain, at least for now, remains superior to AI. For example, we can learn new information by only seeing it once, whereas AI systems need to be trained many more times to learn the same information. Also, we can learn new information while retaining existing knowledge, whereas AI models may degrade older information once they learn new data. Humans possess a rich understanding of the world, including its physical laws, social norms, and causal relationships. AI models do not have this capability.

What makes the human brain so special? According to a paper from researchers at Oxford University's Department of Computer Science and the MRC Brain Network Dynamics Unit, the brain uses a fundamentally different learning principle from AI.[4] The brain first optimizes neuron activity into a balanced state before modifying connections, whereas the AI uses an external algorithm to adjust the synaptic connections to reduce errors. The brain's approach is more efficient by reducing interference and preserving existing knowledge, accelerating learning.[5]

By combining our brains' abilities and AI's neural networks, each can help the other innovate—the brain through its unique mix of intuition and emotion, and AI by processing data in volumes and speeds humans can't match.

Refreshing the Brain is a Must

But if AI is already doing such superb work so quickly on our behalf, why don't we give our brains a rest? Studies suggest that integrating AI tools into creative processes can significantly boost human creativity, surpassing people or AI acting alone.[6]

Here are some examples of effective human-AI creative collaboration:

First, consider architectural design. Architects can use AI to generate multiple design variations based on specific parameters like space requirements, building codes, and environmental factors. The human architect then applies aesthetic judgment, understanding of human needs, and cultural context to refine and customize these AI-generated options into a final design that is both functional and beautiful.

For example, Zaha Hadid Architects used parametric design and machine learning algorithms to create innovative and complex structures. Their work on the Shanghai Tower in China is a prime example. They tapped into AI to create a structure that has enhanced sustainability and structural integrity. The tower is known for energy efficiency, wind resistance, material selection, and construction management.[7]

Second, AI can analyze patterns from thousands of songs in music composition to suggest chord progressions or melodic phrases. The human composer then uses emotional intelligence and artistic sensibility to select, modify, and arrange these elements into a cohesive piece that resonates with listeners.

An example comes from Taryn Southern, an American singer-songwriter and the first pop star to compose and produce an album entirely through an AI, called 'I Am AI.' She used a combination of tools, including IBM's Watson Beat, Amper, AIVA, and Google Magenta. In all cases, AI software composed the notation, and when Amper was used, the AI also produced the instrumentation.[8]

We should add, however, that at the time of writing, there are copyright challenges surrounding AI-generated music. According to Louis Tompros, a Harvard Law expert, AI-generated music raises fundamental questions about authorship. The Copyright Office has determined that works created by AI without significant human intervention cannot receive copyright protection, as only humans qualify as "authors" under the Constitution. Yet the original artists face potential violations on two fronts: the "input" problem (copying works to train AI may infringe copyright) and the "output" problem (whether AI-generated works that mimic an artist's style constitute derivative works). Unlike sampling, which directly copies portions of original works, AI complicates matters by consuming entire catalogs but producing outputs with no directly copied material.[9] This suggests there is a need for the law to protect artists while allowing for technological advancements.

Recent research has extensively compared AI and human creativity, often through 'horse race' experiments where both attempt similar creative tasks. Studies have found that large language models can generate ideas that human evaluators rate equally or more creatively than those from human experts in marketing and product design. However, rather than viewing this as evidence for eventual human replacement, we see it as an opportunity for powerful collaboration. The most promising frontier is not AI or human creativity, but a hybrid creativity that leverages both strengths. Throughout this book, we explore how this partnership approach can elevate creative outcomes beyond what either humans or AI could achieve alone.

Third, in scientific research, AI can process vast amounts of data to identify potential patterns or relationships humans might miss. Scientists then apply their expertise to determine meaningful correlations, develop hypotheses to explain them, and design experiments to test their theories. This partnership between human insight and AI's processing power has led to breakthroughs from drug discovery to climate science.

A real-world example can be found in materials science, specifically in discovering new stable materials. In 2024, Google DeepMind developed an AI tool called Graph Networks for Materials Exploration (GNoME), which identified 380,000 stable materials at low temperatures. It was a task that would be incredibly time-consuming and potentially impossible for humans to do manually. Scientists then applied their knowledge to determine which AI-identified materials could have practical applications. They focused on materials that could enhance energy efficiency, improve materials science, and increase processing power.[10]

In this human-machine partnership, AI remains a tool you use; you drive the results. That means you must ensure your mind remains alert and nimble, able to think dynamically and flexibly. There are several techniques to practice mental agility. One comes from Michael Platt, professor of neuroscience, psychology, and marketing, and the director of the Wharton Neuroscience Initiative at the University of Pennsylvania.

> " **In this human-machine partnership, AI remains a tool you use; you drive the results.** "

Platt describes two mutually opposed networks in the brain. One supports task execution—getting the job done—and the other is for divergent thinking, or unconventional ideas. When one is turned way up, the other is muted, said Platt, one of 60 notable experts sharing their insights in a Coursera course[11] on creativity accompanying this book.

For example, entering numbers into a spreadsheet or responding to email can dial up the task execution part of the brain and suppress the creative side. For this reason, to spark a wave of innovation, it is vital to unplug from routine tasks to unleash creativity. "You just can't be creative when entering numbers into a spreadsheet," Platt said. "You've got to step back, allow yourself to disengage from these routine tasks to be creative."

It may also be true that the desire to overcome the tedium of routine tasks is the spark that ignites creativity. For example, the repetitive nature of data entry spurred the development of older forms of AI tools and Robotic Process Automation (RPA), which automates mundane tasks like form-filling and data validation.

Moreover, boredom with daily chores like adjusting thermostats or turning lights on and off inspired innovations like smart thermostats such as Nest and voice-controlled assistants like Alexa, which streamline routine household tasks. In addition, tedious training methods in education and professional development motivated the creation of gamified learning platforms. For example, language learning apps like Duolingo make acquiring new language skills engaging and enjoyable through game-like elements.

Platt said simple activities can help free your mind from routine thinking, like leaving your desk and going for a walk or moving around the office. It can unleash the brain's "innovation network and allow you to return to your work with a more creative state of mind."

Another technique is to take other people's perspectives—see a situation through their eyes. "Intriguingly, our innovative brains also overlap with part of our social brain network," according to Platt. "Perspective-taking is key to unlocking the creativity available in diverse teams, and diverse teams perform better than teams that are more homogeneous when people on those teams take the perspective of others."

Is It a Rock or a Paperweight?

A standard experiment to gauge creativity is the 'alternative uses test' in which one thinks of as many uses as possible for an everyday household object, such as a pencil. Platt said many people can come up with a dozen or so uses, but some of the most creative people he has met came up with far more. One was the chief marketing officer of Starbucks, who routinely came up with at least 30 uses for everyday objects.

Creativity is key to business success. "Multiple surveys have shown that more creative companies actually have greater market share and growth," Platt said. However, the challenge for companies is that "it is often tough to be creative," adding, "Being creative can be even more challenging when we're under stress."

> " Creativity is key to business success. "

That is why creating an environment that fosters creativity is also crucial. This includes reducing stress, promoting a positive mood, and providing opportunities for diverse experiences. Encouraging behaviors such as taking breaks, engaging in playful activities, and exposing oneself to new and varied stimuli can stimulate the neural pathways involved in creativity.

Beauty and Order

"Environmental factors such as aesthetics also play a key part in creativity. Beauty and order create a sense of wellness and enjoyment in the surroundings where creative minds can flourish. This is the realm of neuroaesthetics, the science of studying the biological basis of aesthetic experiences," said Anjan Chatterjee, founding director of the Penn Center for Neuroaesthetics, a professor of neurology, psychology, and architecture at the University of Pennsylvania, and a neurologist at its School of Medicine.

Chatterjee said that people spend 90% of their time in a world of constructed dwellings or infrastructure, which impacts their state of being. This 'built' space has three characteristics: *coherence*, *fascination*, and *hominess*. Coherence speaks to how organized or logical the space is laid out. Fascination pertains to the complexity of the space that invites one to explore. Hominess is the comfort factor of the built area. Each of these three serves its purpose to give rise to conditions conducive to creativity.

If your mind needs to wander creatively, head to an enjoyable environment. But move into a cohesive space to make those ideas concrete without distraction. The space should be homey and comfortable, a recipe for creativity and productivity. This indicates that there might be different spaces and places where various aspects of your work are better.

Chatterjee also advised being intentional about your surroundings when you're trying to be creative, whether you're in the thinking phase or application stage. "(People's) brains respond to these factors in their environment without even knowing about it."[12]

Beyond location, there is another way to immerse oneself in aesthetics: Gaze at art. "Savoring art slows us down," Chatterjee said. "It allows us to really focus on something that might be challenging, might be pleasurable, might be engaging in a way that could feel unexpected. ... Those are the kinds of things that shake us out of our normal space."[13]

The Case of Jackson Pollock

According to Thom Collins, the executive director and president of the Barnes Foundation, one of the most striking examples of creative transformation in art history comes from the renowned American painter Jackson Pollock's revolutionary shift in artistic expression to abstract expressionism. His journey illustrates how psychological insights and personal transformation can lead to groundbreaking creativity.

In the 1930s, Pollock participated in the Regionalist movement with his "Going West" painting, now in the Smithsonian American Art Museum. He depicted a heroic scene of the significant westward expansion in North America, using recognizable figures set in an illusionistic landscape.

The contrast between his early work "Going West" (1934-35) and his later abstract expressionist pieces like "Lavender Mist" (1950) is stark. "Going West" featured recognizable figures and traditional landscape elements, showing his early connection to regional American art. "Lavender Mist" abandoned all representation in favor of intricate webs of dripped paint, creating a dynamic field of color and movement that expressed pure emotional and psychological states.

Pollock's famous "drip painting" technique, developed in the late 1940s, was inspired by Ukrainian artist Janet Sobel[14] and represented a complete break from traditional painting methods. Instead of using an easel, he laid large canvases on the floor and moved around them, dripping and pouring paint in sweeping gestures. This radical approach emerged from his psychological exploration and engagement with Jungian analysis.

Pollock explored this technique in paintings such as "Number 14," where liquid enamel was applied to unprimed canvas in loose pours that entwine spontaneously produced, fragmented references to the human body, in abstract webs of black paint. Pollock's Jungian influence led him to create psychoanalytic drawings high in symbolism. But these symbolic forms would disappear entirely in the same decade.

"Pollock left symbolic forms derived from his unconsciousness in a quest for a more universal expression," resulting in "dynamic, energetic fields of paint" that were a "visual metaphor for human consciousness more broadly, now fully disordered by the traumas of mid-century."[15]

Five Lessons from Pollock

Concluding his discussion of Pollock, Collins suggests that the artist's journey offers five valuable lessons for creativity across fields:

1. *Embrace experimentation*: Pollock abandoned traditional brush techniques in favor of drip painting, demonstrating that breaking conventions can lead to groundbreaking discoveries. Innovation often comes from daring to try something radically new.
2. *Trust the process, not just the outcome*: His method of action painting emphasized the act of creation rather than just the final product. This teaches us that creativity thrives when focusing on the journey and allowing ideas to evolve organically.

3. *Harness chaos and serendipity*: Pollock's seemingly random drips and splatters were not entirely accidental; they reflected controlled spontaneity. Innovators can learn to use unpredictability as a tool rather than a hindrance.

4. *Go beyond perfectionism*: Pollock's work was not about precision but about raw expression. In creative and technological fields, perfectionism can sometimes stifle innovation. Letting go of rigid constraints can lead to unexpected breakthroughs.

5. *Dare to develop your method*: **Pollock's distinct style set him apart from his contemporaries. In any field, originality comes from developing a unique voice, method, or approach that distinguishes one's work.**

The evolving landscape of human creativity and AI collaboration reminds us of the boundless potential that emerges when we combine the best of both worlds. Neuroscience reveals that creativity thrives in the intricate dance between our brain's networks, fostering innovative thinking and artistic expression. By embracing AI as a complementary force, we unlock new avenues for imagination and problem-solving.

i Exercise

Think about a recent creative activity you engaged in, such as writing, drawing, or problem-solving. Reflect on how each brain network might have contributed to this process. Try to remember where you were when you performed these creative tasks. Write down your reflections, noting how understanding these brain functions and environments can help you enhance your creative processes.

In Summary

1. Your Brain Is Wired for Creativity.
The Default Mode Network generates novel ideas during mind-wandering, the Executive Control Network evaluates and refines them, and the Salience Network balances between both. This scientific foundation means creativity can be developed.

What would change in your creative process if you intentionally gave yourself time to generate wild ideas and critically assess them?

2. Your environment directly impacts your creative capacity.
Spaces with coherence help you focus, fascination encourages exploration, and hominess provides comfort. Be strategic about where you create—switch environments based on whether you're brainstorming or refining ideas.

How might you redesign your workspace to serve different phases of your creative process better?

In Summary (contd.)

---

3. Step Away to Spark Forward.

Your brain struggles to be creative during repetitive work. Simple acts like walking or changing perspectives activate the brain's creative regions.

When did you last have a breakthrough idea while doing something completely unrelated to your work?

4. Human-AI partnerships amplify creativity beyond what either can achieve alone.

From architectural design to music composition, humans provide emotional intelligence and context while AI processes massive datasets at incredible speeds.

How could you leverage AI as a creative partner rather than just a tool?

5. True innovation emerges when you dare to break conventions.

Just as Jackson Pollock abandoned traditional techniques for his revolutionary drip painting method, breakthroughs come from experimentation and trusting the creative process over perfectionism.

What creative "rules" might you need to break to discover your unique approach?

Now that we have learned that anyone can harness their inner creativity, our next chapter looks at how you can utilize AI for a "superpower" edge.

Notes

[1] Kirsten Weir. "The Science Behind Creativity," *Monitor on Psychology* 53, no. 3 (April 1, 2022), American Psychological Association. https://www.apa.org/monitor/2022/04/cover-science-creativity

[2] Ibid.

[3] Adam E. Green, Katherine A. Spiegel, Evan J. Giangrande, Adam B. Weinberger, Natalie M. Gallagher, and Peter E. Turkeltaub. "Thinking Cap Plus Thinking Zap: tDCS of Frontopolar Cortex Improves Creative Analogical Reasoning and Facilitates Conscious Augmentation of State Creativity in Verb Generation," *Cerebral Cortex* 27, no. 4 (April 2017): 2628–2639, published April 13, 2016. https://doi.org/10.1093/cercor/bhw080

[4] University of Oxford. "Study Shows that the Way the Brain Learns Is Different from the Way that Artificial Intelligence Systems Learn," January 3, 2024. https://www.ox.ac.uk/news/2024-01-03-study-shows-way-brain-learns-different-way-artificial-intelligence-systems-learn

[5] Yuhang Song, Beren Millidge, Tommaso Salvatori, Thomas Lukasiewicz, Zhenghua Xu, and Rafal Bogacz. "Inferring Neural Activity before Plasticity as a Foundation for Learning beyond Backpropagation," *Nature Neuroscience*, January 3, 2024. https://www.nature.com/articles/s41593-023-01514-1

[6] Jennifer Haase and Sebastian Pokutta. "Human-AI Co-Creativity: Exploring Synergies Across Levels of Creative Collaboration." arXiv preprint, October 2024, accessed February 26, 2025. https://arxiv.org/html/2411.12527v1.

[7] Ricardo Eloy. "AI in Architecture: 7 Benefits and Examples," Enscape Blog, last modified February 12, 2025, https://blog.enscape3d.com/ai-in-architecture.

[8] Barbican Centre. "12 Songs Created by AI," Google Arts & Culture, accessed March 4, 2025, https://artsandculture.google.com/story/12-songs-created-by-ai-barbican-centre/VwVhbAD7QslgLA?hl=en

[9] Rachel Reed, Harvard Law Today. "AI Created a Song Mimicking the Work of Drake and The Weeknd. What Does that Mean for Copyright Law?" May 2, 2023, accessed April 4 2025, https://hls.harvard.edu/today/ai-created-a-song-mimicking-the-work-of-drake-and-the-weeknd-what-does-that-mean-for-copyright-law/

[10] Softude. "10 Exciting Breakthroughs in Artificial Intelligence," Softude Blog, December 27, 2024. https://www.softude.com/blog/exciting-breakthroughs-in-artificial-intelligence.

[11] Michael Platt. "The Leader's Brain: Enhance Your Leadership, Build Stronger Teams, Make Better Decisions, and Inspire Greater Innovation with Neuroscience" (Wharton School Press 2020). Also in the Coursera course *Creativity in Business and Other Disciplines*, Lesson 1.

[12] Anjun Chatterjee, Interview, Venetian Letters. "We Are Constantly Responding to Our Environment Without being Aware of it", accessed April 4 2025. https://venetianletter.com/2023/06/23/anjan-chatterjee-we-are-constantly-responding-to-our-environment-without-being-aware-of-it/

[13] Ibid.

[14] Noah Charney. *Brushed Aside—The Untold Story of Women in Art* (Rowan and Littlefield, 2023).

[15] Matthew Rampley. "Identity and Difference: Jackson Pollock and the Ideology of the Drip," *JSTOR*, Vol. 19, No. 2 (1996), pp. 83–94 (12 pages), accessed May 13, 2025. https://www.jstor.org/stable/1360731

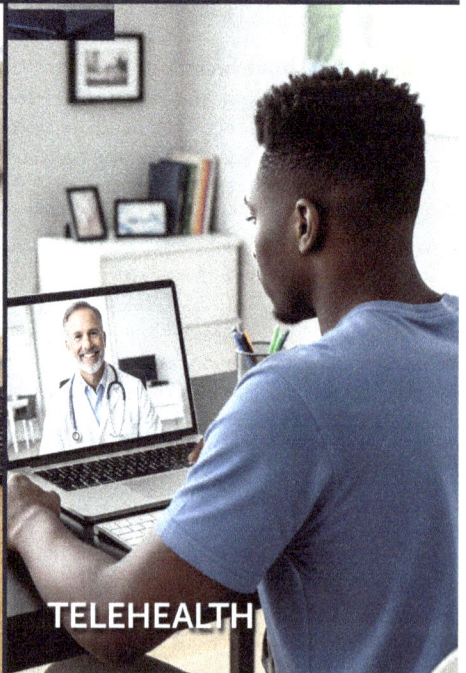

Chapter 3
How AI Can Give You Creative Superpowers

Artificial intelligence is not a substitute for human intelligence;
It is a tool to amplify human creativity and ingenuity.
—Fei-Fei Li, AI pioneer and Stanford professor

A traveler with plans to visit Tuscany, Italy, is looking for guidebooks to the region. Which book cover summary would be the most enticing?

1. *The Tuscan countryside is a captivating blend of natural beauty and timeless charm, where rolling hills stretch as far as the eye can see, draped in shades of green, gold, and terracotta. Vineyards and olive groves dot the landscape, their neat rows interrupted by rustic farmhouses and cypress trees that stand like sentinels against the sky. As the light shifts throughout the day, the hills take on a magical glow, from the soft pastels of dawn to the warm, honeyed hues of sunset. Amid this picturesque setting, small medieval villages perch on hilltops, offering breathtaking views and a taste of Tuscany's rich history and culture.*[1]

2. *The Tuscan countryside of Italy is a magical escape that promises beauty and tranquility for any visitor. Beyond its breathtaking vistas, the region is also home to some of the world's most renowned wines, such as quality-certified DOCGs Chianti Classico, Brunello di Montalcino, Nobile di Montepulciano, and Bolgheri. Explore the medieval churches and art museums of its capital city, Florence; wander through historic towns such as Siena and Pisa, home of the Leaning Tower, for a breathtaking experience.*

3. *Fall in love with Tuscany, Italy, with its captivating blend of natural beauty and timeless charm, where rolling hills stretch as far as the eye can see, draped in shades of green, gold, and terracotta. Vineyards and olive groves dot the landscape, their neat rows interrupted by rustic farmhouses and cypress trees that stand like sentinels against the sky. Beyond its breathtaking vistas, the region is also home to some of the world's most renowned wines, such as quality-certified DOCGs Chianti Classico, Brunello di Montalcino, Nobile di Montepulciano, and Bolgheri. Explore the medieval churches and art museums of its capital city, Florence; wander through historic towns such as Siena and Pisa, home of the Leaning Tower, for a magical experience.*

Which was the most enticing summary addressing the traveler's needs? The first was full of flowery words but didn't say much about the region. Without the words 'Tuscan' or 'Tuscany,' it could be describing Napa Valley, California, or another picturesque countryside. The words sound good, but ultimately lack relevance to the traveler.[2]

The second description was much more helpful, giving visitors ideas of what to do: wine-tasting, enjoying the architecture and museums of Florence, and gazing at the Leaning Tower of Pisa. But the description of Tuscany's magical landscapes could be more artistic and imaginative. The third description blends the best of the first two: It was eloquently imaginative and proactively functional, mindful that its reader is a traveler.

As you might have guessed by now, the first one was written by ChatGPT (GPT-4o version, among the most powerful GPT large language models to date[3]). The second was written by a human writer, and the third was a blend of both. This exercise brings home two big truths about using AI for creativity: First, AI does a terrific job if you give it clear and explicit directions, but your instructions constrain its output. Second, humans do a good job, but a little AI augmentation can go a long way.

There is empirical proof: A March 2024 paper from Boston University researchers found that artists who augment their artwork by using text-to-image AI models like Stable Diffusion, Midjourney, or DALL-E showed a 25% increase in producing artworks on average and a 50% increase in favorable peer reviews by the sixth month. The study, published in Oxford University's PNAS Nexus, used a dataset of over 4 million artworks from 50,000 unique artists.[4]

And yet, for all the amazing things AI can do, experts believe it cannot fully replace human creativity and ingenuity in many fields. In advertising, for example, "big ideas are born from a deep understanding of the hearts, minds and wallets of consumers. Would AI have come up with 'Just Do It' or 'Got Milk?' Can AI think differently? I'm not so sure," according to a member of the Forbes Expert Panel.[5]

AI as Collaborator, Not Replacer

Despite widespread concerns about AI replacing human creativity, the MIT Technology Review Special Issue on Creativity[6] suggests that viewing AI as a creative collaborator is more productive. Technological advances—from oil paints to digital recording—have expanded creative possibilities throughout history without diminishing human

> **The key to artistic achievement is how artists apply technology to express our humanity.**

contribution. As the publication notes, "The key to artistic achievement has never been the technology itself. It has been how artists have applied it to express our humanity."

This collaborative framework reframes the human-AI relationship from competition to partnership. Instead of questioning whether AI possesses "true creativity," we might better consider how it enhances human creativity while maintaining authenticity and meaning. Just as photography created new artistic possibilities rather than replacing painting, AI tools offer novel creative avenues that still require human direction, curation, and purpose.

Adding Constructive Friction to AI-Human Creativity

While commercial AI tools often promise effortless creativity, researchers and artists are discovering value in deliberate friction within AI creative processes. MIT Technology Review documents creative professionals "finding new ways to make art using AI, by injecting friction, challenge, and serendipity into the process."

This approach counters the frictionless convenience that dominates AI marketing narratives. For instance, live coder Lizzie Wilson embraces instances where the technology doesn't perform as expected, considering these moments integral to the creative process. Some artists even explore intentionally challenging relationships with AI, creating performances where humans and machines engage in creative tension.

Design researcher Elisa Giaccardi poses a fundamental question that encapsulates this thinking: "How can we engage in a truly creative process without material that pushes back?"[7] This perspective suggests that meaningful human-AI collaboration requires not just automation but productive resistance and dialogue—elements historically characterized by creative breakthroughs.

Reflection as Critical to AI-Enhanced Creativity

MIT Technology Review highlights reflection as essential to the creative process—a "particular type of focused, deliberate thinking" that occurs when new ideas emerge or assumptions prove incorrect. This reflective component represents the opposite of the instantaneous interactions that characterize many commercial AI tools.

Researchers studying co-creativity are exploring how AI might support reflection by introducing new perspectives or challenging existing assumptions. This approach intentionally adds complexity to human-AI interaction rather than simplifying it. The goal is to develop AI tools that augment human creativity by pushing people to achieve greater heights in music composition, game development, design, and numerous other fields.

This reflective approach offers a more nuanced vision than mainstream generative tools now provide. While existing platforms can produce impressive results, they risk turning humans into passive consumers without the engagement that meaningful reflection fosters. By incorporating reflection into AI-human creative processes, we maintain the essential human elements that give creative work depth and significance.

The Homogenization Risk

As AI becomes increasingly involved in creative processes, MIT Technology Review identifies a potential concern: the homogenization of creative output. Research on AI-assisted writing found that AI-generated content tends to be less distinctive than purely human-created work, as AI models can only draw from their training data.

This effect raises essential questions about creative diversity in an AI-augmented future. If creative industries broadly adopt generative AI, cultural products might become increasingly similar because they would emerge from models trained on similar datasets. Publishing, for example, could lead to increasingly formulaic and derivative works.

This homogenization risk extends across disciplines. As generative models proliferate in music, visual arts, architecture, and other fields, we may witness a narrowing of creative expression unless we deliberately cultivate diversity in AI training data and human-AI collaboration methods. Understanding and addressing this risk represents a crucial challenge as we integrate AI into creative workflows.

How AI Enhances Creativity

AI tools for creativity broadly fall into three functional categories that mirror different phases of the creative process:

AI for Ideation: These tools help generate the initial sparks of inspiration. They include brainstorming assistants suggesting novel concepts, pattern-recognition systems identifying unexpected connections, and prompt-based generators responding to 'what if' scenarios. For example, writers might use Claude[8] to explore different narrative directions, while product designers might use Midjourney to visualize multiple concept variations in minutes rather than days.

AI for Synthesis: These tools help organize, analyze, and combine existing information into meaningful patterns. They excel at summarizing research, identifying themes across datasets, and connecting seemingly disparate ideas. Marketers might use Perplexity[9] and GPT-4[10] to identify emerging customer sentiment patterns across thousands of reviews, while researchers might use it to discover unexpected connections between studies in different fields.

AI for Prototyping: These tools accelerate the creation of drafts, mockups, and testable versions of creative work. Design platforms with generative capabilities can transform rough sketches into polished visuals, while code-generation tools can turn functional descriptions into working prototypes. This rapid prototyping allows creators to test more iterations and refine ideas based on concrete feedback rather than abstract speculation.

But how exactly can AI help? It all depends on what you want to do. Here are a few examples of its capabilities that can give you the creative boost you need to embark on higher levels of creativity.

- **Inspiration and idea generation:** By analyzing troves of data, AI can generate unique concepts or create unexpected connections between diverse concepts to fuel inspiration.[11]
- **Textual creativity:** AI-generated text prompts can kickstart ideas in writers and poets, serving as springboards for narratives.

- **Visual exploration:** AI-generated images and videos can act as catalysts for new creations. These algorithmic creations can also be incorporated into an artist's work.
- **Music composition:** Musicians can use AI to compose melodies, harmonies, or entire pieces of music. AI can also analyze existing compositions to yield new ideas for music genres and styles.
- **Rapid prototyping:** AI can generate design variations considering user preferences, functionality, and manufacturing limitations to enable fast prototyping without extensive manual input.[12]
- **Collaborative tool:** AI enables team collaboration beyond communication and file sharing. It leverages machine learning, natural language processing, and predictive analytics to provide insights, automate routine tasks, and facilitate decision-making.[13]
- **Personalization:** AI can analyze customer data to understand their preferences and behaviors to create personalized products, services, recommendations, and messaging.
- **Augmenting skill sets:** Generative AI augments the capabilities of less skilled workers by making expert knowledge available in real-time during task execution.[14]

Will AI Enhance YOUR Creativity?

After learning about AI's impressive creative capabilities, you might wonder: "This sounds amazing, but will it help ME become more creative?" The answer depends partly on your current creative confidence level, and the research reveals some fascinating insights about how AI affects different people.

A groundbreaking study in Science Advances, which MIT Technology Review reported on, offers an intriguing perspective on AI's impact on creativity: it appears to produce a "leveling effect," significantly boosting the output of less creative individuals while offering more modest benefits to those already highly creative.[15]

In a comprehensive study of AI-assisted creative writing using OpenAI's GPT-4, researchers found that participants with access to AI assistance demonstrated enhanced creativity overall. However, the most significant improvements occurred among participants who initially scored lower on creativity metrics, while those already highly creative showed more modest improvement with AI assistance. As researcher Anil Doshi observes, "We see this leveling effect where the least creative writers get the biggest benefit."[2]

What This Means for You

This leveling effect has profound implications for how you can harness AI in your creative work:

If you've always felt "not naturally creative": AI can be transformational for you. The technology appears to provide the biggest boost to people who struggle with initial idea generation or feel blocked by blank page syndrome. AI can serve as your creative training wheels, helping you build confidence and skills that will serve you even without technological assistance.

If you already consider yourself highly creative: AI won't replace your unique perspective, but it can still enhance your process in meaningful ways. Use it to:

- Rapidly prototype and iterate on ideas
- Explore variations you might not have considered
- Handle routine creative tasks so you can focus on higher-level innovation
- Serve as a creative sparring partner to refine your best concepts

The key insight: Rather than replacing human creativity entirely or enhancing it uniformly, AI functions as an equalizing force that raises the creative baseline. The result is a democratization of creative capacity, with AI helping more people achieve competent creative expression, while highly creative individuals continue to provide distinctive perspectives that AI alone cannot replicate.

> " Rather than replacing human creativity entirely or enhancing it uniformly, AI functions as an equalizing force that raises the creative baseline. "

Practical Applications

Understanding this leveling effect can help with:

1. **Building confidence:** If creativity feels intimidating, start with AI-assisted brainstorming to generate initial momentum, then build from there.
2. **For experienced creators:** Use AI strategically for specific tasks rather than wholesale creative generation—let it handle research, variations, or technical execution while you focus on vision and direction.
3. **For teams:** Leverage AI to ensure everyone can contribute meaningfully to creative processes, regardless of their starting confidence level.

The most significant creative potential lies not in surrendering creativity to machines, but in thoughtfully integrating AI's capabilities with human insight, judgment, and purpose. As we'll see in the following examples, the magic happens when human vision guides AI capabilities toward meaningful outcomes.

Artists, Coca-Cola, and AI

To understand how AI can enhance creativity in marketing, Pagani and Wind's paper examined how machines and humans interact. They conducted two studies: One looked at the practices of creative people, specifically artists, who use generative AI (to create new content) and non-generative AI (to analyze and understand existing content, such as image recognition) in their creations. The second scrutinized how AI systems enhanced the creativity of their users.

Why study artists? Artists are known for pushing creative boundaries and coming up with creative ideas. "Understanding this creative process among artists provides marketers with valuable insights, enabling them to foster a mindset that goes beyond the ordinary and drives innovation," they wrote.

Artists also produce thought-provoking content that challenges societal norms, which could lead to shifts in the culture. Pagani and Wind said marketers can learn from this approach to promote products and services and "engage in meaningful culture dialogues."

They cited Coca-Cola's Real Magic Creative Academy as an example of boundary-pushing efforts. It brings together digital artists, tech firms, and fashion brands to harness AI and create innovative advertisements. Artists who introduced new paradigms or approaches left a lasting impact. Similarly, "truly creative marketers are those who challenge and reshape the status quo," the two authors wrote.

Artists' creative processes often mirror marketers' efforts, offering valuable insights into capturing attention, evoking emotions, and fostering brand loyalty. Since artists increasingly use AI, studying their approaches can teach marketers valuable lessons as they look to integrate AI into their creative flows.

The authors discovered that artists employed AI due to curiosity and for problem-solving. They saw AI as a versatile tool to address artistic challenges and fuel exploration. The paper found that AI plays three major roles in the creative process:

1. **Generative AI as a new resource for technological exploration and artistic expression**
   For example, asking ChatGPT to develop a recipe that infuses Thai flavors into a classic French dish resulted in this entree: Thai-Inspired Coq au Vin. Instead of the traditional wine-based sauce, the dish uses Thai aromatics, coconut milk, and spices for a cross-cultural twist.

2. **Generative AI as a catalyst for imaginative thinking and expanding creative horizons**
   AI can spark divergent thinking by combining things with no apparent connection. For example, ChatGPT was asked to develop business ideas for an aspiring entrepreneur who just finished welding school, loves baking, and lives in Texas. Here are some of the results:

   > **AI is a catalyst for imaginative thinking and expanding creative horizons. Is the human brain superior to AI?**

   - Artisanal metal bakeware: Design and craft custom metal bakeware like cookie cutters, cake molds, and decorative baking tools. Your baking experience can guide you in creating functional and creative products that appeal to amateur and professional bakers.

- Metal art bakery café: Open a boutique café that doubles as a gallery for your metal artwork. Decorate the space with your metal sculptures and offer your own baked goods. This creates a unique ambiance that combines culinary and visual arts.
- Custom cake toppers and event decor: Use your welding skills to create bespoke metal cake toppers, centerpieces, and decorative items for weddings and special events. Your attractive presentation can help in client consultations and event showcases.
- Metalwork for culinary spaces: Offer services to design and fabricate custom metal installations for restaurants and bakeries, such as signage, shelving, and decorative elements. Your understanding of baking environments can help you create practical designs.
- Personalized gifts and keepsakes: Create custom metal gift items like engraved plaques, ornaments, or kitchenware. Offer personalization options to make them special for occasions such as weddings, anniversaries, and corporate events.

3. **Non-generative AI as a tool to help artists understand and deconstruct their creative processes, leading to deeper insights into how creativity happens**

   AI can serve as a sounding board for your creative ideas. For example, AI assistant Claude critiqued business ideas for our welder and baker:

   - Artisanal metal bakeware
     Pros: Combines both skills, unique product offering, potential for online sales.
     Cons: Competition from mass-produced items, potential liability issues
     Feasibility: High. This idea directly utilizes both skill sets and has good market potential

   - Metal art bakery café
     Pros: Unique concept, showcases both talents.
     Cons: High initial investment, complex operations (food service + art gallery)
     Feasibility: Medium. While appealing, it requires significant capital and management skills.

   - Custom cake toppers and event decor
     Pros: High-margin products, growing wedding industry in Texas
     Cons: Seasonal demand, competition from 3D printing
     Feasibility: High. Low startup costs; aligns well with her skills

- Metalwork for culinary spaces
  Pros: High-value contracts, B2B opportunities.
  Cons: Requires networking in the restaurant industry, potential for large, complex projects
  Feasibility: Medium. Good potential, but may require more experience and industry connections

- Personalized gifts and keepsakes
  Pros: Wide market appeal, potential for online sales.
  Cons: Competitive market, may require additional equipment
  Feasibility: High. Good potential for local and online markets

In the second study, Pagani and Wind looked at how AI systems can enhance the creativity of their users. They considered two datasets: AI systems (e.g., Siri and Alexa) and AI models (e.g., ChatGPT). Then, they grouped these into four clusters based on their usefulness and novelty and found three levels of creativity from the four clusters: low, mixed, and high. The paper carefully distinguished between the use of generative and non-generative AI.

The two studies resulted in a framework illustrating three ways AI impacts marketing creativity.

- *Inspire agile methods*: AI streamlines routine tasks, enhances decision-making, and allows marketers to focus on higher-level creative strategy.
  Examples: Delta Air Lines and Walmart use AI for real-time price adjustments based on market conditions.

- *Augment the human creative process*: AI enhances creativity by uncovering new patterns, generating novel ideas, and acting as a creative assistant.
  Example: Zalando uses AI to analyze fashion trends and generate new clothing designs based on customer preferences.

- *Inspire out-of-the-box thinking*: AI challenges conventional thinking and enables marketers to explore bold, unconventional ideas that may not seem possible through traditional methods.
  Example: Nike's AI-designed sneakers let customers create one-of-a-kind designs based on their preferences.

Airbus: A GenAI Case Study

Another example from the corporate trenches comes from Airbus. The European airline manufacturer has a small team of engineers dubbed the 'crazy guys' for their boundary-pushing ideas. Officially called the Emerging Technologies and Concepts group, this team's job is to make their company's innovative visions for the future of commercial aircraft a reality.[16]

The team took on the challenge of designing a cabin partition that is lightweight yet incredibly strong for more eco-friendly planes and would separate the passenger area from the galley in the Airbus A320 cabin. The new partition had to be much lighter than existing ones, be strong enough to anchor two jump seats for flight attendants, have a cutout to pass wide items in and out of the cabin, be at most one inch thick, and be attached to the plane's airframe in just four places. It also needed to meet strict parameters for weight, stress and displacement in case of a crash with a force of 16G. Meeting these design constraints required a significant departure from traditional engineering approaches.[17]

Airbus worked with Autodesk Research to use generative design to develop the 'bionic partition.' Generative design is a technology that mimics nature's evolutionary approach to design. It starts with design goals and explores all the possible permutations to find the best option. This method can cycle through thousands or millions of design choices, testing configurations, and learning from each iteration. "The process lets designers generate new options, beyond what a human alone could create."[18]

To optimize the structural skeleton of the partition, the team developed generative design algorithms that cycled through 10,000 design options. They finally landed on natural growth patterns: slime mold and mammal bones. Slime mold is a single-cell organism that connects multiple points with uncanny efficiency. Meanwhile, the grid structure of mammal bone growth comprises dense points of stress but lighter everywhere else.[19]

After many tries, the final design was a latticed structure that looks random but is optimized to be strong and light, using the least number of materials to build. The result was a 45% lighter partition than those used on Airbus. It was also thinner and stronger.

Consider how music producer Holly Herndon incorporates AI into her workflow. Rather than viewing AI as a replacement, she co-developed an AI system called 'Holly+' that was trained on her vocal patterns. This allows her to create vocal elements that would be physically impossible for a human to sing, while maintaining her distinctive artistic voice. She handles the creative direction, emotional expression, and final editing, using AI as an extension of her artistic toolkit rather than a substitute for her judgment. This collaborative approach exemplifies how creative professionals can leverage AI to expand possibilities while maintaining their essential creative role.

The acceleration of these capabilities is remarkable. Wharton professor Ethan Mollick noted that tasks that took an AI system half an hour to complete in early 2023—generating a product idea, creating a comprehensive marketing strategy, designing a landing page, and drafting social media posts—can now be accomplished in under a minute.[20] This dramatic compression of the creative timeline doesn't eliminate the need for human creativity, but it does fundamentally change how we allocate our creative energy.

Artificially Intelligent

How can AI perform with such uncanny ability? To answer the question, we first have to understand what it is. We have to go back to when and where it started.

AI is a branch of computer science in which machines seek to mimic human intelligence. While its philosophical roots can be traced back centuries, the first truly substantive work in AI came from British computer pioneer Alan Turing in 1936 when he developed the concept of a universal computing machine capable of simulating any algorithmic process. These are now known as universal Turing machines, paving the way for machines operating on and modifying their instructions. Today's computers are essentially universal Turing machines.[21] In 1950, he developed the 'Turing Test' to measure whether a machine could convincingly mimic human conversation.

Computer scientists have attempted to put these theories into practice. In 1956, computer scientist John McCarthy named these efforts artificial intelligence. But it would be decades later when AI's power became clear to the public: In 1996, IBM's 'Deep Blue' supercomputer played against world chess champion Garry Kasparov in a 6-game match—it lost 4–2. The following year, IBM upgraded Deep Blue and beat Kasparov 3.5–2.5.

This was a seminal moment in AI. Deep Blue became the first computer program to defeat a world chess champion.[22] To beat Kasparov, it used 'brute force' computing power where 32 processors performed coordinated, high-speed computations in parallel to evaluate 200 million chess positions per second. Deep Blue's 'brute force' approach differs from machine learning, a subfield of AI in which the computer learns to play strategically independently from examples, with or without human help. This technique was behind the victory of AlphaGo in 2016 against Lee Sedol, who became the world champion in the strategy game of Go.[23]

From the 1950s to today, decades have passed between major AI breakthroughs. These so-called 'AI winters' occurred from 1974 to 1980 and 1987 to 1994 when funding, research, and investment declined because AI didn't live up to the hype, there wasn't enough computing power, and data and storage options were more limited.[24]

ChatGPT and Other Generative AI Models

The generative AI models we use today—such as ChatGPT, Claude, Gemini, DeepSeek, DALL-E, Stable Diffusion, Runway, and others—result from several key developments, particularly in deep learning and neural network architectures. Many of the most prominent generative AI models rely on neural network architectures that, while inspired by the brain's structure, are most effective at learning

> " Where traditional AI is usually domain-specific and rigid, generative AI is highly adaptive. "

and capturing complex patterns in data. (Geoffrey Hinton, who won a Nobel Prize in Physics in October 2024, pioneered a key algorithm to train neural networks.)

After Deep Blue and AlphaGo, the next public seminal moment in AI arrived in November 2022 with the launch of the generative AI model ChatGPT by OpenAI. It quickly went viral: Within two months, it attracted 100 million users, at the time, setting a record for the fastest growth in monthly active users in history.[25]

Generative AI caught people's imagination because of its apparent creativity. It can take a text, voice instruction, or prompt to generate new text or images, audio, video, 3D, and code unlike traditional or narrow AI that performs specific tasks based on pre-set rules, such as playing chess and nothing else, generative AI harnesses data, machine learning and deep learning models to create something novel. Where traditional AI is usually domain-specific and rigid, generative AI is highly adaptive.[26]

Generative AI uses algorithms to scour humongous datasets, such as the internet, and learns how words or groupings of words connect. For example, the word grouping 'hello, how are' often precedes 'you?' These implicit connections become patterns that the generative AI model remembers. Soon, these patterns become implied rules that the model can apply to a new set of data—a process called inference. Large language models, or LLMs, are foundation AI models.

These LLMs are said to be 'pre-trained' on a general dataset's implicit rules. When training is finished, the AI model is ready for inference. However, these general-purpose generative AI models are often not as applicable for the specific needs of an industry or company. That is when these models are retrained, or fine-tuned, on industry- or company-specific data so they can be customized. For example, they can be fine-tuned on financial data, which is the case with the BloombergGPT large language model.

More recently, LLMs have added multimodal capabilities—meaning they can analyze audio, video, and images—and generate the same. However, they are still LLMs with added modes. Some models are natively multimodal, meaning they were built from the ground up to be that way instead of bolting on new capabilities. Google's Gemini is an example of a natively multimodal AI model.

As of this writing, the latest developments in AI models include several significant advances. In February 2025, China's Alibaba unveiled its Qwen 2.5-Max model, claiming it matches or exceeds OpenAI's top-of-the-line GPT-4o across most tasks.[27] DeepSeek, another Chinese AI company, released its R1 reasoning model, which excels at logical reasoning and can solve complex math problems step by step.[28] Other models of note include Grok 3, Claude 3.7 Sonnet, Gemini 2.0, Amazon Nova, and more. A major open-source contender is Meta's Llama family, with improved voice capabilities reportedly coming in Llama 4. French open-source AI startup Mistral has released Mistral OCR 25.03 for document understanding and optical character recognition.

Meanwhile, OpenAI has continued to advance its GPT models to 4.5. It will be the last non-reasoning model from the startup. Months before, it introduced a reasoning model called OpenAI o1, which pauses to reason before answering prompts, aiming to minimize inaccurate answers or hallucinations, the tendency to make things up.[29]

Developers of AI models moved to reasoning to extend the effects of AI scaling laws, which have been slowing down. Previously, the more data a model is trained on, the more capable it becomes. But the pace of advancement has been slowing down. Developers found that other techniques, like making the model go through chain-of-thought reasoning, revive the pace of advancements in AI models. These developments signal a growing focus on enhancing AI's reasoning capabilities, moving beyond simple pattern recognition to more sophisticated analytical thinking.

GPT-5 represents a fundamental shift in AI capability, moving from a tool that requires careful prompting to one that autonomously takes initiative and executes complex tasks. According to Ethan Mollick, a professor of management at the Wharton School and author of the "One Useful Thing" Substack, GPT-5's most significant advancement lies not just in its intelligence, but in its ability to "just do stuff"—automatically selecting appropriate models for different tasks, taking creative initiative, and managing multi-step execution without constant human guidance. The system demonstrates remarkable sophistication by automatically switching between different underlying models based on task complexity, eliminating the common user frustration of selecting the right AI tool for the job. Perhaps most importantly, GPT-5 addresses the second major barrier to AI adoption by proactively suggesting and executing additional relevant tasks, transforming the AI experience from reactive response to proactive collaboration. This shift from passive tool to active agent suggests we are entering a new phase of human-AI interaction where the technology doesn't just answer questions but anticipates needs and takes meaningful action.

Enterprises are increasingly adopting AI agents, software programs that leverage LLMs to do multi-step tasks for users or another system. They can learn, adapt, and make decisions independently. A human employee can have a team of AI agents collect and analyze data, automate workflows, manage projects, and perform other tasks. Instead of simply assisting you, agents can work alongside you or even on your behalf. They can also be tailored to have a particular expertise.[30]

Since generative AI models are probabilistic instead of deterministic, meaning they generate outputs based on likelihoods rather than fixed rules, they can be wildly creative and flexible but also hallucinatory. Moreover, since models are trained on data from the entire internet, they learn from biased and toxic content. Developers use various techniques to mitigate these harms, such as integrating fact-checking systems, but hallucinations continue to be a problem as of this writing.

Privacy is also an issue. Whatever information is fed into a publicly available generative AI model is no longer private. However, for those who want to use AI to help unleash their creativity, these drawbacks are less of an issue because generative AI is a tool to spark novel ideas. The only caveat is not to share proprietary information through public chatbots.

AI Tools for Creativity

There is an ocean of AI tools available sparked by the ChatGPT craze. Note that many of these tools don't train their own models from scratch—a process that can be costly. Instead, they access pre-trained foundation models through APIs to save on costs and development time. APIs let them tap into the capabilities of large models without needing to develop them in-house. Companies that offer customized AI tools, such as for grammar checking, often integrate other computing techniques and optimizations to deliver more precise results tailored to specific tasks.

Here are some of the most popular general-purpose AI chatbots:

1. ChatGPT from OpenAI
2. Gemini from Google
3. Claude from Anthropic
4. Meta AI from Meta
5. Microsoft Copilot (formerly Bing Chat)
6. Perplexity

Except for Microsoft and Perplexity, these companies have developed their own pre-trained, foundation LLMs. (Microsoft, as a major investor in OpenAI, uses its models.) Only Meta's LLM is open source, meaning it can be used or modified freely, subject to the type of license it adopted. Meta's LLM is the Llama family of models, free for academics, researchers, developers, and businesses, unless they have more than 700 million monthly active users. Presumably, this is to prevent Meta's social media competitors like TikTok from using its LLMs.[31] The remaining AI models are proprietary.

All but Meta AI offer paid, premium versions of their AI. Meta AI is free for individuals and businesses, but the latter might need to open a business account. Premium versions are faster, more intelligent, offer more capabilities, and can take in more inputs (depending on the size of their context window) compared to free versions. Context window sizes are expressed in tokens; a token is the whole or part of a word, image, video, audio, or code. A thousand tokens are roughly 750 words.

Another peculiarity about language models is that unless they can access the internet, their information is only as good as the last date of their training data. When ChatGPT was first released, the knowledge cutoff date of its underlying LLM (GPT-3.5) was September 2021. At the time of writing, several gen AI models can access the internet.[32]

A quick summary of their capabilities is presented in Table 3.1.[33] Test a few to see which one suits your needs.

Table 3.1: AI Chatbot Plans Offered to Users and Developers (as of February 15, 2025)

PLAN	ChatGPT	Gemini	Claude	Microsoft Copilot	Meta AI	Perplexity
Text	√	√	√	√	√	√
Audio	Advanced Voice Mode (Plus subscribers)	√	√	√	√	No
Video	Not directly	√	√	√	√	√
Images	DALL-E integration (Plus subscribers)	√	√	√	√	√
Context window	Up to 8k tokens or 6,000 words (Plus); 4K or 3,000 words (free)	Up to 128k tokens or 96,000 words (Pro); undisclosed (free)	Up to 200k tokens or 150,000 words (paid); variable (free)	Up to 128k tokens or 96,000 words	2k tokens or 1,500 words	Up to 200k tokens or 150,000 words (Pro); 4k tokens, or 3,000 words (free)
Access to the internet	Yes (Plus)	Yes	No (data only up to April 2024)	Yes	Yes	Yes
Premium (excluding enterprise accounts)	$20 a month (Plus); $200 a month (Pro)	$20 a month	$20 a month	$20 a month (Pro)	None	$20 a month
LLM Family	GPT-4o, OpenAI o1, o3 (Plus) GPT-3.5 (free)	Gemini 1.5 Pro (paid); Gemini 1.5 (free)	Claude 3.5	GPT-4 Turbo fine-tuned by Microsoft	Llama 3	Various
LLM Developer	OpenAI	Google	Anthropic	OpenAI/ Microsoft	Meta	OpenAI, Anthropic, and other AI companies

Here are some AI tools that have been customized for specific jobs. Be aware that due to the fast pace of AI advancements, some of these could be obsolete by the time you read this, so we encourage you to look for other newer ones:

Ad agencies

- *Adobe Firefly*: A generative AI model that enables users to create images, text effects, and more through simple text prompts, integrated into Adobe Creative Cloud applications
- *Persado*: AI that unearths precise language to inspire customers to engage and act throughout the multichannel shopping experience
- *AdCopy*: Generates high-converting ad copies, leveraging machine learning to create engaging and effective advertising content

Architects and interior designers

- *Spacemaker AI*: Uses AI to analyze and optimize space, allowing architects to design buildings with creative efficiency
- *Autodesk Revit*: Helps architects generate design options and optimize designs for sustainability
- *Morpholio Board*: AI-driven interior design software that helps designers create mood boards and space layouts quickly

Customer support and chatbots

- *Intercom*: Uses AI to automate customer support interactions and provide responses to common queries
- *Zendesk AI*: Helps customer service teams by automating ticket handling, suggesting responses, and analyzing customer feedback
- *Ada*: AI-powered chatbot designed to automate customer service and offer personalized assistance to users
- *LivePerson*: Provides AI-driven messaging tools to help businesses engage with customers in real-time, improving customer service efficiency

Data scientists

- *$H_2O.ai$*: Provides an open-source platform for building AI models, enabling data scientists to experiment with different machine learning algorithms
- *DataRobot*: Automates many aspects of the data science workflow, allowing for rapid model creation and testing
- *IBM Watson*: Offers AI-driven data analysis tools that help extract insights from large datasets and assist in creative data visualization

Fashion designers

- *CLO 3D*: Enables designers to create and visualize garments in 3D, using AI to predict fabric behavior and fit
- *Designify*: Assists fashion designers in generating high-quality visuals and mockups quickly
- *Vue.ai*: An AI-based personalization engine that helps fashion brands design personalized clothing and experiences

Filmmakers and video editors

- *Runway*: Create videos, generate audio, and quickly change a scene's background, characters, etc.
- *Synthesia*: A tool for creating AI-powered videos with avatars, useful for explainer videos and creative content
- **Adobe Firefly Video Model:** Allows users to generate and edit videos from text descriptions or images, offering features like camera angle adjustments and scene transformations

Financial analysts and accountants

- *Kensho*: AI-driven financial analysis tool used by financial professionals to generate reports and predictions from large datasets
- *Zest AI*: Helps financial institutions make creative underwriting decisions using AI-powered risk assessment
- *AlphaSense*: AI-driven search engine for financial research, allowing analysts to explore investment opportunities creatively

Graphic designers and artists

- *Adobe Firefly:* Adobe's generative AI model integrated into Creative Cloud applications like Photoshop and Illustrator, enabling users to create images and text effects through simple text prompts
- *Stable Diffusion*: An open-source AI model that generates images from text prompts, widely used for creative exploration and integrated into various design tools
- *RunwayML*: An online platform offering AI-powered tools for video editing, image generation, and creative workflows

Health care and medical diagnostics

- *IBM Watson Health*: Uses AI to analyze medical data and provide insights for personalized treatment plans, medical research, and diagnostics
- *PathAI*: Leverages AI to assist pathologists in making more accurate diagnoses by analyzing medical images
- *Aidoc*: Provides AI solutions to analyze medical scans and flag critical issues, helping radiologists improve speed and accuracy in diagnosing conditions

Human resources professionals

- *HireVue*: AI-driven video interview platform that helps HR professionals screen candidates based on facial recognition and natural language processing
- *Pymetrics*: Uses AI to match candidates to job roles based on their emotional and cognitive abilities
- *Eightfold.ai*: AI-powered platform for talent acquisition and management that suggests creative recruitment strategies

Journalists and content creators

- *Wordtune/Grammarly*: AI writing assistants that help journalists and content creators enhance their storytelling by suggesting better ways to phrase ideas
- *Description*: AI-powered transcription and video editing tool for podcasters and video creators
- Otter.ai: AI-powered audio transcription and meeting assistant

Lawyers and legal professionals

- *Harvey AI*: AI-powered legal research and contract analysis designed to help law firms with drafting, reviewing, and interpreting legal documents
- *Luminance*: AI-powered legal document analysis tool that assists lawyers in contract review and due diligence
- *Robin AI*: Provides AI tools that suggest edits to contracts and delves into thousands of legal documents to answer queries

Marketers

- *Jasper AI*: Helps marketers create ad copy, social media posts, and blog content
- *Phrasee*: Generates optimized email subject lines and social media ads using AI
- *Canva*: Provides AI-based design suggestions and templates, streamlining the creative process for marketers

Musicians and composers

- *AIVA*: Create new songs in more than 250 styles in seconds or revise existing audio.
- *Amper Music*: An AI music platform that lets users create and customize original music from over one million individual audio samples.
- *Magenta Studio*: Developed by Google, it provides tools to create new melodies, harmonies, and rhythms using machine learning.

Photographers

- *Luminar Neo*: AI photo editing software that helps photographers enhance images automatically while still allowing creative control
- *Topaz Labs*: Uses AI to sharpen, denoise, and upscale images without losing quality
- *Lensa*: AI photo editor for touch-ups and adjustments, great for quick creativity boosts

Product managers and entrepreneurs

- *Notion AI*: Assists with task management, brainstorming product ideas, and summarizing documents

- *Miro*: A collaborative whiteboard tool that uses AI to help with brainstorming sessions and product design
- *Copy.ai*: Generates marketing and product descriptions, perfect for e-commerce and business owners to create content quickly

Psychologists and mental health professionals

- *Woebot*: AI-driven chatbot designed to help individuals with mental health issues through cognitive behavioral therapy
- *Replika*: An AI companion that helps people explore their emotions and thoughts, offering a creative therapeutic tool

Scientists and researchers

- *Atomwise*: Uses AI to help chemists and researchers discover new drug molecules
- *Zebra Medical Vision*: An AI tool for medical imaging, assisting radiologists and healthcare professionals in diagnosing diseases creatively and efficiently

Software developers

- *GitHub Copilot*: Helps developers write code faster by suggesting code snippets and auto-completing functions
- *Tabnine*: An AI code completion tool that suggests various programming languages.
- *DeepCode*: An AI-based tool that reviews code and suggests improvements, helping developers write more efficient code

Teachers and educators

- *Socratic by Google*: Uses AI to help educators create engaging lesson plans and visual aids
- *Eduaide.ai*: Simplifies lesson planning, resource creation, and student feedback
- *Quizlet*: AI-powered flashcard and quiz tool to help teachers create engaging study aids for students

Writers and authors

- *Grammarly/Hemingway*: AI assistants to improve writing by correcting spelling and grammar and suggesting style improvements
- *Sudowrite*: Designed for fiction writers, aids in plot generation, character development, and editing
- *Quillbot*: Helps with paraphrasing and improving sentence flow. It includes a plagiarism checker and translator

Tip: Ask ChatGPT or another AI model to craft your prompts. OpenAI, Anthropic, and Gemini websites offer guides for better prompting. There are also online prompt libraries—essentially a database of prompts—to help you along. Try the one from Anthropic.[34]

Practice co-creating with AI

Let's practice how to innovate with AI as your smart assistant.

Step 1: Set a challenge or goal. It can be a creative task, such as writing a short story about an unexpected event, solving a real-world problem, or tackling a product design challenge like making a device more eco-friendly.

Step 2: Set rules. It can be anything from a 30-minute time limit to a product restriction, such as it must be inexpensive.

Step 3: Brainstorm without AI individually or as a group. Write down as many ideas as possible, no matter how outlandish they may seem. Evaluate the ideas for feasibility, innovativeness, and likely attractiveness to your target market.

Step 4: Brainstorm with AI, choosing the appropriate tool for your challenge. Adjust your prompts as necessary to get different results.

Step 5: Compare the results of your brainstorming session with and without AI. Did the AI suggest new ideas you or your group didn't think of? Which AI ideas could be combined with human ideas for a more innovative solution?

Step 6: Reflect on your exercise (or gather feedback if you're in a team)

- Did AI introduce ideas that were unexpected or outside your typical thought patterns?
- Were you surprised by any of the answers? Did it make you think creatively in a new direction?
- How might AI help you break rigid mental models to unleash creativity?

Step 7: Choose the most promising ideas from the human and AI lists and refine them. Use AI to develop specific concepts further or run multiple iterations to refine the details of particular ideas.

Step 8: Create a prototype based on the refined ideas. Ask AI for feedback.

Avoiding Overreliance on AI

As you discover the benefits of using AI, it's easy to become over-reliant on these assistants. This change in habits highlights the importance of maintaining a balance—using AI as an enhancement tool while continuing to develop and exercise our creative capabilities with or without the help of the various approaches described in Part 2 of this book.

The risk of automated complacency represents one of the most significant challenges in human-AI creative collaboration: when users become overly dependent on AI systems, accepting their outputs without critical evaluation or creative elaboration. Research shows this can lead to several creativity-inhibiting patterns:

1. **Anchoring bias:** Initial AI suggestions can unduly influence subsequent thinking, narrowing rather than expanding creative exploration.
2. **Novelty illusion:** The perceived novelty of AI-generated content can mask its derivative nature, as these systems fundamentally recombine patterns from existing data.
3. **Creative outsourcing:** Gradually delegating more creative thinking to AI systems can atrophy our creative capabilities over time.
4. **Homogenization risk:** When people use the same AI systems, creative work across different fields may begin to look and sound alike.

To counter these tendencies, we recommend approaching *AI as a creative provocateur rather than an oracle*, using its suggestions as starting points for your divergent thinking rather than endpoints. Deliberately modifying, combining, or challenging AI outputs helps maintain human creative agency while benefiting from computational assistance.

A 2024 study from the University of Pennsylvania and Stanford University found that excessive reliance on AI tools can impair learning and skill development. The research showed that students who used AI for all their writing tasks showed decreased improvement in their writing abilities compared to those who used AI more selectively as a learning aid.[35]

Despite some evidence suggesting that using AI could impair cognitive abilities, we believe this risk is minimal when AI is used to augment the various approaches to enhance creativity outlined in this book and treated as a series of interactions with a smart research assistant. Recent studies, including research from MIT that found students using ChatGPT exhibited markedly lower neural activity in brain regions associated with creative functions and attention, raise important questions about AI's long-term cognitive effects.[36]

However, these concerns primarily emerge when AI is used as a replacement for human thinking rather than as a collaborative tool. The approaches presented in this book are specifically designed to maintain human agency in the creative process, using AI to expand possibilities rather than to provide final answers. When you engage with AI as a thinking partner—challenging its suggestions, iterating on ideas, and maintaining critical evaluation of outputs—you preserve the cognitive engagement that drives both learning and creativity.

Navigating the Global AI Landscape

Given the enormous speed and magnitude of advances in AI, staying current with global AI developments is crucial for creative professionals and innovators. The AI landscape is rapidly shifting beyond traditional Western-centric perspectives, requiring us to broaden our information sources and understanding.

As we were preparing for this book's publication, the global AI research landscape has undergone significant transformation. *China now produces approximately 26.5% of the world's AI research publications, compared to the US at 19.8%* (Nature Index 2025). This shift represents more than academic statistics since research leadership often translates to commercial advantage within three to five years.

China's AI research output leads the world, with increased patent filings and commercial applications spanning everything from autonomous vehicles to creative content generation. This leadership extends beyond quantity to encompass breakthrough applications in areas like generative AI for traditional art forms, AI-powered urban planning, and innovative human-AI collaboration frameworks.

Meanwhile, other regions are positioning themselves strategically in this evolving landscape. Singapore has launched a $1 billion AI investment fund and implemented streamlined visas for AI talent, positioning itself as neutral ground for US-China collaboration and innovation exchange.

Implications for Creative Professionals

This global redistribution of AI innovation has practical implications for anyone seeking to harness AI for creative work:

Diversify Your Information Sources: Relying solely on US-based AI publications and platforms may limit your understanding of emerging capabilities and applications. Incorporate research and insights from Chinese AI labs, European research institutions, and innovative hubs in Singapore, South Korea, and Israel.

Monitor Cross-Cultural AI Applications: Different cultural contexts often drive unique AI applications. Chinese AI companies are pioneering applications in social commerce and community-driven content creation, while European developers focus heavily on privacy-preserving AI creativity tools.

Prepare for Rapid Capability Shifts: The three- to five-year timeline between research breakthroughs and commercial availability means today's academic papers from leading global institutions preview tomorrow's creative tools. Following international AI research helps you anticipate and prepare for capabilities before they become mainstream.

Staying Current in a Fast-Moving Field

To effectively navigate this global AI landscape:

1. **Follow International AI Research**: Subscribe to publications and conferences from major AI research centers worldwide, not just in Silicon Valley
2. **Experiment with Global AI Platforms**: Test AI tools developed in different countries to understand varying approaches to creativity and human-AI collaboration
3. **Engage with International AI Communities**: Participate in global forums and online communities where practitioners share insights across cultural and geographical boundaries

4. **Track Policy and Investment Trends**: Government AI investments and policies often signal where breakthrough applications will emerge next

The democratization of AI development means that your next creative breakthrough might come from understanding how AI is being applied in contexts and cultures different from your own. By maintaining a global perspective on AI innovation, you position yourself to harness the full spectrum of AI's creative potential rather than limiting yourself to familiar, local applications.

As we've seen throughout this chapter, AI's greatest strength lies in its ability to combine unexpected elements and perspectives. The same principle applies to our approach to AI itself—the most innovative applications often emerge from the intersection of different technological traditions, cultural approaches, and creative philosophies from around the world.

Era of Augmented Intelligence

If the possibilities of human co-creating with machines opened your eyes, be aware that this is just the beginning of the coming AI tsunami. More tools and techniques at increasing levels of sophistication are being developed to catapult human creativity to heights yet unseen.

Tolga Kurtoglu, the CTO of Lenovo, got it right when he said that we are entering the era of "augmented intelligence," where machines have the unprecedented power to enhance human capabilities.[37]

He sees three types of human intelligence converging with digital tools and capabilities: *Cognitive intelligence,* sensory intelligence, and 'connectional' intelligence. AI can help shoulder cognitive complexity and free our brains to do what we do best as humans: Be creative. *Sensory intelligence,* digital tools track and analyze our biometrics, with AI enhancing tracking and diagnoses. *Connectional intelligence,* or the human capacity to make social connections, will reach new levels as machines reinvent socialization.

Artificial intelligence is advancing so rapidly that talk about AI becoming as capable as humans in general tasks—a capability called artificial general intelligence or AGI—could be here as soon as 2029, according to Nvidia CEO Jensen Huang. He defines AGI as AI that can match humans in tests, whether the bar exam, pre-med, economic tests, and the like.[38] Meanwhile, OpenAI is developing an even higher level of computing called artificial superintelligence (ASI), which is when AI becomes more intelligent than humans.

As these tools become more sophisticated, many creators wonder: If AI can do this, what role remains for human creativity? However, as noted by Professor Mollick earlier, the accelerating pace of AI development creates exciting possibilities. Rather than seeing AI as a threat, consider it an invitation to ask yourself: 'What aspects of my creative process do I most value and want to deepen personally? What tasks drain my creative energy that I might offload to technology?' The most successful creators are developing symbiotic relationships with AI—using it to handle routine aspects of creation while focusing their human capacity on judgment, emotional resonance, cultural context, and meaning-making that remains distinctly human. This efficiency liberates creative professionals to focus more deeply on uniquely human contributions.

Professor, author, and authority on technology, Shelly Palmer,[39] argues that while AI isn't replacing human creativity, it is revolutionizing content production. AI delivers comparable results at a fraction of the cost and time for routine creative tasks where efficiency matters more than originality.

This shift mirrors what happened with music quality after the iPod: technical compromises that experts noticed went completely undetected by most listeners. Similarly, A/B tests now show AI-generated content performing equal to or better than human-created alternatives across advertising platforms.[40]

AI excels at executing technical tasks while humans remain uniquely capable of originality and emotional depth. Embrace this partnership. Let AI handle the repetitive production work, freeing your human creativity for what's truly magical, the inspired ideas only you can bring to life. The tools have changed, but your creative spark remains irreplaceable.

Imagine how much more creativity AGI can unleash in you once it arrives. But it is still only your able assistant; you can be original and creative. Just look at AI-generated images. Once you've made a few, you start seeing a sameness about them: the same with text. With our emotional depth, flashes of inspiration, gut instinct, and imagination, we are still the founts of unique creativity that no machine can sustainably match.

More recently, Palmer identified five tasks that LLMs and reasoning engines appear to do[41]—but should be left strictly to humans:

1. *Original insight.* AI can synthesize research, but drawing fresh conclusions, making lateral connections, and deciding what matters most remains human work.
2. *Taste.* AI can mimic a style guide, yet it cannot judge elegance, know when less is more, or sense when a bold stroke beats a safe one.
3. *Emotional context.* AI does not feel. It lacks the intuition to choose restraint or celebration, irony or sincerity, in the moment.
4. *Strategic judgment.* AI will forecast scenarios, but it will not bet the brand, kill a beloved project, or abandon sunk costs. Strategy is a choice, not a prompt.
5. *Ethics.* AI can debate principles, but it has no moral compass. Only people decide what "right" means for their organizations.

These gaps will narrow over time, but they currently mark the boundary between automation and leadership. Knowing what AI can't do is just as important as knowing what it can do.

The 12 approaches discussed in Part 2 of this book are designed to unlock your inner creativity. AI will help you develop more and better ideas and act as your smart, impartial analyst to help you succeed.

🔋 Exercise

*   Do you use AI in your creative work? _____.
*   If yes, how do you use AI? _____.
*   Did it enhance your creativity? _____.
*   If yes, in what way? _____.
*   If no, why not? _____.
*   The limitation that I have observed so far in using AI is _____.
*   What have you learned from your experience using AI? _____.

In Summary

1. AI sparks your imagination in unexpected ways.

You can use AI as a catalyst for imaginative thinking to expand your creative horizons, by, for example, using AI to combine unrelated concepts to trigger new business ideas.

What unexpected combination of your skills and interests might lead to your next breakthrough if you let AI help you connect these dots?

2. Deliberately challenging AI keeps your work unique and original.

Creative professionals find new ways to make art using AI by injecting friction, challenge, and serendipity into the process.

What deliberate challenges could you introduce to your AI interactions to maintain diversity and distinctiveness in your creative output?

3. AI streamlines your routine tasks so you can focus on bigger thinking.

Companies like Delta and Walmart already use AI for real-time price adjustments, freeing their teams to concentrate on higher-level creative strategy.

What routine tasks could you offload to make room for your most brilliant work?

4. AI helps you understand your creative process better.

By serving as a sounding board for your ideas, AI can help you deconstruct and gain deeper insights into how creativity happens. It can critique your concepts with surprising objectivity, highlighting strengths and weaknesses you might miss.

What creative blind spots might AI help you discover about yourself that could unlock your next level of innovation?

In Summary (contd.)

> **5. Your AI assistant enables boundary-pushing innovation that wasn't possible before.**
>
> Just look at Airbus engineers who used generative design to create a bionic partition that's 45% lighter, stronger, and thinner than existing models. Their AI-powered algorithm cycled through 10,000 design options to land on nature-inspired patterns from slime mold and mammal bones.
>
> *What revolutionary designs could you create with AI's computational power behind you?*

Our next chapter analyzes common obstacles to creativity and innovation and how you can overcome them.

Notes

[1]   ChatGPT prompt: You are a travel writer. Write a one paragraph description of the Tuscan, Italy countryside with its delightful rolling hills.

[2]   To be sure, more detailed instructions in the prompt would have resulted in a list of activities as well. But a human travel writer would have intuitively known to include it without any specific instructions.

[3]   GPT-4o is the most powerful of OpenAI's large language models in the GPT series. OpenAI did debut a reasoning LLM called OpenAI o1 that falls under a new series of LLMs.

[4]   Zhou, Eric, and Dokyun Lee. "Generative Artificial Intelligence, Human Creativity, and Art." *PNAS Nexus*, Vol. 3, no. 3 (March 2024). https://academic.oup.com/pnasnexus/article/3/3/pgae052/7618478

[5]   Forbes Expert Panel. "Why AI Will Never Fully Replace Humans in 19 Agency Service Areas," *Forbes*, May 10, 2023. https://www.forbes.com/councils/forbesagencycouncil/2023/05/10/why-ai-will-never-fully-replace-humans-in-19-agency-service-areas/

[6]   *MIT Technology Review*. "How Creativity Became the Reigning Value of Our Time," April 18, 2025, accessed May 12, 2025. https://www.technologyreview.com/2025/04/18/1114478/cult-of-creativity-samuel-franklin-book-technology-ai/

[7]   ResearchGate. "Foundations of Materials Experience: An Approach for HCI," Elisa Giaccardi and Elvin Karana, April 2015, Conference: CHI'15 Proceedings of the 33rd Annual ACM Conference on Human Factors in Computing Systems, pg. 2447-2456. https://www.researchgate.net/publication/270586693_Foundations_of_Materials_Experience_An_Approach_for_HCI

[8]   Claude.ai an AI assistant by Anthropic.

[9]   Perplexity.ai.

[10] Chat GPT-4, https://openai.com

[11] Andres Fortino. "Embracing Creativity: How AI Can Enhance the Creative Process." *NYU School of Professional Studies*, November 2, 2023. https://www.sps.nyu.edu/homepage/emerging-technologies-collaborative/blog/2023/embracing-creativity-how-ai-can-enhance-the-creative-process.html

[12] Rokk3r. "AI-Powered Prototyping: Accelerating Innovation." Rokk3r, https://www.rokk3r.com/insights/ai-powered-prototyping-accelerating-innovation

[13] "AI-Powered Collaboration: Transforming Ideation into Implementation with Smart Tools." Medium, March 20, 2024. https://medium.com/@xtn13/ai-powered-collaboration-transforming-ideation-into-implementation-with-smart-tools-86b754df322a

[14] Beatriz Sanz Sáiz. "How to Augment People with AI to Build a Better Working World," *EY*, January 18, 2024. https://www.ey.com/en_ae/insights/ai/how-to-augment-people-with-ai-for-a-better-working-world#:~:text=GenAI%20augments%20less%20skilled%20workers,tended%20to%20drive%20inequality%20wider

[15] A.R. Doshi, and O.P. Hauser. Generative AI Enhances Individual Creativity but Reduces the Collective Diversity of Novel Content. *Science Advances*, 10(28), eadn5290, 2024, accessed June 10, 2025. https://www.technologyreview.com/2024/07/12/1094892/ai-can-make-you-more-creative-but-it-has-limits/amp/

[16] "Reimagining the Future of Air Travel," *Autodesk*, accessed October 16, 2024. https://www.autodesk.com/customer-stories/airbus

[17] Ibid.

[18] Ibid.

[19] Ibid.

[20] Ethan Mollick. One Useful Thing, "Superhuman: What can AI do in 30 minutes?", accessed April 13 2025. https://www.oneusefulthing.org/p/superhuman-what-can-ai-do-in-30-minutes

21 Encyclopedia Britannica. "History of Artificial Intelligence," accessed October 5, 2024. https://www. britannica.com/science/history-of-artificial-intelligence

22 Gil Press. "The Brute Force of IBM Deep Blue and Google DeepMind." *Forbes*, February 7, 2018. https:// www.forbes.com/sites/gilpress/2018/02/07/the-brute-force-of-deep-blue-and-deep-learning/

23 Google DeepMind. "AlphaGo," accessed October 12, 2024. https://deepmind.google/research/breakthroughs/alphago/

24 Kathleen Walch. "Are We Heading for Another AI Winter Soon?" *Forbes*, October 21, 2019. https://www. forbes.com/sites/cognitiveworld/2019/10/20/are-we-heading-for-another-ai-winter-soon/

25 Krystal Hu. "ChatGPT Sets Record for Fastest-Growing User Base—Analyst Note." Reuters, February 2, 2023, accessed February 26, 2025. https://www.reuters.com/technology/chatgpt-sets-record-fastest-growing-user-base-analyst-note-2023-02-01/

26 Artificial Intelligence Board of America. "Generative AI vs. Traditional AI: Key Differences and Advantages." October 19, 2023. https://www.artiba.org/blog/generative-ai-vs-traditional-ai-key-differences-and-advantages

27 Zhou Xin. "Alibaba Launches New AI Model That It Says Outperforms DeepSeek, China's Hottest Start-Up," *South China Morning Post*, January 29, 2025. https://www.scmp.com/tech/big-tech/article/3296737/alibaba-launches-new-ai-model-targeting-rival-deepseek-chinas-hottest-start

28 DeepSeek. "DeepSeek-R1 Release," *DeepSeek API Documentation*, January 25, 2025. https://api-docs. deepseek.com/news/news250120

29 OpenAI. "Introducing OpenAI o1-Preview," September 12, 2024. https://openai.com/index/introducing-openai-o1-preview/

30 Susanna Ray. "AI Agents—What They Are, and How They'll Change the Way We Work." *Microsoft Source*, February 22, 2024. https://news.microsoft.com/source/features/ai/ai-agents-what-they-are-and-how-theyll-change-the-way-we-work/

31 Meta AI. *LLaMA 3.0 License*. GitHub, accessed October 12, 2024. https://github.com/meta-llama/llama-models/blob/main/models/llama3_2/LICENSE

32 As of October 12, 2024.

33 As of October 12, 2024.

34 Anthropic. "Prompt Library." *Anthropic Documentation*, accessed February 22, 2025. https://docs.anthropic.com/en/prompt-library/library

35 Hamsa Bastani, Osbert Bastani, Alp Sungu, Haosen Ge, Özge Kabakcı and Rei Mariman., Generative AI Can Harm Learning. The Wharton School Research Paper, July 15, 2024, accessed April 4, 2025. https:// ssrn.com/abstract=4895486 or http://dx.doi.org/10.2139/ssrn.4895486

36 "Will AI Make You Stupid?" *The Economist*, July 16, 2025.

37 Tolga Kurtoglu. "Lenovo Innovation Brings Hybrid AI to All," *Lenovo Tech World '24*, Bellevue, Washington, October 15, 2024.

38 Haje Jan Kamps. "Nvidia's Jensen Huang Says Hallucinations are Solvable, Artificial General Intelligence is Five Years Away," *TechCrunch*, March 19, 2024. https://techcrunch.com/2024/03/19/agi-and-hallucinations/

39 Shelly Palmer. "If You Can't Tell the Difference, There Is No Difference," December 1, 2024, accessed April 6, 2025, https://shellypalmer.com/2024/12/if-you-tell-the-difference-there-is-no-difference/

40 Ibid.

41 Shelly Palmer. "What ChatGPT Can't Do." May 2025, https://shellypalmer.com/2025/05/what-chatgpt-cant-do/

Overcoming the Obstacles
PERFECTION
RESOURCES
FEAR
RIGIDITY

Chapter 4
Overcoming Obstacles to Creativity and Innovation

The only use of an obstacle is to be overcome.
—US President Woodrow Wilson

When Microsoft CEO and co-founder Steve Ballmer resigned in 2014, it was a time of stagnation at the company. Back then, many had written off the software giant as a twentieth-century has-been resting on the laurels of its Windows monopoly on PCs. The company was stodgy, slow to change, and its stature was declining.

The board replaced the brash Ballmer—and Bill Gates' confidante—with Satya Nadella, a thoughtful and mild-mannered engineer. Nadella had a tough challenge: He was untested in the C-suite and tasked with turning around a behemoth that was famously resistant to change.

How would he tackle this gargantuan problem? Nadella decided to go on a listening tour. He set aside entrenched management practices that had defined Microsoft for decades and solicited honest employee feedback instead. They described an atmosphere lacking collaboration, and employees feared taking risks.

This was Nadella's 'a-ha' moment.

"They came to Microsoft with big dreams, but it felt like all they did was deal with upper management, execute taxing processes, and bicker in meetings," Nadella wrote in his book, *Hit Refresh*.[1] "We needed to rediscover the soul of Microsoft, our reason for being. ... My primary job is to curate our culture so that one hundred thousand inspired minds—Microsoft's employees—can better shape our future."

Nadella's opening up of the culture also extended to taking its business toward a new trajectory: Microsoft's once-closed ecosystem that resisted partnerships began to open up its platforms, supporting rival operating systems, Linux, and Apple's iOS. The company also invested in small tech firms at the forefront of innovation, bringing in valuable external talent. Meanwhile, it redoubled its focus on areas already growing fast, like cloud computing.

Nadella then shook up Microsoft's business lines, buying category pioneers such as LinkedIn for $26 billion and popular code repository GitHub for $7 billion, among others. It was an early investor in OpenAI before ChatGPT was introduced to the world. Today, Microsoft is not just known for its Windows operating system but also its cloud, and sits at the forefront of AI productivity tools with its Copilot software suite. As of this writing, it is one of the most valuable companies in the world, worth $3.1 trillion.

Nadella's transformation of Microsoft exemplifies not just one but several of our creativity approaches working in concert. He challenged the entrenched mental model of Microsoft as primarily a Windows company, embraced an interdisciplinary perspective by bringing cloud computing expertise to their business software strategy, cultivated curiosity throughout the organization, and persistently iterated their products based on customer feedback. This interconnectedness highlights an essential truth about creativity: These approaches aren't isolated techniques but complementary facets of a holistic creative mindset. As you explore the approaches in subsequent chapters, look for opportunities to combine them, recognizing that their power multiplies.

Yes, We Can

This book introduces a range of approaches and tools designed to unlock creativity within each of us. Ordinary people can achieve extraordinary outcomes when driven by a clear and compelling vision using techniques and tools that enhance their creativity. To do so, be ready to summon grit, dedication, and courage as you challenge outdated mental models and embrace transformative new ideas.

> "
> **Ordinary people can achieve extraordinary outcomes when driven by a clear, compelling vision.**
> "

As with any journey, the path of creativity is not without its bumps. Many of the obstacles listed in this chapter may not even be evident until mentioned. The goal is to help you identify these blockers, equipping you with strategies to prevent or overcome them. This process of self-discovery is essential for reaching new heights both personally and professionally.

It's worth noting that many obstacles are interconnected. The examples we provide often illustrate multiple points, and you are encouraged to think about how these and related factors might intertwine in your own experiences. This exploration gives you the clarity and tools needed to unleash your full creative potential.

Common Roadblocks

1. Resistance to change

When people are comfortable and doing well, they may lack the motivation to explore new possibilities or challenge existing assumptions. Trying something new brings risk and discomfort, with no certainty of success. Newness also brings the possibility of costly mistakes. Hence the saying, "if it ain't broke, don't fix it."

But not rocking the boat because everything seems fine is illusory since change is constant. Relying on familiar approaches can narrow one's perspective as well, reducing exposure to diverse viewpoints and creative thinking. And the longer people stay in the same mindset, the harder it is to change their mental models.

Example: The rise of Disney+ online streaming

Disney, the owner of film studios and TV and cable channels, resisted entering into online streaming for years because it didn't want to cannibalize its business in traditional cable TV.[2] It had long profited from conventional media channels and movie theaters. Even as Netflix began to gain market share, Disney stuck to its old ways. Its foray into streaming was limited to a partial ownership of online channel Hulu it had largely neglected.

But as more people canceled their cable subscriptions, Disney was forced to confront its resistance to change to protect its business. In 2018, it finally took the plunge with ESPN+, the online subscription version of its cable channel. The following year, Disney rolled out Disney+ and took complete operational control of Hulu from its partners. In November 2023, Disney acquired the entirety of Hulu. In its fiscal fourth-quarter 2024 results, Disney reported having 174 million Disney+ and Hulu bundled subscriptions and more than 120 million Disney+ only subscribers.[3]

How to overcome resistance to change

Powerful questions can shift the dynamic when facing resistance, whether from others or within ourselves. Instead of dismissing resistance as stubborn opposition, ask: 'What evidence would convince me (or them) that change is necessary?' or 'What aspects of the current approach am I most attached to and why?' These questions help identify whether resistance stems from valid concerns, emotional attachment to the status quo, or a lack of compelling evidence for change. By acknowledging and exploring the roots of resistance, you can address the underlying issues rather than merely pushing harder against the opposition.

2. Ignoring or being unaware of the forces of change

Staying unaware of changing trends, interests, and situations can carry significant risks, such as obsolescence, missed opportunities, and a diminished ability to make optimal decisions because one is reactive, not proactive. Meanwhile, others are advancing, improving, and adapting. It might be too late to rebound if a crisis forces a change.

Example: BlackBerry's decline

BlackBerry's fall is a cautionary tale of failing to adapt to shifting market trends and technological innovations. In the mid-2000s, BlackBerry was a dominant force in the mobile phone market, renowned for its secure email services and QWERTY keyboards. However, the company underestimated the impact of the smartphone revolution ushered in by Apple's iPhone in 2007.[4]

While Apple and other competitors embraced touchscreens, app ecosystems, and consumer-friendly interfaces, BlackBerry remained focused on its enterprise audience, neglecting the broader consumer shift toward devices that combined functionality with entertainment. This lack of foresight allowed rivals like Apple and Samsung to capture significant market share.

Moreover, BlackBerry's operating system, BlackBerry OS, failed to compete with the app ecosystems of iOS and Android. Developers flocked to Apple's App Store and Google Play, leaving BlackBerry's app offerings stagnant and outdated. Consumers increasingly gravitated toward ecosystems that provided better functionality, a wide array of apps, and seamless integration with other devices.

The company's leadership further compounded these issues by resisting change and failing to respond quickly to emerging trends. BlackBerry dismissed the iPhone as a niche product and underestimated the growing demand for touchscreens and app-driven platforms.

By the time the company attempted to pivot with its BlackBerry 10 operating system in 2013, it was too late—Android and iOS had already cemented their dominance. This inability to adapt to consumer demands, coupled with leadership's failure to anticipate market shifts, led to BlackBerry's dramatic fall from market leader to a niche player focused on enterprise software and cybersecurity. BlackBerry's story highlights the importance of staying attuned to market trends and being willing to move fast.

How to stay abreast of changes

How do you currently stay informed about changes in your field or industry?

3. Fear of failure

The fear of failure can stem from personal insecurities, organizational cultures that penalize mistakes, or discomfort with uncertainty. When people fear failing, they are less likely to take risks or propose new ideas. The result is what is called 'analysis paralysis.' But this inaction may result in one missing a significant opportunity or pushing a problem down the road.

> " **When people fear failing, they are less likely to take risks or propose new ideas.** "

Example: Nokia's fearful culture

Nokia was once the smartphone brand of choice worldwide, but when the iPhone gained popularity and ate into its market share, this instilled such fear in the company that coordination froze between the top and middle managers.[5]

This led to company-wide inertia, making Nokia unable to respond effectively to the iPhone's rise. They knew their operating system, Symbian, was inferior to Apple's iOS, but they were too afraid to publicly acknowledge it and appear defeatist before investors, suppliers, and customers.

"Nokia's top managers should have encouraged and role-modelled more authentic and psychologically safe dialogue, internal coordination, and feedback mechanisms to understand the true emotional picture in the organization," according to INSEAD Knowledge.[6]

Instead, fear paralyzed them from pivoting quickly to address the threat. Nokia would pay the price by seeing its smartphone business erode and eventually sell this unit to Microsoft in 2013, which later killed the product. "When fear permeated all levels, the lower rungs of the organization turned inward to protect resources, themselves, and their units, giving little away, fearing harm to their careers," INSEAD's authors wrote.

While stories like Blackberry and Nokia's fall have become classic cautionary tales of innovation failure, similar patterns continue to emerge in today's business landscape. Consider Peloton's recent struggles after revolutionizing home fitness during the pandemic. The company failed to anticipate shifting consumer preferences as restrictions lifted, resulting in overproduction, layoffs, and a 95% stock value decline from its 2021 peak. This demonstrates how even contemporary innovation leaders can become trapped by their initial success, illustrating that resistance to change remains a persistent creative obstacle.

How to overcome the fear of failure

To transform how we approach potential failure, consider implementing pre-mortems—a strategy where you imagine a project has already failed and work backward to identify what went wrong. Unlike post-mortems that analyze past failures, pre-mortems proactively identify vulnerabilities before they manifest. Ask your team: 'If this initiative fails, what will be the most likely cause?' This exercise surfaces potential pitfalls and reduces the psychological burden of discussing risks, since you're analyzing a hypothetical future rather than assigning blame for actual mistakes.

4. Lack of resources

Innovation often requires time, money, and access to technology and information. A shortage of these resources can severely limit creative potential. Organizations that do not invest in research and development or cut budgets for creative projects hinder their capacity to innovate to solve problems.

Example: NASA's space shuttle program

In 2011, NASA terminated its space shuttle program because a series of budget cuts going back to the 1970s had compromised the safety of the shuttles, culminating in the 1986 Challenger explosion and the 2003 Columbia accident. "In the aftermath of Columbia, people realized that the vehicle was riskier than generally thought," said NASA's chief historian Bill Barry. "And most of the reasons for that were because of compromises made back in the 1970s when the shuttle was being designed due to cutbacks in the budget."[7]

Since terminating the shuttle program, NASA's astronauts would hitch a ride on the Russian Soyuz spacecraft to go to the International Space Station (ISS). In 2020, tech billionaire Elon Musk would stake his fortune to build a commercial space exploration company that launched the first NASA-certified commercial human spacecraft system in history, bringing American astronauts to the International Space Station instead of relying on another nation.[8] SpaceX would also introduce reusable rockets to lower the cost of space travel.

Notably, organizations may hinder their efforts to raise resources in the following ways: being reluctant to engage in strategic alliances or acquisitions that may lead to more resources but will change the nature of their operations; continuing to hire full-time employees instead of designing a workforce portfolio of open talent, consultants and employees to meet business needs of the moment; being slow to automate, which can increase productivity and free additional resources.

Other organizations may have the resources but are unwilling to reallocate them to new and uncertain endeavors. Many hesitate to challenge the current way of doing things and explore new ways, to their detriment and sometimes even their demise.

How to manage limited resources

What resources do you currently have that can be better utilized for innovation? Are there untapped resources or partnerships you can explore?

5. Organizational rigidity

Traditional hierarchical organizational structures can stifle creativity by imposing rigid rules and limiting the flow of ideas. Bureaucratic red tape and excessive control can deter employees from thinking outside the box or experimenting with new approaches.

But organizational rigidity spans more than structure. It also includes a culture resistant to change, processes that hamper innovation, outdated technology, a complacent workforce, and performance metrics and incentives that reward maintaining the status quo instead of risk-taking endeavors.

Example: Knowledge@Wharton

In 1998, the Wharton School at the University of Pennsylvania hired one of this book's co-authors, Mukul Pandya, to start a new management publication to compete with *Harvard Business Review* or MIT's *Sloan Management Review*. He came up with an innovative idea: Instead of publishing a traditional print magazine, establish the world's first online-only business school journal to stay at the cutting edge of the dot-com boom at the time. Pandya called the journal *Knowledge@Wharton*.

He outlined his idea in a 14-page proposal. But management resisted the change and barely acknowledged it for three months. A key turning point came from his mentor, who said, "At Wharton, things happen when enough faculty members want them to happen. Why don't you speak to our faculty colleagues about your idea?" This advice gave Pandya a glimmer of hope.

Pandya met with 40 faculty members who read his proposal and gave him feedback. After incorporating their comments, his proposal evolved from an untested journalist's idea to a collective vision. This caught the attention of the vice dean in charge of Pandya's department. The project went forward with strong faculty support. *Knowledge@Wharton* would eventually serve 3.5 million readers globally.

How to overcome organizational rigidity

How rigid is your organizational architecture, including structure, culture, processes, people, technology, and incentives? What steps can you take to make it more flexible and conducive to innovation?

6. Inadequate support systems

Creativity thrives in environments where individuals feel supported and valued. A lack of encouragement from management, inadequate feedback mechanisms, the absence of incentives and rewards, and an unsupportive workplace can demotivate employees and stifle innovative thinking.

Example: Richard Williams, the father of Serena and Venus Williams

Tennis prodigies Serena and Venus Williams, African Americans who grew up in the rough Los Angeles neighborhood of Compton, Calif., would not have succeeded without the perseverance of their father and coach, Richard Williams. The family lived far away from competitive tennis, an upper-class sport. The sisters came from a working-class family and had to sweep the courts before they could practice.[9]

Their father, Richard Williams, was a visionary who pushed his daughters to persevere. Without money to pay for professional coaches or training facilities, he had to be creative to keep his daughters in the sport. The self-taught coach watched instructional videos and read tennis books so that he could teach his daughters. He made them practice on cracked, uneven public courts using old tennis balls and homemade equipment.[10]

But it paid off. In 1997, Venus Williams became the first African American to reach the final of the US Open since 1958. Serena Williams has won 23 Grand Slam titles and is considered the greatest female tennis player of all time.[11] Their father's vision, resilience, and belief in his daughters' prowess in the face of seemingly insurmountable odds are legendary.[12]

How to gain support

What support systems currently exist in your environment? How can you strengthen or create new support systems to foster creativity and innovation?

7. Lacking a culture of experimentation

Creativity can quickly be stifled without a culture or support system that encourages experimentation. Innovation thrives by trying new things and learning from both successes and failures.

> " **Innovation thrives by trying new things and learning from both successes and failures.** "

Example: Amazon's experimentation culture

Traditional organizational structures often favor large teams and long development cycles. But Amazon implemented a culture of constant experimentation, running thousands of experiments each year. This approach has led to numerous innovations, from the Amazon Prime subscription service to the Alexa voice assistant.

Amazon's approach is characterized this way by Tom Soderstrom, who leads the AWS Public Sector Technologists unit.[13] He said that fostering a culture of experimentation is about creating a structured framework that enables innovation while managing risk. The key lies in starting small, focusing on real business problems, and maintaining a straightforward, methodical approach to testing solutions.

Soderstrom said it is critical to define what constitutes an experiment in your organization, then target business challenges that can be addressed within two weeks. This rapid iteration approach keeps momentum high while minimizing resource investment. Rather than isolating innovation in a specialized department, seek out natural experimenters across all functions of your organization. These individuals often already possess the skills and drive to innovate.

Share successes through demonstrations, recorded presentations, and internal communications to build momentum. This approach helps create buy-in and generates enthusiasm for future experiments. The goal is continuous improvement—even a 10% enhancement in a business process, when repeated consistently, can lead to transformative change. This approach drives innovation and creates an engaging workplace that attracts and retains talent.

How to develop a culture of experimentation

How does your organization currently approach experimentation? What lessons can you draw from companies with strong experimentation cultures to foster a more experimental culture in your context?

8. Short-term focus that destroys value

When organizations become too focused on short-term gains, they can lose sight of their core purpose: creating value for their stakeholders. This shift in focus can lead to a downward spiral, eroding trust and ultimately harming the organization's ability to innovate and compete.

Example: The challenges of Boeing

The venerable Boeing has fallen on hard times. Its focus on prioritizing short-term gains at the expense of long-term value has led to significant safety oversights culminating in two fatal crashes involving the 737 MAX aircraft in 2018 and 2019, which has put a substantial blemish on the storied reputation of the company.[14] It faces problems in design and production with its newest jumbo jet, the 787

Dreamliner. In late 2024, it suffered a public humiliation when its Starliner rocket left two astronauts stranded on the International Space Station because it was not safe enough for the return voyage.

Boeing's failures stemmed from two decisions made by former CEO Philip Condit: Acquiring rival McDonnell Douglas in 1997, which focused on cost-cutting and upgrading older airplanes rather than developing new aircraft, compared to Boeing's culture of engineering excellence, and moving the headquarters to Chicago from Seattle, separating leadership off from its engineering and product teams. The successor CEO, Harry Stonecipher, elected to maximize profits and buy back stock. He lasted only two years. The CEO that followed, Jim McNerney, also prioritized short-term gains and cost savings by upgrading the 737 to the 737 MAX instead of redesigning a new aircraft to replace it. Flaws in the software design that took flight control away from the pilots led to the two 737 MAX crashes.[15]

As of this writing, Boeing remains mired in difficulty. It remains to be seen whether the company can regain its former glory.

How to stay focused on value creation

How does your organization balance focusing on financial performance with creating value for customers and other stakeholders? Are there areas where a renewed focus on value creation can drive innovation and improve overall performance? As an individual, don't limit yourself to immediate, measurable results. Creative exploration, learning, and experimentation are all valuable aspects of value creation, which often become apparent later. Permit yourself to pursue promising ideas, even if the payoff isn't immediately obvious.

Key strategies across levels

While we hope you identified specific approaches to overcome your obstacles, we must recognize that many of these challenges are interrelated. Here, we present a set of individual, organizational, and societal approaches that can help address various combinations of these. These approaches will help implement the 12 sets of approaches we discuss in the subsequent chapters.

Individual level approaches:

1. *Cultivate a Growth Mindset:* Embrace challenges as opportunities for learning and growth. View failures as stepping stones to success.
2. *Practice Continuous Learning:* Stay curious and seek new knowledge and experiences. This can help you stay aware of changes and spark creative ideas.
3. *Build a Personal Network:* Surround yourself with diverse, supportive individuals who can offer different perspectives and encouragement.
4. *Develop Resilience:* Learn to bounce back from setbacks and maintain enthusiasm in facing obstacles.

5. *Set Clear and Measurable Stretch Goals and Take Calculated Risks:* Define what you want to achieve and be willing to step out of your comfort zone to pursue these goals. Note that minimal goals such as 10% improvement are a call for no change.
6. *Practice Creative Thinking Techniques:* Regularly engage in brainstorming, mind mapping, or lateral thinking exercises to enhance your creative abilities.

Organizational level approaches:

1. *Foster a Culture of Innovation:* Make innovation a core value of the organization and reward creative thinking at all levels.
2. *Implement Flexible Structures:* Design organizational architectures for rapid decision-making and cross-functional collaboration.
3. *Invest in Employee Development:* Provide resources and opportunities for continuous learning and skill development. Implement policies like Google's "20% time," which encourages employees to spend 20% of their work time exploring projects they are passionate about outside their regular work responsibilities. This enables them to foster innovation and creativity.
4. *Encourage Experimentation:* Create safe spaces for trying new ideas and learning from failures. Microsoft hosts an annual, company-wide Hackathon, bringing together employees globally, virtually, and in-person, to encourage creative, innovative solutions and idea-sharing.[16]
5. *Leverage Open Innovation:* Engage with external partners, customers, open talent, and competitors to source new ideas and solve complex problems.
6. *Set Up Measurable Stretch Objectives and Align Incentives with Innovation:* Set up stretch objectives, develop reward systems that recognize and compensate innovative efforts, not just successful outcomes.
7. *Promote Interdisciplinary Perspectives:* Build teams with diverse backgrounds and perspectives to enhance creativity and problem-solving capabilities.
8. *Implement Effective Knowledge Management:* Create systems for capturing, sharing, and leveraging organizational insights and learnings.

Societal level approaches:

1. *Prioritize Education:* Invest in educational systems that foster creativity and curiosity, critical thinking, and adaptability from an early age.
2. *Support Research and Development:* Implement policies and funding mechanisms to encourage basic and applied research across various fields.
3. *Create Innovation Ecosystems:* Develop innovation hubs, incubators, and accelerators that unite diverse stakeholders to solve complex problems.
4. *Implement Supportive Policies:* Design regulations and incentives that encourage risk-taking, entrepreneurship, and long-term value creation.

5. *Foster a Culture of Lifelong Learning:* Promote and support continuous education and skill development throughout individuals' careers.
6. *Encourage Cross-Sector Collaboration:* Create platforms and incentives for collaboration between academia, industry, government, and non-profit sectors.
7. *Invest in Infrastructure:* Ensure widespread access to technology and resources that enable innovation, such as high-speed internet and shared research facilities.

The journey to unlocking creativity and innovation is often fraught with challenges, yet these barriers are not insurmountable. By embracing failure as a learning opportunity, cultivating mental flexibility, and fostering environments that nurture creative thinking, individuals and organizations can transform obstacles into powerful catalysts for innovation that can drive meaningful change on personal, organizational, and societal levels.

> **The journey to unlocking creativity and innovation is often fraught with challenges, yet these barriers are not insurmountable.**

The key lies in adopting the proper perspective. Look at each obstacle not as a roadblock, but as an invitation to think differently, stretch boundaries, and discover uncharted possibilities. The road to transformative ideas is seldom smooth, but it is in navigating these very obstacles that true innovation is born.

i Exercise

1. The comfort zone challenge
   Objective: Spot your resistance to change and step outside your comfort zone.
   Tasks:

   - Write down three habits, routines, or beliefs you strongly believe.
   - Choose one to challenge this week—try a new perspective, routine, or activity that disrupts it.
   - Reflect: How did it feel? What did you learn?

2. Reverse your thinking
   Objective: Challenge ingrained mental models
   Tasks:

   - Take a belief or assumption you hold about your work or personal life.
   - Write down the exact opposite of that belief.
   - Imagine how that opposite belief could be true. List three scenarios where it could work.
   - Reflect: What does this reveal about your thinking patterns?

3. The "What if" expansion
   Objective: Train the mind to embrace uncertainty and possibility.
   Tasks:

   - Pick a project, idea, or problem you're working on.
   - Ask yourself "What if…" and complete the sentence five different ways (e.g., "What if I did the opposite?" "What if I made it funnier?" "What if it were three times bigger?").
   - Choose one "What if" idea and explore how you might implement it.

4. The creativity role swap
   Objective: Overcome resistance by shifting perspectives.
   Tasks:

   - Identify a problem or challenge you're facing.
   - Imagine how five different people would approach it:
     - A child
     - An artist
     - A scientist
     - A comedian
     - A historical figure you admire
   - Write down their hypothetical approaches and choose one to try.

5. The "kill the resistance" letter
   Objective: Address subconscious resistance directly.
   Tasks:

   - Write a letter to "Resistance."
   - Start with "Dear Resistance, I know you're here because…"
   - Explain why it's holding you back and what you will do to move past it.
   - End with a commitment to action.

In Summary

1. Change is inevitable, but our resistance is optional.
Microsoft's transformation under Satya Nadella shows how listening, opening up, and embracing new directions can revitalize even the most entrenched organizations.

What one thing are you resisting right now that might be your most significant opportunity?

In Summary (contd.)

---

2. Staying alert to market shifts prevents obsolescence.

BlackBerry's tragic decline from market leader to footnote happened because they ignored the smartphone revolution happening right before their eyes.

How are you actively monitoring the changes in your industry, and what emerging trend might you be dismissing too quickly?

3. Fear paralyzes innovation just when you need it most.

Nokia's culture of fear prevented honest communication about the iPhone threat, ultimately destroying their smartphone business.

When was the last time fear of failure stopped you from taking action, and what would you do differently if success was guaranteed?

4. Resource constraints can spark creative solutions.

Richard Williams created tennis champions without fancy facilities or coaching, using determination and unconventional methods instead.

What untapped resources or partnerships exist around you that could fuel your next breakthrough?

5. Short-term thinking destroys long-term value.

Boeing's focus on immediate profits at the expense of engineering excellence led to catastrophic failures and damaged trust.

Are you sacrificing tomorrow's success for today's convenience, and what one change could realign your focus toward creating lasting value?

The next section of the book, Part 2, unveils 12 powerful approaches to help you tap into your creative potential.

Notes

[1] Satya Nadella. *Hit Refresh: A Memoir by Microsoft's CEO*, (William Collins, 2018).

[2] Josef Adalian. "Why Disney Plussed Itself," *Vulture*, August 14, 2024. https://www.vulture.com/article/disney-plus-streaming-tech-company.html

[3] Michelle Chapman. "Disney Q4 Bolstered by Strong Results from Streaming, 'Inside Out 2' and 'Deadpool & Wolverine,'" *Associated Press*, last modified November 14, 2024, 8:33 a.m. CST. https://apnews.com/article/disney-iger-gorman-6ae9c3f7355ad53cec02e7c87fb1fb09

[4] *The Guardian*. "BlackBerry: From Status Symbol to Crashed and Burned." Published October 15, 2023. https://www.theguardian.com/technology/2023/oct/15/blackberry-smartphone-status-symbol-then-crashed-and-burned

[5] Quy Huy and Timo Vuori. "Who Killed Nokia? Nokia Did," INSEAD Knowledge, September 22, 2015, https://knowledge.insead.edu/strategy/who-killed-nokia-nokia-did

[6] Ibid.

[7] Aristos Georgiou. "Why Did the Space Shuttle Program End?" May 21, 2020. https://www.newsweek.com/why-space-shuttle-program-end-1505594

[8] "NASA's SpaceX Crew-1 Astronauts Headed to International Space Station." NASA.gov, November 16, 2020. https://www.nasa.gov/news-release/nasas-spacex-crew-1-astronauts-headed-to-international-space-station/

[9] Lesa Cline-Ransome. *Game Changers: The Story of Venus and Serena Williams* (New York: Simon & Schuster, 2018). https://www.juniorlibraryguild.com/game-changers-the-story-of-venus-and-ser-9781481476843j

[10] "History of the Williams Sisters," April 17, 2023, https://www.slazengerheritage.com/williams-sisters-2/

[11] Utathya Nag. "Serena Williams: The All-conquering Grand Slam Tennis Queen," August 25, 2022. https://olympics.com/en/news/serena-williams-grand-slam-tennis-women

[12] Julie Miller. "King Richard: Understanding the Real Richard Williams, Father and Coach to Venus and Serena," *Vanity Fair*, November 19, 2021. https://www.vanityfair.com/hollywood/2021/11/king-richard-williams-serena-venus-true-story

[13] Tom Soderstrom. "How Can You Build a Culture of Experimentation?" *AWS Enterprise Strategy Blog*, May 9, 2024. https://aws.amazon.com/blogs/enterprise-strategy/how-can-you-build-a-culture-of-experimentation/

[14] Bill George. "Why Boeing's Problems with the 737 MAX Began More Than 25 Years Ago," *Working Knowledge, Harvard Business School*, January 24, 2024. https://www.library.hbs.edu/working-knowledge/why-boeings-problems-with-737-max-began-more-than-25-years-ago

[15] Wikipedia, James McNerney. https://en.wikipedia.org/wiki/James_McNerney

[16] Microsoft Hackathon Innovation and Contribution, accessed April 24, 2025, https://techcommunity.microsoft.com/blog/mvp-blog/microsoft-global-hackathon-2024-innovation-and-contribution/4266737

Part 2

12 Sets of Approaches to Enhance Creativity

1. Challenge Your Mental Models

2. Create New Paradigms

3. Morphological Analysis

4. Analogies and Benchmarking

5. Engage In Interdisciplinary Collaboration

6. Rules and Tools

7. Extract Insights from Trends

8. Embrace Experimentation and Iteration

9. Foster Curiosity and Imagination

10. Leverage Emerging Technologies

11. Customize Your Own Toolkit

12. Cultivate Courage and Persistence

Part 2

12 Powerful Approaches to Enhance Creativity

You can't use up creativity. The more you use, the more you have.
—Maya Angelou

The second part of this book explores 12 transformative approaches to unlocking your inner creativity, each enhanced by AI tools designed to elevate your potential to new heights. Every chapter introduces a set of approaches, turbocharged by AI, weaving together inspiring real-world examples with practical exercises to help you or your team unleash creativity with confidence.

Chapter 5: Approach #1—Challenge Your Mental Models

Mental models are powerful frameworks that guide how we interpret and navigate the world. While they provide structure, they can also entrench rigid thinking, stifling creativity and adaptability. As circumstances change, mental models must be challenged and, if needed, changed. This foundational approach cultivates the flexibility required to challenge the status quo, embrace change, and harness the full potential of the other creativity approaches outlined in this book. Look out for examples across different industries, such as:

- How the founders of Uber challenged the assumption that taxis must have professional drivers in designated vehicles and created a new industry that has redefined how we commute.
- How Patagonia challenged the business model that profit must be a company's primary goal, creating one where sustainability drives decisions rather than simply influencing them.

AI tools can help identify subconscious assumptions by offering alternative perspectives and generating counterfactual scenarios that push beyond our habitual thinking patterns.

Chapter 6: Approach #2—Create a New Paradigm

Innovation often starts with a vision—a dream that inspires exploration and fuels resilience in the face of challenges. True innovators are people with extraordinary ideas who dare to create entirely new paradigms. This approach encourages dreaming boldly as a catalyst for unlocking creativity and transforming setbacks into stepping stones. Look for examples such as:

- How Spotify revolutionized the consumption of music by changing music from a physical product into a streaming service.

- How Minerva University created a new educational paradigm that earned it the #1 ranking as the most innovative university in the world, according to the World University Ranking for Innovation.

AI tools can serve as a catalyst to generate provocative 'what if' scenarios that expand the boundaries of what you believe possible as a compass to navigate the uncertainty inherent in paradigm-shifting journeys, and to prototype concepts through rapid iteration.

Chapter 7: Approach #3—Use Morphological Analysis

Morphological analysis dissects complex problems and their solutions into their core elements, enabling systematic exploration of combinations and variations to uncover innovative solutions. By embracing this structured method, you could unlock possibilities that might otherwise remain hidden. Look out for examples such as:

- An analysis of Airbnb and how it revealed an untapped market for a new travel accommodation.
- An analysis of Spotify's business components and how reassembling them created the revolutionary streaming service we all know and enjoy.

Incorporating AI with morphological analysis allows you to expand your exploration, receive initial assessments of feasibility and attractiveness, and rapidly iterate your ideas.

Chapter 8: Approach #4—Employ Analogies and Benchmarking

Analogies can provide fresh perspectives by letting you view a problem through an entirely different lens. For instance, improving an operating room's workflow might draw inspiration from the efficiency of a race car pit stop. Similarly, benchmarking looks at best practices from top performers, offering insights that can be adapted and refined for your challenges. Look for:

- How IDEO took inspiration from the Formula One pit stop to redesign the operating room for speed and efficiency.
- How the Cleveland Clinic transformed patient experience, drawing inspiration from seemingly unrelated organizations—Ritz-Carlton hotels, Apple stores, Southwest Airlines, and Disney.
- What leadership insights CEOs can glean from orchestral conductors.

AI tools can dramatically expand your search for powerful analogies by rapidly identifying patterns and connections across diverse domains that might take humans weeks of research to discover.

Chapter 9: Approach #5—Engage in Interdisciplinary Collaborations

Collaboration across disciplines sparks novel ideas, drawing from unexpected intersections of knowledge and expertise and open innovation—crowdsourcing ideas or solutions from the wider world—and provides fresh angles for tackling even the most challenging problems. Leveraging your networks by tapping into insights and expertise within your professional and personal networks can challenge assumptions and ignite creativity that might not emerge in isolation. Look out for examples such as:

- How NASA tapped a global community of experts to solve a network security challenge in space.
- How Pixar creates groundbreaking films by integrating experts across multiple disciplines—artists, animators, computer scientists, storytellers, psychologists, and sound engineers—as collaborators and unified creative teams.

AI can be used to synthesize seemingly disparate fields into a cohesive strategy that no single discipline could develop independently.

Chapter 10: Approach #6—Adopt Rules and Tools

This section introduces a variety of techniques that address different aspects of the creative process. Some of the tools we present cover more than one of the categories:

Problem Definition Tools—For Framing Challenges

- SWOT Analysis—Assessing Strengths, Weaknesses, Opportunities, and Threats to frame strategic challenges

Ideation Tools—For Generating Ideas

- Brainstorming
- Random Word/Image Generators, Mood and Inspiration Boards
- SCAMPER (Substitute, Combine, Adapt, Modify, Put to other uses, Eliminate, Rearrange)
- Six Thinking Hats—Structured parallel thinking from different perspectives
- Blue Ocean Strategy—Creating uncontested market spaces
- Seligman's Five Types of Creativity—Integration, Splitting, Figure/Ground Reversal, Distilled Imagination, Discovery
- Out-of-the-Box and Inside-the-Box Thinking—Both unconstrained and constraint-based ideation

Evaluation Tools—For Assessing and Selecting Ideas

- Six Thinking Hats (Evaluation Phase)
- AI-Powered Critique—Using AI to assess pros/cons and feasibility of ideas

Implementation Tools—For Turning Ideas Into Action

- Redesign Principles—Eliminate steps/interfaces/inefficiencies, design for quality
- Democratizing Creativity Tools—Using accessible platforms (Meta, Google tools, etc.) for implementation

AI can be used to enhance, challenge, and expand on the results of your approaches, either with generative AI to produce new content or analyze what you have created.

Chapter 11: Approach #7—Extract Insights from Trends

Analyzes shifting consumer preferences and behaviors, cultural trends, business trends, and technological advancements to develop innovative and relevant solutions. Mixing and matching ideas from these domains can lead to groundbreaking outcomes. Look out for examples such as:

- How Warby Parker transformed eyewear by acting on converging trends in online shopping behavior, creating a direct-to-consumer business model.
- How Netflix disrupted the DVD industry by analyzing consumer behavior, providing streaming and on-demand entertainment.

AI-driven analytics can enable you to proactively make key decisions to quickly adapt to consumer preferences, behavior, and other trends to identify new growth opportunities.

Chapter 12: Approach #8—Embrace Experimentation and Iteration

Creativity doesn't stop at the first solution. Iteration and experimentation refine ideas, uncovering bold and innovative paths. Experimentation is the key to establishing causal links between strategies and outcomes and is the must-have tool for any creative person or organization. Look for examples such as:

- How FarmBot, an open-source precision farming robot, evolved through continuous iteration using community feedback to develop a system that automatically plants, waters, and weeds.
- What you can learn from failed experiments, such as Google Glass, Humane's AI Pin, Kodak, Blockbuster, and Nokia.

AI can dramatically compress experimentation by creating virtual simulations of products, services, or entire business models that can be tested thousands of times under varying conditions before physical implementation.

Chapter 13: Approach #9—Foster Curiosity and Imagination

Creativity thrives on curiosity and imagination. Engage in activities stimulating these qualities, such as playing creativity-boosting games, reading science fiction, watching futuristic films, or exploring imaginative art. These practices open doors to new perspectives and ideas. Look for:

- How Disney's Imagineering division taps curiosity and imagination to design its theme parks, resorts, and cruise ships.
- How Elon Musk questioned why rockets couldn't be reusable, leading to the SpaceX revolution and creation of Falcon 9, the first reusable orbital class rocket.
- Look for practical ways to foster a mindset that is curious and imaginative.

AI tools can amplify these efforts.

Chapter 14: Approach #10—Leverage Emerging Technologies

Expand your creative boundaries using generative AI tools and leverage other scientific and technological advances, such as AR/VR/MR, cloud, blockchain, etc. Given the speed and impact of these scientific and technological advances, continuously monitoring and evaluating the relevance of these developments is a must. Look for:

- How artists use generative AI to push their creative work in new directions
- How Boeing and Siemens use AR to visualize assembly instructions and maintenance steps to improve efficiency and reduce errors
- How Louis Vuitton uses Blockchain technology to provide proof of authenticity to combat counterfeit fraud
- How the University of Maryland uses quantum computing for cross-disciplinary creativity
- How precision medicine leverages AI and other technologies to bring personalized care to patients

Chapter 15: Approach #11—Customize Your Own Toolkit

Experiment with the approaches discussed and adapt them to have a customized portfolio of approaches and processes. Whether you adopt a proven method, modify an existing one, or forge a new path, your personalized portfolio will be your unique toolkit for generating and evaluating ideas effectively. Your portfolio will most likely change over time, reflecting your unique experience and circumstances. Some additional examples of approaches you might consider including in your toolkit are:

- IDEO Design Thinking: a human-centered approach focusing on user needs. Learn how H&M used this approach to eliminate plastic packaging, developing a paper system that cut 2,000 tons of plastic.
- Front2Back Transformation: focusing on customer needs. Learn how Mphasis helped a life insurance company improve by focusing on customer experience rather than just simplifying core systems

- Growth-focused strategies: If interested in growth, consider any of the many frameworks that generate growth strategies.

AI can be used to expand and adapt your personalized toolkit to your specific context and challenges.

Chapter 16: Approach #12—Cultivate Courage and Persistence

- After customizing your portfolio of approaches, persistence and courage are key to creating and implementing bold innovations. These character traits often make the difference between succeeding and failing. Courage fuels the willingness to take risks and embrace uncertainty, while persistence keeps you moving forward despite the obstacles. By harnessing both, you can turn your seemingly impossible dream into reality. Look for examples such as:
    - Art and Design: Learn from pioneers in their fields, such as Impressionist Claude Monet, architect Zaha Hadid, and publicist Ava DuVernay
    - Business and Technology: Oatly, which transformed plant-based milk from a niche alternative to a cultural norm or Glossier, which has a community-first approach to innovating new beauty products
    - Music and Performing Arts: Draw inspiration from Lin-Manuel Miranda's reimagining of history with the stage production of Hamilton.
    - Political and Social Movements: Malala Yousafzai as an advocate for female education despite threats

There are other examples of courage and persistence throughout the book and throughout history. We encourage you to look for them and take inspiration from them.

Are you ready to unlock the full potential of your creativity and shape a future fueled by bold ideas and powerful tools?

This journey is about transforming how you think, work, and lead in a world redefined by technology. Let's dive deeper to keep experimenting, and let curiosity and courage guide you as you create what's next.

Mental Models and Lessons from the Gorilla Experiment

Chapter 5
Approach #1: Challenge Your Mental Models

*We cannot solve our problems with the same thinking we used when
we created them.*
—Albert Einstein

It is late at night, and you're walking alone in an underground parking garage. You hear footsteps behind you. Recalling that there has been a series of recent assaults in the area, you quicken your pace as you head to your car. But as you pass a lighted area, you glance behind you and see an office colleague who had also been working late. Immediately, you relax. The stress inside you instantly evaporates.

What just happened? Your mind created a mental model of a dangerous situation with just one small piece of information—footsteps behind you—and you filled in the rest: This is not surprising, as you're in an underground garage late at night, and you recalled recent news about assaults. Your mental model triggered stress, fear, and action—you walked faster toward your car to safety.

But when more information emerged, your mental model changed. You weren't being followed by hooligans after all; the footsteps belonged to your co-worker, who was also heading to their car after a long day at work. This whiplash of changing mental models occurred subconsciously and in a split second. But they evoked starkly different responses in you.

Every day, we operate in one mental model or another. We develop mental models from what we perceive with our senses, as informed by experiences, beliefs, education and situations. This becomes our reality—and it is a good thing. Without the ability to parse through the trillions of data points that surround us, we would be overwhelmed and unable to function in life.

> **Creativity is stifled when we stay in our mental status quo, especially if we're not even aware that we're operating in it.**

But creativity is stifled when we stay in our mental status quo, especially if we're not aware that we're operating in it. So, we work and live conflating what we 'see' with what we believe we see. That means most of what we 'see' is in our minds.[1]

In *The Power of Impossible Thinking*,[2] by Jerry Wind and former Citicorp CTO Colin Crook, they discuss a well-known psychological study that demonstrates a phenomenon called 'inattentional blindness': when people are so focused on a specific task, they can fail to notice unexpected events. In the experiment, participants are shown a video of people passing basketballs and are asked to count how many times the players in white shirts pass the ball. While viewers concentrate on this task, a person in a black gorilla costume walks through the scene, pounds their chest, and exits. Remarkably, more than half of the viewers did not notice the gorilla at all. The experiment is used as a metaphor for how individuals and organizations can become so fixated on their current models or tasks that they overlook major changes or opportunities, what they refer to as the "gorilla in our midst." The lesson is to question what "gorillas" might be passing through our own fields of vision, unnoticed because of our intense focus on specific goals or assumptions. Within organizations, these mental models become even more complex as our view of the world mingles with others' views, coalescing into 'groupthink'[3] that becomes institutionalized.

Wind and Crook also explain that our mental models function like cognitive operating systems that interpret incoming information according to existing beliefs and expectations. These models create efficiency but also blind spots—we literally cannot see what doesn't fit our current understanding of how the world works. Recognizing that all models are inherently limited is the first step toward more flexible thinking. The authors suggest four key practices: becoming aware of your current models, testing their limitations, overcoming inhibitors to change, and transforming your world by reshaping these foundational thought patterns. This process is the practical foundation for innovation, adaptability, and creative problem-solving in a rapidly changing world.

Think Differently: Challenge your Mental Models

The first thing to do is also the most important: Take stock of your existing mental models related to your goals and actively challenge them. To solve a problem at work, consider your mental model around workflows, processes, organizational values, and other factors. Consider how you approach sales and customer experience if you need entrepreneurial inspiration. If you have a personal creative goal, like writing your first novel, challenge mental blocks that tell you you're not good at communicating.

Question why things are done a certain way and see if the reasons remain valid. Analyze and evaluate your prevailing mindset. To find new ideas, seek diverse perspectives from non-traditional sources.

If you need help identifying your existing mental model, use an all-purpose AI tool such as ChatGPT, Claude, or Gemini to help you. Get responses from each of them and pick the most relevant answers for your goal. The more specific you are in your prompt, the more relevant the answers will be for you. (In Chapter 3, we have tips on how to craft the best prompts.)

Sample prompt to ChatGPT: *If I want to solve a problem in my workflow at work, what mental models could be holding me back?*

Answers (edited for conciseness):

1. *Status quo bias:* The assumption that the current way of doing things is the best or only way, even if it's outdated or inefficient.
2. *Fixed mindset:* A belief that skills and systems are static or rigid vs. the belief that skills, processes, and systems can evolve.

3. *Over-reliance on expertise:* Past experiences or industry best practices can make you overlook innovative solutions.

4. *Incrementalism at the expense of radical innovation:* A focus on making incremental improvements rather than a complete overhaul. People can often be stuck in a cycle of small changes rather than rethinking the workflow for greater effectiveness.

5. *Anchoring on past successes:* This mindset can create an "if it's not broken, don't fix it" mentality.

6. *Tunnel vision on existing tools:* You believe specific tools are "right" for the job, so you ignore new methods or technologies.

7. *Confirmation bias:* A tendency to favor information supporting the current workflow, even if evidence suggests that a change is necessary. Be open to data and feedback.

8. *Sunk cost fallacy:* If significant time or resources have been invested in the current process, it can feel wasteful to change direction. Make decisions based on current and future needs, not past investments.

9. *'Not invented here' syndrome:* This is a reluctance to adopt ideas or tools that didn't originate within your team or organization. Embrace external ideas to broaden your problem-solving toolkit.

10. *Linear thinking:* Thinking linearly means approaching problems step-by-step without considering lateral or non-sequential solutions. Creative problem-solving often requires a nonlinear approach, such as breaking down the workflow, rearranging steps, or integrating parallel processes.

Entering the same prompt to DeepSeek yields three similar answers (now removed) and seven different ones, displayed below. Now you have an expanded set of hurdles you can consider as inhibiting your creativity:

1. *Anchoring bias:* Relying too heavily on the first piece of information you encounter when making decisions. This can limit your ability to explore other options or adjust your thinking.

2. *Overconfidence bias:* Overestimating your knowledge, skills, or ability to predict outcomes. This can lead to poor decision-making or overlooking potential risks.

3. *Black-and-white thinking:* Viewing situations in extremes (e.g., all good or all bad) without considering nuances or middle ground. This can limit your ability to find balanced or creative solutions.

4. *Analysis paralysis:* Overanalyzing a problem to the point where you become stuck and unable to take action. This can delay progress and prevent you from testing potential solutions.

5. *Groupthink:* Prioritizing harmony or consensus within a team over critical thinking or dissenting opinions. This can stifle innovation and lead to suboptimal decisions.

6. *Availability heuristic:* Relying on readily available or recent information, rather than seeking comprehensive or accurate data to learn for yourself. This can lead to skewed perceptions and poor problem-solving.
7. *Fear of failure:* Avoid risks or new approaches because you fear making mistakes. This can prevent you from experimenting with solutions that could significantly improve your workflow.

To overcome these and other mental blocks, practice self-awareness, seek diverse perspectives, and challenge your assumptions. Tools like brainstorming, root cause analysis, and feedback loops can help you break free from limiting thought patterns.

Remember that challenging and changing your mental models are keys to developing innovative solutions.

Now Comes the Fun Part

Apple's famous 'Think Different' ad is an ode to innovators: "Here's to the crazy ones. The Misfits. The rebels. The troublemakers. The round pegs in square holes. The ones who see things differently. They're not fond of rules and have no respect for the status quo. ... And while some may see them as the crazy ones, we see genius. Because the people who are crazy enough to think they can change the world are the ones who do."[4]

> " *The people who are crazy enough to think they can change the world are the ones who do.* "

But how exactly can you think differently? How do you take off the blinders that may have been there for years? Here are some ways to change mental models that may be holding you back. AI tools can also give you ideas, but we narrowed it down to the most salient ones backed by research.

• **Question the current way of doing things**
Routines are comforting in their familiarity. But depending on them can be disastrous, as they reinforce habitual thinking, bypassing consideration of new and potentially better approaches to a problem or situation. Being stuck on a routine puts the brain on autopilot—creativity will not flourish.

Routines also seal you from novel experiences that can lead to new ideas. It makes your day predictable, leaving little room for spontaneity that can lead to 'eureka' moments. Routines are often established to improve efficiency and productivity. But focusing on getting things done quickly can discourage experimentation and exploration of new ideas.

Marketing and consumer behavior research shows that both individual and corporate buyers often go on autopilot when making purchases. For example, after deciding on a brand of coffee, the shopper will continue repurchasing it automatically without even looking at other brands in the supermarket aisle.

To get out of established ways of thinking, question your routines. Is this the best way to accomplish a task or goal? See how other people are tackling similar tasks to spark new ideas on how to approach your own situation—then mindfully change routines.

Even a simple change can be impactful. For example, this book's main author suggested to a major financial services firm that they replace the traditional conference room with bar-height round tables to encourage more open and collaborative discussions among decision-makers. They spent too much time in meetings, with nearly all lasting an hour. The less formal set-up led to shorter meeting times, creating a more dynamic environment that promoted creativity and interaction.

- **Look for and listen to people from other disciplines, cultures, professions, and generations**
  Combining disparate disciplines can lead to big innovations. For example, the Wake Forest Institute for Regenerative Medicine combined its medical expertise with engineering disciplines to develop the field of 3D bioprinting. The groundbreaking innovation came from biologists and engineers bringing together their disparate fields to enable the 3D printing of organs.[5]

  Biologists provided information about cellular structures, tissue regeneration, and knowledge of how organs worked. Engineers brought in expertise in 3D printing and material science to develop 3D printers capable of precisely layering biomaterials and living cells to create complex structures.

  By working together, they were able to create functional 3D printed tissues and organ prototypes such as skin, cartilage, and even kidneys. Their advances opened the door to a future where transplants would no longer require donors. It revolutionized medicine by providing a solution to donor organ shortages, mitigating organ rejection with custom organs.

- **Embark on a journey of discovery**
  Take a breather from daily routines and go on an adventure. It can refresh your mind and lead to new breakthroughs. Travel, try a new cuisine, take a class different from your current field and make friends from other professions, cultures and beliefs. Look at the world with a new perspective.

Pizzeria Beddia

That's how Joe Beddia was transformed from an ordinary pizza-loving guy into the chef behind the best pizza in America as proclaimed by *Bon Appetit* magazine in 2015.[6] The Philadelphian took his inspiration from his travels abroad. While in Japan, he noticed that in many restaurants, there was often only one person making the main dish, and with great attention to detail.

Once back in America, "I took that same attention to detail and just put it to a pizza," said Beddia. His insight was this: "What if I try to make every single pizza perfect?" In 2013, he opened a modest 300-square-foot pizza shop in the working-class neighborhood of Fishtown in Philadelphia. Beddia handmade the pizzas, using only the best ingredients, churning out only 40 pies a day. It was a smash hit, culminating in Bon Appetit's accolade two years later. Today, Beddia is a well-known restaurateur and author.

- **Look at advances in science and technology**
  New developments in science and technology are often a source of new ideas. Think of how these new technologies can offer opportunities or solutions. Stay up-to-date on emerging trends by reading publications such as the MIT Technology Review, which releases an annual list of 10 Breakthrough Technologies; scientific journals, tech blogs, and innovation forums. Attend conferences, meetups, and similar events to hear about new ideas.

Zoom

Eric Yuan, the founder of Zoom, capitalized on the growing demand for remote communication as businesses expanded internationally, hired workers abroad, or outsourced their operations to other countries. He realized that current video conferencing solutions were often clunky, unreliable, and hard to use. Yuan should know. He was vice president of engineering at Cisco Webex, a video conferencing service.

"The year before I left Webex, I did not see a single happy Webex customer," Yuan told Forbes.[7] "They complained about so many things: ease of use, video quality, mobile support." He left the company when it was unwilling to rebuild Webex into something new and more user-friendly.

By keeping up with advancements in cloud computing, video compression, and AI technologies, Yuan knew to move away from traditional video conferencing platforms that used on-premises infrastructure, which made scaling expensive and complex. Instead, he built Zoom as a cloud-native application—meaning it was built from the start to optimize cloud computing—allowing it to scale more easily to accommodate both individual users and teams.

This enabled Zoom to support massive surges in demand, which was especially useful during the COVID-19 pandemic when people switched to working remotely. He also tapped into cross-platform technologies to enable Zoom services on smartphones, tablets, and PCs. Further, Yuan used advanced compression algorithms to optimize audio and video streaming when the internet was slow.

Most recently, Zoom has embraced AI and pledged to deliver an AI-first platform. In 2023, the company unveiled AI Companion, a generative AI assistant that will help meeting participants become more productive.[8] For example, if they are late to a meeting, they can discreetly submit questions to the AI assistant to catch up on what they missed. In October 2024, Zoom upgraded the AI Companion to detect, track, and complete actions while operating with more advanced contextual understanding. Zoom also introduced a new subscription plan: For $12 per user per month, users can customize the AI Companion by doing such things as grounding the model on their business data.[9]

- **Monitor the changing business environment**
  Understanding the evolving business landscape is critical to challenging mental models that may have worked in the past but are becoming obsolete. These include patterns of globalization such as increased international competition and the emergence of regional and global customers and resource markets, continuous M&A and strategic alliances that alter the competitive landscape of many industries, and the changing demographics, values, expectations, and behavior.

  Add to the mix the scrutiny of business decisions by governments and the public with a greater focus on ethical dimensions including most recently, the changing US Government attitudes toward diversity, equity and inclusion; changes in business practices such as downsizing, outsourcing, reengineering, and reliance on open innovation and open talent; working from home as part of the future of work; and the shift to a stakeholder orientation, which changes the social/business contract of firms with their employees, customers and other stakeholders. In addition, consider the backdrop of global risk factors ranging from terrorism and cybersecurity to pandemics, wars, and other uncertain geopolitical conditions, and government actions.

- **Recognize your barriers**
  Do an honest self-assessment: What mental blinders inhibit you from considering other scenarios? Is it fear, complacency, an aversion to change, lack of vision, or another reason? Let's say you've always wanted to start your own business but are reluctant to leave a steady paycheck from an employer. What will get you to take the leap?

  > **What mental blinders inhibit you from considering other scenarios?**

Amazon

Amazon founder Jeff Bezos faced a similar dilemma before starting the e-commerce giant. In 1990, he became the youngest senior vice president at hedge fund D.E. Shaw, climbing the ladder quickly after graduating summa cum laude from Princeton University.[10] While researching potential business opportunities, he stumbled across this fact: The web was growing at 2,300% a year. He thought about capitalizing on the trend by opening an online bookstore.

He had to leave a high-paying job for an uncertain venture to become an entrepreneur. But he overcame this mental barrier that valued stability and certainty. "I pictured myself at 80 years old, thinking back on my life in a quiet moment of reflection," he said in 2020.[11] "Would I regret leaving this company, in the middle of the year, and walking away from my annual bonus? All of those things that, in the moment, can be very confusing."

Ultimately, Bezos chose the risky route: "I wanted not to have regrets."

- **Envision multiple futures**
  Conduct scenario planning. What are the potential future pathways for your endeavor? What mental models will be needed to succeed in each scenario?

Khan Academy

Consider Sal Khan, the founder of Khan Academy. He studied math, electrical engineering, and computer science at MIT, followed by an MBA from Harvard Business School. He started working in finance as a hedge fund analyst. When he began tutoring his cousin in math remotely, other relatives heard about it and participated. Khan began filming the tutorials and uploading them to YouTube in 2006 to meet demand.[12]

Khan was faced with two scenarios. If he continued working in finance, he would have high earnings, stability, and a clear career path. Another scenario was to use his engineering skills to develop an educational platform that would democratize learning for people worldwide. It was highly risky since there was no guarantee of success, and classes would be free.

In 2009, he quit his finance job to run the nonprofit full-time. Today, Khan Academy is one of the most influential education platforms that offers free, world-class education to millions of people worldwide. Among its supporters are the Bill and Melinda Gates Foundation and Google.

The examples of innovation we've explored demonstrate that creativity is accessible to everyone, whether you consider yourself a gifted individual or not. The approaches shared in this book provide a structured and time-tested framework for tapping into your wellspring of creativity, enhanced by AI.

IKEA

Mental model disruption drives innovation across diverse industries, not just technology. Consider how IKEA fundamentally challenged assumptions about furniture retail by shifting from fully assembled, expensive pieces to flat-packed, self-assembled furnishings. This mental model shift—that customers would trade convenience for affordability and that logistics could be reimagined around compact packaging—revolutionized the industry.

elBulli

Similarly, Spanish restaurant elBulli redefined fine dining not as perfect execution of classic techniques but as systematic experimentation with food science, turning a restaurant into a creativity laboratory that closed for six months each year to develop new culinary concepts.

Grameen Bank

In finance, Grameen Bank upended traditional banking models by questioning the assumption that collateral was necessary for lending. Using peer accountability instead, they created microfinance systems that extended credit to previously 'unbankable' populations and sparked economic development in underserved communities. These examples demonstrate that challenging mental models can transform any field, not just cutting-edge technology sectors.

The distinction between market-driven and market-driving innovation, as conceptualized by Jaworski and colleagues, provides another lens for understanding the impact of mental model transformation. Market-driven innovation responds to customer needs and conditions, resulting in incremental improvements. Market-driving innovation, however, fundamentally reshapes market structures and customer behaviors by challenging industry assumptions—exactly what happens when mental models are successfully transformed.

AI can play a pivotal role in shifting innovation efforts toward more market-driving approaches by helping organizations identify and question their deepest assumptions. For example, generative AI tools can systematically produce counterfactual business scenarios that challenge existing mental models: 'What if our biggest competitive advantage became irrelevant overnight?' or 'What if our customers' priorities reversed completely?' By engaging with these AI-generated provocations, teams can develop the cognitive flexibility needed for more radical innovation pathways.

ℹ Exercise

The following exercises will help you identify and overcome limiting mental models:

1. Identify paradigm-shifting products

   Choose three products and services that are critical to your daily life. Identify the mental models their inventors had to change to develop these paradigm-shifting ideas.

2. Strategic brand challenge

   This exercise helps you identify your brand's key mental models by challenging them. Get a small group of co-workers from various disciplines and areas of expertise. Give them 24 hours to develop a strategy to destroy their brand. Then, the results can be used to proactively develop strategies to protect the brand.

3. Use 'What if' scenarios

   Ask a 'what if' question related to your goal. For example, 'What if we had unlimited resources?' Then, responses can be made without looking at current limitations. Further refine these ideas to make them practical and adaptable to current challenges.

4. Ask the five 'Whys'

   Identify the root cause of your assumptions by asking 'why' five times. With each successive 'why,' you will dig deeper into yourself to find the mental models you didn't realize you had.

   For example, if you believe you're not creative, ask, "Why do I believe I'm not creative?" If the answer is, "Because I've never been good at coming up with new ideas," ask why you haven't been good at coming up with new ideas. If the answer is "Because I don't know where to start and often feel stuck," ask why you feel stuck.

   If you say, "Because I worry my ideas won't be original or good enough," ask why you worry about it. If the answer is "Because I compare myself to others who seem more creative than me," ask why you compare yourself to others this way. You answer, "Because I think creativity is something you're either born with or not."

   This last revelation, that you believe you must be born creative, is not entirely true. Research shows that creativity is a combination of innate tendencies and learned skills. Everyone has a degree of creativity, but they can nurture it through experiences and practice. You can dismantle mental hurdles that stop you from being creative by realizing that your base assumption that creativity is inborn is invalid.

5. Reverse roles

   Think of a person or entity whose opinion you respect and actions you admire. Imagine how they would tackle your problem or challenge. This exercise may reveal new ways of thinking.

6. Flip your mental model

   Take five minutes to identify one mental model that shapes your work or personal life. This might be an assumption like 'meetings should last one hour,' 'customers won't pay for [X],' or 'creativity requires unstructured time.' Now, deliberately flip this assumption and explore the implications: What if meetings never exceeded 25 minutes? What if customers would pay significantly more for [X] under certain conditions? What if creativity flourished within tight constraints? Don't worry about whether the flipped model is 'correct'—instead, use it as a lens to see your situation from a radically different angle. What new possibilities become visible when you temporarily adopt this contrary perspective?

In Summary

---

1. Shake up your mental models and shatter the status quo.

Your brain creates frameworks that shape how you see reality, but these frameworks can trap your thinking. Challenge your deepest assumptions about how things "should" work.

What long-held belief might you need to abandon to move forward?

2. Leverage the power of diverse perspectives.

The most groundbreaking innovations happen at the intersection of different disciplines, cultures, and generations. Your next breakthrough might come from combining seemingly unrelated ideas into something entirely new.

Who could you invite into your process that sees the world differently than you do?

3. Step boldly outside your comfort zone.

Travel to unfamiliar places. Immerse yourself in new experiences. Learn about advances in science and technology outside your field. Remember: the edge of comfort is where growth begins. Every successful innovator made their mark by pushing past limiting beliefs about what's possible.

What uncomfortable action could you take today that might lead to tomorrow's breakthrough?

4. Identify and overcome your innovation barriers.

Whether you're held back by fear of failure, sunk cost fallacy, or confirmation bias, the first step is recognizing these mental blocks exist. Create "what if" scenarios that challenge your thinking and try role reversal exercises to see problems through fresh eyes.

Which mental block has been holding you back the longest, and how will you finally break through it?

5. Future-proof your thinking with scenario planning.

Envision multiple possibilities for your projects and aspirations. This forward-thinking approach builds adaptability and resilience into your creative process, ensuring you're never caught off guard by change.

What mental models would help you succeed in each scenario?

Our next chapter explores how challenging your mental models can lead to you creating new paradigms.

Notes

[1]   Yoram (Jerry) Wind, Colin Crook, *The Power of Impossible Thinking* (Philadelphia: Wharton School Publishing, 2006).

[2]   Ibid.

[3]   Ibid.

[4]   "Apple—Think Different—Full version." YouTube. September 30, 2013. Video, 1:09. https://www.youtube.com/watch?v=5sMBhDv4sik

[5]   Wake Forest University, School of Medicine website, accessed August 8, 2024. https://school.wake-health.edu/research/institutes-and-centers/wake-forest-institute-for-regenerative-medicine

[6]   Andrew Knowlton. "This Is the Best Pizza in America (Yep, We Said It)," *Bon Appétit*, June 23, 2015. https://www.bonappetit.com/people/chefs/article/beddia.

[7]   Joanne Chen. "American Dreamers: Zoom Founder Eric Yuan On Making His Mark in Silicon Valley," July 11, 2022, https://www.forbes.com/sites/joannechen/2022/07/11/american-dreamers-zoom-founder-eric-yuan-on-making-his-mark-in-silicon-valley/

[8]   "Zoom Introduces Zoom AI Companion—Available at No Additional Cost with Paid Zoom User Accounts," *Zoom* (press release), published September 5, 2023. https://news.zoom.us/zoom-ai-companion/

[9]   "Zoom introduces AI Companion 2.0 and the ability to customize AI Companion with a new add-on," *Zoom*, published October 9, 2024. https://news.zoom.us/zoom-introduces-ai-companion-2-0/

[10]   "Jeff Bezos, American Entrepreneur," Britannica Money, August 5, 2024, https://www.britannica.com/money/Jeff-Bezos

[11]   "Jeff Bezos Speaks at Amazon India Event." YouTube. January 14, 2020. Video, 25:57.

[12]   Richard Adams. "Sal Khan: The Man Who Tutored His Cousin—and Started a Revolution," *The Guardian* newspaper, April 23. 2013 https://www.theguardian.com/education/2013/apr/23/sal-khan-academy-tutored-educational-website

The Power of New Paradigms

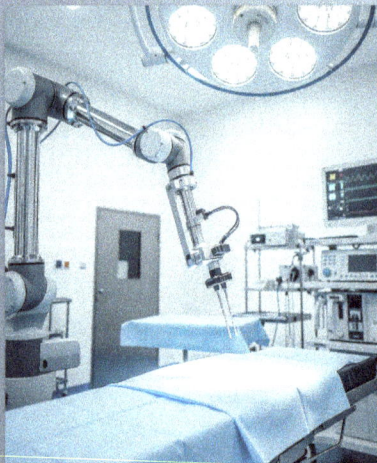

Chapter 6
Approach #2: Create New Paradigms

Some men see things as they are and say, why; I dream things that never were and say, why not.
—Robert F. Kennedy, US Attorney General 1961–1964

To unlock creativity, you must challenge your mental models. When you do it the right way, it can lead to new paradigms. A paradigm is a collection of mindsets, beliefs, and patterns of thinking that have the power to reshape entire industries, cultures, and societal norms. When a new paradigm arrives, the old one often atrophies or dies off. Critically, chasing your dreams can fuel innovation by igniting passion in what you're doing. It also fosters resilience so you can push the boundaries of creativity.

When you pursue your deepest passions, you may find yourself in new territory where innovation can thrive and new possibilities emerge. Be courageous in pursuing what's important to you, which can disrupt old patterns, foster fresh perspectives, and lead to transformative change. Paradigms—mindsets, beliefs, and thinking patterns—shape how entire industries, cultures, and societies operate. When you create new paradigms, you fundamentally alter what people do and how they feel about what is possible. This approach complements challenging mental models but operates at a more fundamental level. It's about having a bold vision and systematically bringing it to life despite seemingly insurmountable obstacles.

> **Be courageous in pursuing what's important to you.**

Transformative Examples of Paradigm Shifts

Technology and computing

- The internet and digital connectivity revolutionized how we communicate, work, and access information
- Cloud computing shifted from local storage to networked resources
- Mobile computing moved computing from desktops to everywhere
- Touchscreen interfaces eliminated physical keyboards and buttons

Business and economics

- Sharing economy (Airbnb, Uber) transformed asset utilization
- E-commerce replaced many brick-and-mortar retail experiences
- Subscription models replaced ownership in many industries
- Blockchain decentralized financial and data transactions

Science and medicine

- Genomics and CRISPR technology revolutionized medicine and agriculture
- Quantum physics superseded classical Newtonian physics
- The heliocentric model replaced the geocentric understanding of our solar system
- Germ theory replaced miasma theory in medicine

Art and design

- Digital art and NFTs transformed creation, ownership, and distribution
- Cubism and abstract expressionism broke from representational art
- 3D printing shifted manufacturing from subtractive to additive processes
- Streaming media replaced physical media formats

Transportation

- Electric vehicles challenged internal combustion engine dominance
- Ride-sharing services transformed urban mobility
- Self-driving technology is redefining vehicle operation
- Commercial space travel is expanding beyond government agencies

Social and political

- Social media transformed information sharing and public discourse
- Digital privacy concerns have changed how we think about personal data
- Nonviolent resistance movements redefined political change
- Remote work shifted workplace dynamics and geography

Let's explore some specific examples of paradigm shifts in greater detail.

Spotify

An example of a company that brought in a new paradigm was Spotify. Created in 2006 in Sweden, its founders, Daniel Ek and Martin Lorentzon, wanted to create a platform that offered a

> " Spotify disrupted the way music is consumed and distributed for everyone. "

superior user experience while mitigating piracy.[1] Spotify's most fundamental shift was changing music consumption from a product to be owned to a streaming service with a subscription. This challenged the traditional music model of buying albums or singles and changed the habits of hundreds of millions of music lovers forever.

Unlimited listening: The streaming model offered listeners access to millions of songs for a flat monthly fee, dramatically increasing the value proposition compared to purchasing individual albums or tracks.

Personalization and discovery: Spotify's algorithms and curated playlists transformed how people discovered new music.[2] This shifted the power of music curation from traditional gatekeepers (radio DJs, music critics) to a mix of algorithms and user-generated content.

Socialization: Features like shared playlists and the ability to see what friends are listening to transformed music consumption into a more social, connected experience. In 2023, it unveiled Jam, a personalized, real-time listening session for friends, colleagues, or relatives.[3]

Monetization model: Spotify's 'freemium' model, offering free streaming with ads or a paid subscription without ads, created a new way to monetize music, addressing piracy concerns while providing a no-cost option.

Podcast integration: By incorporating podcasts into its platform, Spotify diversified its audio products. It is now one of the most popular podcast platforms in the world.[4]

International expansion started in Europe but expanded to the US, Latin America, and Asia.[5] Easy access to music worldwide accelerated the globalization of music tastes and the rise of international hits.

Spotify disrupted the way music is consumed and distributed for everyone. These changes fundamentally altered how people think about music consumption and distribution. Notably, Spotify's model compensated artists based on streams rather than the old way of album purchases.

Today, music streaming makes up 89% of the music industry revenue, a seismic shift from traditional music revenue sources such as physical sales and digital downloads. This trend underscores how streaming has revolutionized how music is distributed, accessed, and monetized.[6]

The Minerva project

Another example of a paradigm shift comes from Minerva, which has been named the most innovative university in the world. Founder Ben Nelson believes that universities are crucial institutions for society, but they have been mired in traditional practices that have not changed for decades, leading them to lose sight of their original purpose. Their pedagogy is neither memorable nor valuable, churning out students who do not learn anything long-lasting but just want a graduation certificate.[7]

His alma mater is not exempt from this charge. Nelson said the curriculum he took 30 years ago as an undergrad, which was not brand new then, is still the one his university uses today. He said this indicates that all university education is a repeat of approaches that have been proven ineffective for decades. Colleges do not teach students the know-how they need post-graduation, such as how to do business in different countries, industries, and other contexts.

But the core failing of current universities is not teaching systematic thinking—learning holistically, considering the big picture—for better decision-making. "I realized that a traditional university education, where every professor comes up with their class, and they're disconnected from one another, doesn't enable systematic thinking," Nelson said. "Creating education that is practical and usable is an imperative."[8]

In 2012, he established a university that would correct what he felt were missed opportunities forsaken by higher education. "This was really the heart of what the Minerva reform was, which was thinking about how to teach systematic thinking in an interconnected way, with students that are deeply engaged and retain what it is they've learned," Nelson said in a video for a Coursera course on unlocking creativity and innovation.

Minerva's educational approach starts with a core curriculum, coupled with a pedagogy called 'fully active learning' delivered digitally, where students apply what they have learned. Students live together in San Francisco for a year, and then in six different countries for the six semesters. They learn to apply systematic thinking from course to course and country to country.

"Systematic thinking isn't just what a computer does. In fact, it is quite the opposite. It is being able to take a problem and break it down into its component parts, but creatively thinking through what kinds of solutions can come out of them," Nelson said.

Most recently, the university has embraced generative AI applications in education. Its AI Consensus student group infused the students' perspective in the experiment because most conversations around AI in higher education are dominated by teachers and administrators who focus more on theoretical frameworks than practical implementation.[9]

At the time of writing, Minerva University has been recognized as the most innovative university in the world for the third year in a row by the World University Rankings for Innovation (WURI).[10] A thousand students are enrolled as undergraduates from 100 countries.

Israel's first private, not-for-profit university

Thirty years ago, Uriel Reichman set out to do what seemed impossible: Establish a nonprofit, private university in Israel. At the time, higher education was controlled by seven government-sponsored universities, which had to approve the creation of another university. Reichman thought it was essential to build a private university, to open the gates to higher education for more people. It was an ambitious dream, but Reichman was determined to pursue it.

"I was able to do it, first and foremost, by having an obvious plan of what I wanted to accomplish," he recounts in a video for a Coursera course on unlocking creativity that accompanies this book. As dean of a law school, university professor, and founder of a movement to establish a constitution for Israel, he had the connections and experience to execute his plan. He persuaded his leading academic friends to join his endeavor, even though they had scarce resources. "We didn't have any money. We didn't have, in the beginning, any accreditation to grant academic degrees. The road was very tough."

But with a big dream and determination, he succeeded. In 1994, Reichman founded the Interdisciplinary Center (IDC) Herzliya (Israel). As an interdisciplinary university from the start, it offered degree programs in Hebrew and later, English, that attracted enrollees from over 90 nations. Its ideology is summed up by two words: Freedom and responsibility.

"We try to educate our students not to wait for the government to solve their problems, but rather to show entrepreneurship and initiative," along with a spirit of responsibility, upholding the values upon which Israel was founded. "What was the most important element in our success was having a clear idea where we were aiming, what we wanted to do, what is our vision," Reichman said. "We were able to walk our way independently and bring about a change in higher education in Israel."

In 2022, the IDC college was recognized as a university, and its name was changed to Reichman University in honor of its founding president. In the same year, the university added the Google high-tech school. In 2024, they added a new medical school in collaboration with the country's leading hospitals and healthcare providers.

The university has 8,400 students and more than 24,000 alumni.[11] The success of Reichman University demonstrates several key creativity lessons:

- Having a bold vision and dream despite seemingly insurmountable obstacles
- Being persistent in the face of endless challenges from governing institutions
- Having the courage to challenge the status quo and the established monopoly
- Focusing on students as co-producers and at the center of the initiative
- Designing innovative interdisciplinary programs that create more attractive graduates for employers to hire
- Challenging the revenue model by rejecting government support and instead relying on tuition and philanthropic contributions
- Building networks of supporters from industry in Israel and abroad, government officials, and leading faculty

Uber

Some ideas are so revolutionary that they create a significant paradigm shift that affects entire industries. Consider the creation of Uber, the ride-hailing app. Founders Travis Kalanick and Garrett Camp could not get a taxi in Paris on a cold winter evening in December 2008. It sparked the idea that there must be a better way to get a ride.[12]

They questioned the status quo—in most cities, one can only hail a cab at taxi stands or outside airports and train stations. What if there were a way to make rides ubiquitous by paying regular people to transport the public using their private vehicles, at any time and place?

Kalanick and Camp knew they would disrupt the long-standing taxi industry, which had stood unchallenged since the horse-drawn carriages for hire of the 17th century.[13] In March 2009, the two developed a smartphone app to connect riders with drivers, and changed the mental model of mobility forever. They created a system of on-demand public transportation and flexible employment now known as the modern 'gig economy.'

Tesla

Another company that challenged the industry's status quo is Tesla. When it decided to enter the global auto industry, Tesla faced the might of entrenched automobile manufacturers in Detroit, Germany, Japan, and South Korea, whose highly competitive moat made it difficult for new rivals to gain traction.

Tesla shattered the perception that electric vehicles were underpowered. The Tesla Roadster, the company's first production car, could accelerate from zero to 60 mph in under four seconds, competing with high-end sports cars. Tesla also challenged the stereotype that eco-friendly vehicles always look utilitarian. It created sleek, modern cars that appealed to luxury consumers.

Tesla also sold cars differently. It adopted a direct-to-customer sales model rather than using third-party car dealerships, delivering a more streamlined, transparent process. It also disrupted the auto supply chain model by vertically integrating battery and car production at its 'Gigafactories.'

Tesla reimagined cars as computers on wheels, where new features could be downloaded over the air.[14] They have large touchscreen interfaces and advanced driver assistance features (such as Autopilot) that position the cars as high-tech devices rather than just transportation. It also developed a network of charging stations to scale electric vehicle adoption.

By challenging these established norms, Tesla not only changed perceptions about electric vehicles but also forced the entire auto industry to consider the viability of electric cars and reconsider its approach to automotive design, technology, and sustainability. This shift in mental models rippled beyond car enthusiasts and influenced public policy, urban planning, and people's daily energy consumption.

BYD Auto

China's electric vehicle makers have also been trailblazers. One that stands out as the most innovative is BYD Auto, which is leading the industry in China with groundbreaking technologies and strategic advancements. Founded in 1995, BYD has evolved from a battery producer into a global automotive powerhouse, selling more than three million vehicles in 2023. This remarkable growth is primarily attributed to its proprietary 'Blade Battery,' known for its cost-effectiveness, safety, and durability. The Blade Battery's design enhances energy density and thermal management, setting new standards in EV battery performance.[15]

In addition to battery innovation, BYD has revolutionized vehicle intelligence with its self-driving system. This advanced driver-assistance technology offers features such as remote parking and autonomous overtaking, and is being integrated across BYD's vehicle lineup, including the affordable $9,500 Seagull model. By making high-level autonomous features accessible in entry-level vehicles, BYD democratizes advanced automotive technology, challenges industry norms, and sets new benchmarks for competitors.[16]

Patagonia

While Uber and Tesla represent powerful examples of paradigm shifts driven by technological innovation, equally transformative paradigm shifts have emerged from mission-driven visions. Consider Patagonia, which challenged the fundamental business paradigm that profit maximization must be a company's primary goal. By prioritizing environmental stewardship—even discouraging unnecessary purchases of their products—the company created a revolutionary business model where sustainability drives decisions rather than merely influencing them. Founder Yvon Chouinard ultimately transferred ownership to a trust and nonprofit dedicated to fighting climate change, creating a new corporate-purpose paradigm.

Creating new paradigms revolves around having a bold vision and chasing that dream, rather than finding a million reasons why it won't work. Many individuals and companies have done the seemingly impossible and improbable; why can't you? It starts with having a deep passion about something and then working systematically to make it real.

There's an essential distinction between refining an existing paradigm and creating a genuinely new one. While incremental improvements have their place, they rarely lead to breakthrough innovation. When faced with significant challenges or opportunities, beware the temptation

> **"**
> AI can serve as both a catalyst and a compass when pursuing paradigm-shifting visions.
> **"**

to make safe, modest adjustments to the status quo. True paradigm shifts require courage to imagine fundamentally different outcomes, even when they initially seem impossible or impractical. Netflix didn't try to make video rental stores marginally better—they envisioned an entirely different way to access entertainment. When developing your vision, ask whether you're merely improving the existing game or changing the rules entirely. Sometimes, the latter is necessary to achieve the transformation you seek.

The Role of AI in Creating New Paradigms

AI can serve as both a catalyst and a compass when pursuing paradigm-shifting visions. As a catalyst, AI tools can generate provocative 'what if' scenarios that expand the boundaries of what you believe possible. For example, prompting an AI system to envision ten radically different futures for your industry can reveal ambitious directions that conventional thinking might miss.

As a compass, AI can help navigate the uncertainty inherent in paradigm-shifting journeys. Predictive models can simulate potential outcomes of different strategic approaches, while natural language processing can analyze vast amounts of case studies to identify patterns in successful paradigm shifts across industries. This evidence-based guidance helps balance visionary ambition with practical implementation strategies.

Additionally, AI's ability to rapidly prototype concepts through text descriptions, visual renderings, or simulated outcomes allows visionaries to refine their ideas through rapid iteration long before significant resources are committed. This accelerates the journey from initial dream to viable paradigm shift.

Tome

Consider Tome, an AI-powered platform that reimagines presentations as living, evolving narratives. Instead of spending hours formatting decks, users input an idea or prompt, and Tome co-creates a polished presentation in minutes, complete with structured storytelling, visuals, and layout.

Tome was co-founded in 2020 by Keith Peiris and Henri Liriani, two former Instagram leads who worked on AR and product storytelling.[17] At Instagram, they witnessed firsthand how content creation tools could empower everyday users. They asked themselves a paradigm-shifting question: What if storytelling tools were so intuitive and intelligent that anyone could craft a world-class narrative without design or tech skills?

Traditional presentation software treated visuals as separate from ideas, requiring users to be part writers, designers, and technicians. Tome makes creating presentations more accessible by embedding large language models and design intelligence into the creative flow.

Tome's Paradigm Shift

1. The storyteller is the visionary, not the technician: It empowers users to focus on what they want to say, not how to build it. The shift from tedious formatting to seamless storytelling allows more voices to share bold ideas without barriers.

2. Design becomes dynamic: Unlike static slides, Tome presentations adapt. They can be updated in real time with new data, content, or structure, all guided by

AI. This makes communication feel less like publishing and more like a live dialogue.

3. Communication becomes iterative: With rapid prototyping built in, users can instantly test different narrative flows or visual approaches. Feedback becomes part of the creative cycle, not something tacked on after.

4. In short, Tome challenges the assumption that storytelling belongs to the technically skilled.

Canva

To truly understand the power of creating new paradigms, consider Canva, the graphic design platform Melanie Perkins co-founded with her partner Cliff Obrecht and Cameron Adams in Australia in 2012. At the time, Perkins was a university student teaching peers how to use complex design tools like Adobe Photoshop and InDesign, and noticed that most people found these tools intimidating because of their notorious steep learning curve.[18]

She wondered: What if anyone, regardless of skill or training, could easily create beautiful designs? Under the leadership of the founding trio, Canva has grown to over 200 million monthly active users and has achieved a valuation of $32 billion.[19]

Perkins' rethinking of graphic design was a paradigm shift of design itself. Traditional design tools assumed a high barrier to entry: expensive software, steep learning curves, and years of training, built for professionals. Canva made graphic design accessible to everyone.

Canva's Paradigm Shift

1. Democratization of design: Canva made design accessible to students, marketers, entrepreneurs, teachers, and everyone else through a reasonably priced, intuitive, drag-and-drop interface paired with thousands of templates, beautiful fonts that can be purchased separately, and stock photographs from subsidiary companies Pixabay and Pexels. Professional-looking visuals were no longer the domain of experts. Design became part of an everyday toolkit.

2. Design as a collaborative act: Before Canva, design was often a siloed task outsourced to a specialist graphic designer or illustrator. Canva's cloud-based platform introduced real-time collaboration, allowing teams to co-create, iterate, and publish all in one space, mirroring what Google Docs did for documents or Excel for spreadsheets. This was a new way of thinking about who participates in the creative process.

3. Visual communication becomes universal: Visual storytelling is now an essential part of our lives, whether we want to pitch a business idea, provide visuals when teaching a class, rally support for a cause, or just simply design invitations for a party. Canva recognized this early on, positioning itself as more

than a graphic design tool but a visual communication platform. This shift has empowered users in 190 countries to tell their stories visually.

4. The mission drives the model: Perkins has said from the start that Canva's mission is "to empower the world to design." That clarity of purpose helped the company stay focused on inclusion and simplicity even as it scaled. Canva is used by everyone from rural students to Fortune 500 brands. It was designed for universal access, not elite functionality.

Canva reminds us that you don't need to start with the biggest team or the most resources. You need a bold vision that solves a problem others accept as permanent. This is what paradigm shifts look like: They don't just improve the rules, they change the game. Perkins saw a world where highly skilled professionals no longer gatekeep design. She envisioned one where design was a language everyone could speak, and her dream became a platform that has now redefined visual communication across industries.

With AI now embedded in platforms like Canva and Tome, the visual design and storytelling paradigm is still evolving.

Ask yourself: What tools or paradigms do you accept as fixed, simply because that's how it's always been? Or what barriers seem immovable? What if the opposite were true?

⚡ Exercise

1. Reflection: Identifying Broken Paradigms. What assumption about your work, industry, or life seems increasingly broken or outdated? Which accepted 'truths' create friction, inefficiency, or frustration for you or those you serve? Identifying these pain points can reveal opportunities for paradigm shifts. For example, before Airbnb, the paradigm that accommodations required purpose-built hotels seemed obvious—until someone questioned why unused living spaces couldn't become temporary lodging. What similar opportunities might exist in your environment? What if the opposite of today's dominant approach were true? Allow yourself to explore these possibilities without immediately judging their feasibility.

2. Reverse your excuses
    - List the top 3 reasons you can't pursue your dream.
    - Now, write a counterargument for each excuse as if you were advising a friend.
    - This trains your mind to challenge limiting beliefs and see opportunities where you saw roadblocks.

3. Letter to your future self
   - Write a letter to yourself from your future self who has achieved your dream.
   - Describe your life, how you overcame obstacles, and what advice you would give yourself today.
   - This exercise strengthens your vision and connects you to your dream.

4. The bold experiment
   - Identify one small but bold action you can take this week that aligns with your dream (e.g., reaching out to a mentor, launching a test version of an idea, or applying for a relevant opportunity).
   - Set a deadline and commit to doing it, no matter how imperfect.
   - Reflection: After completing it, write down what you've learned and what your next step should be.

5. Obstacle mapping
   - Take a blank sheet of paper and write your dream in the center.
   - Around it, list all potential obstacles that could get in your way.
   - Next to each obstacle, brainstorm at least one creative way to overcome it.
   - This trains you to proactively solve problems instead of being paralyzed by them.

6. One-year action blueprint
   - Break your dream into four major milestones for the next year.
   - For each milestone, list three actions that will help you achieve it.
   - Assign deadlines to each action step and put them on your calendar.

Having a structured plan makes your dream feel more achievable and keeps you accountable.

In Summary

1. **Chase your wildest dreams instead of listing reasons why they won't work.**
Like Spotify's founders who transformed music from a product to a service, or Uriel Reichman who created Israel's first private not-for-profit university against all odds, your passionate pursuit of what seems impossible can reshape entire industries and cultures.
What dream have you been dismissing as unrealistic?

2. **Question the fundamental assumptions everyone else takes for granted.**
Tesla challenged the belief that electric vehicles must be underpowered and utilitarian. Uber questioned why we needed designated taxis when anyone could provide rides.
"What if the opposite of today's dominant approach were true?"

In Summary (contd.)

---

3. Focus on systematic implementation, not just the vision.

Minerva University methodically built a revolutionary alternative with active learning pedagogy, global immersion, and cross-disciplinary approaches.

How might you map your obstacles and create a structured action plan with specific milestones to transform your dream into reality?

4. Look for pain points that signal broken paradigms.

Melanie Perkins noticed how frustrating design software was for beginners and created Canva, a platform that democratized visual communication for 200 million users.

What friction or inefficiency in your world might be an opportunity for transformation rather than an unchangeable reality?

5. Use AI as a catalyst and compass for paradigm shifts.

AI tools can generate provocative "what if" scenarios that expand your thinking beyond conventional boundaries while helping you navigate uncertainty through predictive models and rapid prototyping.

What hidden insights might emerge if AI challenged your most fundamental assumptions about your business model?

Our next chapter will explore a structured approach to making your idea a reality.

Notes

1   Pablo Nastar. "Spotify: A Story of Innovation, Automation, and Success," LinkedIn, May 8, 2024. https://www.linkedin.com/pulse/spotify-story-innovation-automation-success--mrkjf/

2   Ibid.

3   "Spotify Unveils Jam, a New, Personalized Way to Listen With Your Entire Squad," Spotify corporate website, September 26, 2023. https://newsroom.spotify.com/2023-09-26/spotify-jam-personalized-collaborative-listening-session-free-premium-users/

4   Pablo Nastar. "Spotify: A Story of Innovation, Automation, and Success," LinkedIn, May 8, 2024 https://www.linkedin.com/pulse/spotify-story-innovation-automation-success--mrkjf/

5   Ibid.

6   Anna Durrani. "Top Streaming Statistics in 2024," Forbes, June 13, 2024. https://www.forbes.com/home-improvement/internet/streaming-stats/

7   "Revolutionizing Higher Education: A Conversation with Ben Nelson, Founder of Minerva University," YouTube, September 29, 2023, video, 16:09. https://www.youtube.com/watch?v=69SQpKTZqg4

8   Ibid.

9   Leo Wu, Jan Bartkowiak, and Maia Lortkipanidze. "Students@AI: What Does It Mean to Be a Student in the Age of AI?" March 25, 2024. https://www.aiconsensus.org/

10 Minerva University. "Minerva University Earns Title of Most Innovative University in the World for Third Straight Year," university press release, June 10, 2024, https://www.prnewswire.com/news-releases/minerva-university-earns-title-of-most-innovative-university-in-the-world-for-third-straight-year-302168445.html; S.M. Kosslyn and B. Nelson (Eds.). *Building the Intentional University: Minerva and the Future of Higher Education* (MIT Press, 2017).

11 Reichman University. "About Reichman University," accessed November 12, 2024. https://www.runi.ac.il/en/about/

12 Uber website. "The History of Uber," accessed August 8, 2024. https://www.uber.com/newsroom/history/

13 Robert Tate. "A Brief History of Taxicabs 1907-1968," MotorCities. https://www.motorcities.org/story-of-the-week/2018/a-brief-history-of-taxicabs-1907-1968

14 Nathan Furr and Jeff Dyer. "Lessons from Tesla's Approach to Innovation," *Harvard Business Review,* February 19, 2020. https://hbr.org/2020/02/lessons-from-teslas-approach-to-innovation

15 Marina Lopes. "Wang Chuanfu," *TIME100 Climate 2024, Time,* November 12, 2024. https://time.com/7172564/wang-chuanfu-climate/

16 Tom Carter. "China's BYD Goes All-In on Self-Driving, with Even Its $9,500 EV Getting 'High-Level' Autonomous Features," *Business Insider,* February 11, 2025. https://www.businessinsider.com/byd-self-driving-expansion-cheap-seagull-ev-high-level-features-2025-2

17 AI-powered storytelling tool catches fire with Gen Z, Reed Albergotti, July 19, 2023, Semafor, accessed April 28, 2025. https://www.semafor.com/article/07/19/2023/tome-an-ai-powered-slideshow-tool-catches-fire-with-gen-z

18 Melanie Perkins—Canva, by Kit Warchol, Career Contessa, accessed April 28, 2025. https://www.careercontessa.com/interviews/canva-founder-melanie-perkins/

19 Canva, Wikipedia, accessed April 28, 2025. https://en.wikipedia.org/wiki/Canva

Chapter 7
Approach #3: Use Morphological Analysis

Creativity is the process of having original ideas that have value.
It is a process; it's not random.
—Ken Robinson, British author

Creativity often flourishes when structure meets imagination. This chapter explores a systematic method for categorizing complex problems and solutions into their fundamental components, called morphological analysis. This allows you to reimagine solutions through new combinations and configurations.

Morphological analysis was first developed in the 1940s by Fritz Zwicky at Cal Tech. The first applications were in astrophysics, but the power of the approach was recognized in many other domains. The classic book on the topic, *Discovery, Invention, Research through the Morphological Approach*, was published by Zwicky in 1969.[1]

Morphological analysis proves especially valuable for complex, multi-variable challenges where traditional brainstorming might miss non-obvious combinations. When designing a new product, service, or business model, the number of potential configurations often exceeds what intuitive thinking can explore. The morphological analysis approach breaks down the challenge into distinct dimensions to help you systematically evaluate combinations.

It shines particularly when you are addressing problems with multiple stakeholders, technical constraints, and competing objectives—situations where finding the optimal configuration requires examining numerous possibilities rather than settling for the first workable solution. To conduct morphological analysis:

> **Morphological analysis shines particularly when you are addressing problems with multiple stakeholders**

Step 1: Identify your goal or aspiration.
Step 2: Break down the parts of the solution.
Step 3: Recombine these elements in new ways.

For example, consider a nonprofit organization aiming to develop an effective fundraising strategy. By applying morphological analysis, the organization can break the challenge into interconnected components: identifying the target audience, crafting a compelling positioning strategy, determining the most effective ways to engage the audience, and selecting the optimal context for the fundraising effort. This structured approach allows for a comprehensive exploration of possibilities, ensuring the strategy is innovative and well-rounded.

The table below illustrates options for the nonprofit's fundraising effort:

Table 7.1: Morphological Analysis of a Nonprofit's Fundraising Efforts: Step 1

Assume that the objective is funding a nonprofit organization. To do so the organization must develop a strategy that at the minimum includes four elements:

Segment	Positioning	Approach by	Context
• Foundations	• Education	• Head of institution	• One-on-one
• Government	• Future building	• Trustee	• Dinner
• Trustees	• Capital campaign	• Development	• Breakfast
• Local members	• Endowment	• Friends	• Conferences
• Other prospects		• Crowd	• Emails
• Crowd		• Celebrities	• Telephone

Assuming you are satisfied with the four categories and the list of strategic options under each, the next step is to crisscross entries under each category to mix them up. This will result in many combinations that could turn into potential strategies.

For example, a fundraising strategy could reach out to foundations like the Bill and Melinda Gates Foundation (Segment: Foundations) with a pitch to improve education (Positioning: Education) for the children of incarcerated parents. The nonprofit's trustee (Approach by: Trustee), who knows some folks at the Gates foundation, will approach. The appeal will be made in a personal phone call (Context: Telephone) since some rapport has already been established. (See the Green line in Table 7.2.)

Table 7.2: Morphological Analysis of a Nonprofit's Fundraising Efforts: Step 2

Assume that the objective is funding a nonprofit organization. To do so the organization must develop a strategy that at the minimum includes four elements:

Segment	Positioning	Approach by	Context
• Foundations	• Education	• Head of institution	• One-on-one
• Government	• Future building	• Trustee	• Dinner
• Trustees	• Capital campaign	• Development	• Breakfast
• Local members	• Endowment	• Friends	• Conferences
• Other prospects		• Crowd	• Emails
• Crowd		• Celebrities	• Telephone

Another potential strategy is to ask local members to donate to a building project. The nonprofit's executive director will make the outreach through the monthly email (Red line). An out-of-the-box strategy could be tapping crowdsourcing to fund a capital campaign using celebrities to amplify the message at a breakfast rally (Blue line).

How AI Can Take It to the Next Level

Continuing with the nonprofit example, use ChatGPT, Claude, or the Gemini AI assistant to help you do the following:

- Identify more categories to add to the four.
- Identify more elements within each category.
- Create comprehensive combinations of these elements.
- Evaluate the feasibility and attractiveness of combinations from the morphological analysis

Our prompt to ChatGPT, focusing on the last three points, was, "Come up with a morphological analysis of a nonprofit seeking to raise funding. It must create a fundraising strategy. Create a morphological matrix and combinations of possible strategies."

Using AI to expand the elements of our nonprofit example, we add two new suggestions under Segment: high-net-worth individuals and community groups, such as clubs, churches, etc. Under Positioning, it added 'research and innovation funding' and 'program-specific funding.' For Approach By, it added email newsletters and online ads. In Context, the AI added galas, auctions, membership programs, personal tours, and networking events.

The AI assistant came up with the following suggested strategies:

1. Develop an exclusive membership program where wealthy donors receive personal tours and networking opportunities, with contributions to growing the nonprofit's endowment.
2. Approach foundations with a targeted direct mail campaign, highlighting media stories about a capital campaign to construct a new community center, offering naming rights to major donors.
3. Send personalized letters and emails highlighting heartwarming stories of impact. Utilize strong visuals, testimonials, and clear calls to action.
4. Launch an annual corporate matching program where businesses match employee donations. Regular executive meetings maintain relationships with company names featured on projects.
5. Empower supporters to fundraise through their networks using social media campaigns, supported by monthly giving programs and regular impact updates.
6. Let's say you want to implement the first strategy. But you want to know the pros and cons of each. You can ask the AI assistant to assess it.

Pros and Cons

Prompt (to ChatGPT): What are the pros and cons of this strategy? Develop an exclusive membership program where wealthy donors receive personal tours and networking opportunities, with contributions to growing the nonprofit's endowment.

Pros: Sustainable funding, strengthens donor relationships, attracts high-impact donors, showcases transparency (personal tours), leverages networking, and enhances reputation

Cons: High costs, limited accessibility (might alienate smaller donors), risk of overdependence, long-term commitment, perception issues (exclusivity, hints of elitism), complex management of an endowment

Feasibility Rating

Table 7.3: Feasibility Rating

Factor	Rating (High/Medium/Low)	Key Notes
Target Audience Availability	High	High-net-worth individuals value exclusivity
Organizational Capacity	Medium	Staff and resources may limit implementation
Financial Investment	Medium	Upfront costs require careful budgeting
Endowment Readiness	Medium	Expertise is needed for setup and management
Donor Engagement Expertise	High	Strong donor relationships enhance success
Alignment with Mission	Medium	Exclusivity must align with the brand
Long-Term Benefits	Medium	Immediate needs may compete with long-term goals

Attractiveness: These fundraising strategies are highly attractive because they offer a mix of high-impact, relationship-driven approaches and scalable, grassroots engagement methods. They cater to donor segments—wealthy individuals, corporate partners, foundations, and the general public—maximizing the nonprofit's reach and potential funding sources. By balancing exclusivity with broad-based appeals and leveraging emotional storytelling and financial incentives, these strategies create multiple entry points for donors to contribute. The key to success lies in tailoring the approach to the nonprofit's mission, resources, and audience, ensuring a sustainable and diversified revenue stream.

Verdict: Feasible and attractive with conditions

This strategy is feasible and attractive if the nonprofit has access to high-net-worth donors, sufficient resources for execution, and aligns the strategy with its mission. Success depends on careful planning and balancing immediate operational needs with long-term financial security.

Try experimenting with other AI platforms like Claude, Gemini, or DeepSeek for different perspectives and insights. Each model may provide unique strategic ideas based on their training data and capabilities.

Expanding upon Airbnb's model

Airbnb is a disruptor that has introduced a new paradigm into the well-entrenched hospitality industry. In 2007, Brian Chesky and Joe Gebbia were broke and looking to make money from rent in San Francisco. At the time, a design conference was coming to town, but hotels were all booked. So they rented out air mattresses in their apartment to attendees, added a little city tour on the side, and called their place 'Air Bed and Breakfast.'[2] When they later decided to turn it into a business, people thought they were crazy. Investors would not meet with them, predicting guests would murder their Airbnb hosts.

But to the founders' surprise, the people who stayed with them were not hippie backpackers, but budget-minded folks like them who wanted to rent those air mattresses. People would send in their resumes and LinkedIn profiles to prove they were not security risks.[3]

In March 2009, the startup changed its name to Airbnb. As of January 2025, it is a publicly held company with more than eight million listings globally in more than 100,000 cities and towns, and has served more than two billion guests. Hosts have earned a total of $250 billion worldwide.[4]

At 17 years old, Airbnb is now a mature business. How could it further innovate?

To truly understand the power of morphological analysis, the table on next page breaks down the key variables and their possible values.

Entrepreneurs or business owners can discover unexplored market opportunities by systematically exploring combinations across these variables. For instance, the combination of 'Unique spaces' (Accommodation Type) with 'Event attendees' (Target Market) might suggest a specialized service for renting unusual venues for weddings or corporate retreats—a different business than Airbnb's core offering, but discoverable through this analytical approach.

> **Entrepreneurs or business owners can discover unexplored market opportunities by systematically exploring combinations across variables.**

Table 7.4: Morphological Analysis of the Airbnb Business Model

Morphological Analysis of Airbnb Business Model

Accommodation Types	Booking Duration	Property Ownership	Target Markets	Revenue Models
• Entire homes/ apartments • Private rooms • Shared rooms • Unique spaces • Office spaces • Storage spaces	• Hourly • Daily • Weekly • Monthly • Long-term leases	• Individual homeowners • Property managers • Hotel/hostels • Universities • Corporations	• Budget travelers • Business travelers • Luxury seekers • Digital nomads • Event attendees	• Commission-based • Subscription-based • Advertising-based • Freemium model • Membership fees

Booking Process	Trust & Safety	Additional Services	Technology	Geography
• Instant booking • Request-to-book Bidding system • Long-term matching	• User reviews • Identification verification • Security deposits • Insurance offerings • Property vetting	• Cleaning services • Local experiences • Transportation • Concierge services • Property management	• Mobile app • Web platform • Smart home integration • Virtual reality tours • AI-powered matching	• Local • National • International • Special locations

Practice morphological analysis

1. Product reinvention challenge: Choose a common, everyday item such as table, sofa, or book and break it down to its key components in terms of material, color, shape, function, etc. List variations for each attribute (material could be wood, cloth, metal, for example). Experiment with combining elements from each of the attributes to create a new version of the product.

2. Combine contradictory attributes: Select an object or service and list its characteristics and opposite attributes. Examples are 'large, but portable,' and 'fragile, yet durable.' This method can lead to new designs, features, or reimagined products. A glass manufacturer, for example, can aim to develop fragile yet durable wine glasses.

3. Attribute evolution: Pick a classic version of a product or service. List its main attributes and imagine alternative versions in the next few decades. For example, 'battery-powered' could become 'solar-powered energy harvesting.' The goal is to imagine future product versions to avoid obsolescence from a competitor.

4. Business concept reinvention: Generate ideas for a new business by combining attributes from unrelated industries. Start by picking two sectors, for example, health care and entertainment. List key characteristics of each. For health care: patient care, technology, privacy; for entertainment: storytelling, audience engagement, visual appeal. Combine attributes across industries to create a new business idea.

Make sure to pose the challenge to different AI assistants and compare their responses. Pick the best answers from each for optimal results. You could also ask one AI assistant to critique the work of another.

The Role of AI With Morphological Analysis

Morphological analysis is an opportunity to use one of the generative AI models to explore any of the following:

- Systematically explore solution spaces you might otherwise overlook
- Generate truly innovative ideas by combining elements in unexpected ways
- Evaluate the feasibility and attractiveness of different approaches before investing in resources
- Break free from linear thinking to discover breakthrough innovations
- Build simple tables that map out all key aspects of your problem and potential solutions
- Identify gaps in existing approaches that competitors may not have yet explored
- Test multiple concepts without the high costs of full implementation
- Balance structured thinking with creative exploration
- Develop a shared language for teams to discuss innovation possibilities
- Borrow successful ideas from other fields to solve your specific challenges
- Question whether certain features or elements truly need to work together
- Find new competitive edges by mixing and matching existing components in surprising ways

This approach efficiently reimagines existing products, services, or strategies and designs new solutions to complex problems. By incorporating AI assistants, you can expand your exploration, receive initial assessments of feasibility and attractiveness, and rapidly iterate on your ideas.

In Summary

> **1. Break down complex problems into their basic building blocks.**
> Just as Airbnb's business model can be analyzed across ten dimensions from accommodation types to technology integration, you can dissect any challenge into its core components and discover hidden opportunities.
>
> *What hidden opportunities might you find out by mapping the ten key dimensions of your current challenge?*

In Summary (contd.)

---

2. Create robust solutions by connecting unexpected elements.
Don't just stick with obvious combinations. The most innovative strategies emerge when you deliberately pair elements that aren't typically connected, like using celebrities to promote crowdfunding breakfast events for capital campaigns.

Which unusual combination of resources or ideas could create your next breakthrough?

3. Follow a structured framework for systematic innovation.
Start by clearly defining your goal, then map out all possible components and variations in a simple grid. This organized approach helps you generate innovative combinations that intuitive thinking alone would miss.

How might a simple grid approach reveal combinations your intuition has overlooked?

4. Supercharge your analysis with AI tools.
Ask AI assistants to expand your categories, generate comprehensive combinations, and evaluate the feasibility of your most innovative ideas before investing resources.

What seemingly impossible ideas could become feasible with the proper AI evaluation?

5. Practice with everyday challenges.
Try reinventing everyday products, combining contradictory attributes, or mixing elements from unrelated industries to develop your morphological thinking muscles for larger business challenges.

What new value could you create by mixing elements from completely unrelated industries?

The next chapter shows how you can learn from the success of others to draw fresh perspectives and then combine them with morphological analysis to deepen your study of an innovative idea.

Notes

[1] F. Zwicky. *Discovery, Invention, Research—Through the Morphological Approach* (Toronto: The Macmillan Company, 1969).

[2] "The Inside Story Behind the Unlikely Rise of Airbnb," Knowledge@Wharton, April 26, 2017. https://knowledge.wharton.upenn.edu/podcast/knowledge-at-wharton-podcast/the-inside-story-behind-the-unlikely-rise-of-airbnb/

[3] Ibid.

[4] Airbnb. "About Us." *Airbnb Newsroom,* accessed January 25, 2025. https://news.airbnb.com/about-us/

Analogies for the Rescue

Chapter 8
Approach #4: Employ Analogies and Benchmarking

If I have seen further, it is by standing on the shoulders of giants.
—Isaac Newton

A fourth approach to unlocking creativity is Analogies and Benchmarking, learning from the successes and, at times, failures of others. Finding analogies to which you can compare your situation can spark newfound ideas, especially if the analogy differs from your context. Look at other professions, disciplines, industries, and cultures to teach you new lessons and give you new frameworks.

For example, IDEO, the pioneering design firm that helped shape Stanford's Hasso Plattner Institute of Design, or 'd.school,' was charged with redesigning an operating room where speed was critical. It took inspiration from an analogy as far-flung from medical care as possible: a Formula One pit stop. But what's beautiful about this pairing is that it worked wonders: Analyzing the efficiency of the pit stop crew in a small space centered around a race car gave IDEO valuable lessons in how an operating room can similarly function efficiently, given design changes in the workflow.[1]

Consider also how Broadway stage crews and surgical teams share remarkable parallels: both operate under intense pressure, require flawless coordination among specialists, maintain sterile/organized environments, follow carefully choreographed procedures, and cannot afford

> " **Solutions to your challenge may already exist in seemingly unrelated fields.** "

mistakes. Healthcare innovators studying Broadway's rapid set changes between scenes have improved operating room turnover times and team communication protocols. Similarly, forward-thinking CEOs draw inspiration from orchestra conductors, who harmonize diverse specialists without micromanaging them, communicate through subtle gestures rather than constant intervention, and create collective experiences greater than any individual contribution. These analogies reveal that high-performance coordination principles transcend specific domains and that solutions to your challenges may already exist in seemingly unrelated fields.

Another example is the Marriott Bonvoy loyalty program, which drew heavily from tech platform designs rather than traditional hospitality models, creating a digital ecosystem resembling Amazon's customer experience more closely than a conventional hotel rewards program. Cross-industry learning helped Marriott build stronger digital guest relationships and increase direct bookings. Similarly, Amazon's fulfillment centers have borrowed extensively from fast-food operational models, particularly McDonald's emphasis on standardized processes, consistent quality metrics, and optimized flow. By studying quick-service restaurants rather than traditional warehouses, Amazon developed distribution systems optimized for speed and accuracy rather than mere storage efficiency. These examples demonstrate that the most valuable benchmarking often crosses industry boundaries, finding inspiration in sectors that have already solved similar challenges in different contexts.

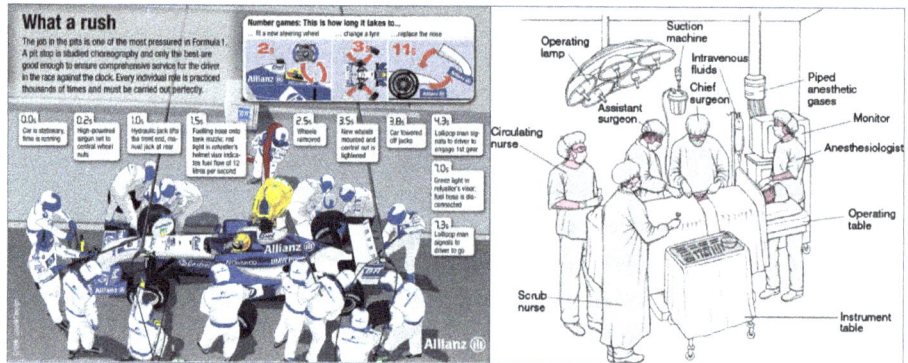

Figure 8.1. IDEO's redesigned operating room takes a page from Formula 1

AI-assisted Analogical Thinking Prompt:

AI tools can dramatically expand your search for powerful analogies. Consider prompting ChatGPT or another AI assistant with questions like:

'What systems in nature or other industries face challenges similar to [your specific challenge]?' or 'What other processes require [key attribute of your process] and have solved it elegantly?' For example, a retail executive might ask, 'What systems outside of retail excel at predicting highly variable demand patterns?' and discover relevant models from electricity grid management or hospital emergency departments.

The AI can rapidly identify patterns and connections across diverse domains that might take humans weeks of research to discover. While you'll need to evaluate these suggestions critically, they can provide a rich starting point for analogical thinking that breaks you out of industry tunnel vision.

Finding Your Analogies

Identify a specific challenge you currently face in your work or personal life. Now, rather than looking for solutions within your domain, ask yourself:

'Who would be world-class at handling this challenge, even in a different context?'

You might look to emergency response teams if you're struggling with rapid decision-making. You might study museum curators or library scientists if you need to organize complex information. If you're working on customer experience, you might examine luxury hotels or theme parks. Identify one organization or field that excels in your fundamental challenge, and schedule time to study their approach in depth. What principles could you adapt to your context?

These analogies offer creative frameworks for approaching a complex social challenge. Try using AI to generate analogies for your challenges and see how they inspire new solutions.

i Exercise

Choose a challenge or goal and pair it with an analogy from which you can view the situation through a new lens. What did you learn?

For example, consider this prompt to Claude: "What strategies can be used to resolve ideological divides in society? Please illustrate your answer using analogies from different fields." Claude responded with the following analogies that provide fresh perspectives on addressing ideological divides:

1. Bridge engineering: Like connecting two separate land masses, resolving ideological divides requires structural support (shared values), multiple connection points (diverse dialogue channels), and flexibility to withstand stress (adaptable frameworks that accommodate different viewpoints).
2. Ecosystem restoration: Similar to healing damaged ecosystems, bridging divides requires understanding the entire system, introducing "keystone species" (respected bridge-builders), creating buffer zones (neutral discussion spaces), and recognizing that recovery takes time and patience.
3. Musical harmony: Just as different notes create harmony when properly arranged, diverse viewpoints can create social harmony through structured dialogue, recognizing that dissonance (disagreement) can lead to resolution, and that a skilled conductor (mediator) helps keep everyone 'in time.'

Benchmarking as a Creative Tool

Using benchmarks is another way to develop creative ideas or solutions. This technique requires finding an individual or organization accomplishing a similar goal excellently and then learning from their example.

Xerox used this method to significant effect. The technology giant learned from a retailer how to cut the cost of invoicing. Xerox found out, for example, that the entire purchase invoice of a retailer was lower than its billing cost alone. The stark comparison prompted Xerox to rethink its invoicing processes completely.[2]

Benchmarking is typically used to measure performance against industry standards or com-

> **Benchmarking can be leveraged to stimulate creative solutions.**

petitors, but it can also be leveraged to stimulate creative solutions. Here's how you can use benchmarking to foster creativity:

- Cross-industry benchmarking
  - Look at best practices from unrelated industries
  - Adapt innovative ideas from other sectors to your field

- Identify performance gaps
  - Pinpoint areas where your organization lags behind benchmarks
  - Use these gaps as opportunities for creative problem-solving

- Reverse engineering
  - Study top performers' processes and outcomes
  - Brainstorm ways to achieve similar results through different methods

- Best practice adaptation
  - Analyze why certain practices work well in other contexts
  - Creatively modify these practices to fit your unique situation

- Trend analysis
  - Examine patterns and trends across benchmarked organizations
  - Predict future developments and innovate proactively

- Combination of ideas
  - Take elements from various benchmarked practices
  - Combine them in novel ways to create unique solutions

- Challenge assumptions
  - Question why benchmarked practices work
  - Explore alternative approaches that could yield better results

- Stretch goals
  - Set ambitious targets based on top performers
  - Encourage creative thinking to achieve seemingly impossible goals

- Collaborative benchmarking
  - Partner with other organizations to share insights
  - Use diverse perspectives to spark new ideas

- Customer-centric benchmarking

  - Study how top performers meet customer needs
  - Innovate ways to exceed customer expectations

Using benchmarking as a springboard for creativity rather than a rigid comparison tool, you can generate novel solutions beyond simply matching industry standards.

How AI can Help with Benchmarking

AI can significantly enhance creativity through benchmarking by streamlining the process of identifying, analyzing, and adapting best practices from various fields.

> " AI can significantly enhance creativity through benchmarking by identifying, analyzing and adapting best practices from various fields. "

- Broadening the search for inspiration: AI-powered tools can quickly sift through vast amounts of data, identifying successful strategies, innovative solutions, and emerging trends across diverse domains. This expansive reach ensures that benchmarks are not limited to your immediate industry, opening the door to cross-disciplinary creativity.
- Highlighting patterns and insights: AI algorithms identify patterns and correlations within datasets. By analyzing benchmarks, AI can uncover underlying principles or strategies contributing to success, offering actionable insights that can be adapted and reimagined for your specific context.
- Customizing benchmarks: AI tools can tailor recommendations to your unique goals, challenges, or creative projects. This targeted approach ensures relevance and maximizes the potential for innovative applications.
- Speeding up the iterative process: Benchmarking often involves trial and error. AI accelerates this process by simulating outcomes or suggesting optimized iterations, allowing teams to refine creative ideas more efficiently.
- Visualizing and testing ideas: AI tools can create visualizations, prototypes, or simulations based on benchmarked ideas, enabling teams to explore creative concepts more tangibly. For instance, a company might use generative AI to visualize how a successful architectural design could inspire their next product.
- Sample prompt to AI: How might a small local restaurant apply the benchmarking principles of high-performing businesses outside the food industry? We prompted Claude to provide three examples. Claude responded with the following:
  - Apply Disney's queue management techniques to waiting areas: Study how Disney designs lines to feel shorter and more engaging. Transform your waiting area with elements that create perceived value during wait times, such as digital menu previews, storytelling elements about your ingredients' origins, or interactive elements that build anticipation for the meal experience.
  - Adopt Apple Store's customer service approach: Observe how Apple creates memorable retail experiences. Train staff to greet customers immediately upon entry, provide tableside tablet ordering, and implement a "genius bar" concept for special menu recommendations or wine pairings. Create an open kitchen design that showcases your culinary team's expertise, similar to how Apple displays its products.

    – Implement IKEA's customer flow design: Study how IKEA guides customers through a carefully designed journey in each of its stores. Create a restaurant layout that subtly guides diners through different experience zones—from a welcoming entrance area to intimate dining sections and a dessert or coffee station. Use lighting, music, and decorative elements to create distinct atmospheres within your space that encourage a complete dining experience.

The Cleveland Clinic Story

In the early 2010s, the Cleveland Clinic, a world-renowned academic medical center, used creative benchmarking to improve patient experience dramatically. Instead of only comparing themselves to other hospitals, they looked to different industries to learn about improving customer service.[3]

The clinic studied premier hospitality brands like Ritz-Carlton hotels to learn about creating memorable customer experiences and retailers like Apple for their approach to customer-facing technology. They also examined Southwest Airlines' staff communication practices and Disney's methods for managing guest flow and creating positive experiences in high-traffic environments.[4]

This cross-industry benchmarking led to concrete innovations at the Clinic:

- Redesigned waiting areas with more comfortable seating, better lighting, and clearer signage
- Implementation of a hotel-style "concierge" service for patients and families
- Streamlined check-in procedures modeled after efficient retail experiences
- Enhanced staff training focused on empathetic communication, similar to high-end hospitality
- Patient journey mapping to identify and remove friction points in the experience

The clinic changed the belief that only medical outcomes mattered at hospitals; patient satisfaction was critical, too. In 2007, it hired its first chief experience officer.

The Cleveland Clinic initiative led to a remarkable transformation in patient experience. After implementing hospitality-inspired benchmarking practices, their patient satisfaction scores rose dramatically from below average to ranking among the national top performers. This success established them as industry leaders in patient experience innovation, with their model being studied and adopted by healthcare organizations worldwide.

The key lesson for restaurants is clear: by measuring results and staying committed to cross-industry inspiration, businesses can achieve measurable improvements that elevate them from average performers to industry benchmarks others seek to emulate.

Companies that excel in customer service offer customer experience training programs to other businesses. For example:

- The Ritz-Carlton Leadership Center offers onsite and virtual training programs that teach businesses how to create exceptional customer experiences using the same principles that have made the Ritz-Carlton legendary for service. These programs are available to professionals from any industry looking to elevate their customer service standards.[5]
- The Disney Institute, the professional development and external training arm of The Walt Disney Company, trains and advises professionals by providing unique insights into Disney's best practices in business. The institute offers various formats that include onsite programs at Disney destinations, live courses, and self-paced online training. All are designed to showcase Disney's approach to leadership, employee engagement, and service excellence.[6]
- Zappos, an American online shoe and clothing retailer now owned by Amazon, created a dedicated division called Zappos Insights that shares its exceptional customer service expertise with other businesses. Zappos Insights trains companies that want to change their own culture through better employee recruitment, onboarding, and training, by offering immersive training camps, tours, and speaking engagements.[7]

These three companies have recognized that their expertise in customer experience is valuable to other businesses and have developed formal training programs to share their methodologies. This is a perfect example of how companies can use benchmarking—looking outside their industry to learn the best practices from recognized leaders. Which company outside your industry would your customers wish you operated more like? What service experience made you say 'wow' recently, and how could you bring that magic to your business? Who solves challenges similar to yours, but in a completely different context? Or, what business do you enjoy interacting with, and how can you emulate their best ideas?

⚡ Exercise

As you move forward, experiment with these approaches and some of the questions posed above in addressing one of your primary personal or professional challenges. Draw parallels from unexpected sources and adapt proven practices to your unique challenges. Remember that AI can be your partner in this journey, helping you expand your creative horizons and implement your ideas more effectively.

Creativity thrives when curiosity meets action—so embrace these approaches, harness AI tools, and let your imagination and ingenuity lead the way to innovative solutions that make a difference in your work and life.

In Summary

1. Look beyond your field for inspiration.
The most powerful creative solutions often come from unexpected places. IDEO revolutionized operating room design by studying Formula One pit crews, proving that seemingly unrelated domains can solve similar challenges.
What unconventional field might hold the key to your most pressing problem?

2. Cross-industry benchmarking beats competitor analysis.
Cleveland Clinic transformed patient satisfaction by studying Ritz-Carlton hotels, Apple stores, and Disney parks instead of looking at other hospitals. This approach unlocked innovations that conventional healthcare thinking may not have produced.
Which industry with exceptional customer service could revolutionize your approach?

3. Find structural similarities in different systems.
Surgical teams and Broadway crews both operate under time pressure with specialized roles. Recognizing these patterns helps you transfer winning strategies across domains.
What unexpected field mirrors the core challenges in your work?

4. Use analogies to reframe complex problems.
When facing ideological divides, think outside the box: like a bridge engineer, an ecosystem restorer, or an orchestra conductor—you will be surprised how these fresh perspectives can break through entrenched thinking.
How would an entirely different expert tackle your biggest challenge?

5. AI can supercharge analogical thinking.
Use AI tools to rapidly identify relevant patterns across diverse domains, simulate outcomes, and visualize creative applications of benchmarked ideas. This will dramatically expand your search for powerful analogies.
What patterns might AI help you discover that human thinking alone might miss?

In our next chapter, we will see how opening challenges to an interdisciplinary perspective and outside innovators can solve unique problems quicker and cheaper.

Notes

[1] Pit Stop for Doctors, TED Blog, August 31, 2006, accessed May 4, 2025. https://blog.ted.com/pitstop_for_doc/

[2] Hoan Nguyen. "The Evolution of Quality at Xerox." *Hoan Nguyen's Blog*, January 27, 2019. accessed February 26, 2025. https://hoannhct.wordpress.com/2019/01/27/the-evolution-of-quality-at-xerox/

[3] James Merlino, Ananth Raman. "Health Care's Service Fanatics," *Harvard Business Review,* May 2013 edition. https://hbr.org/2013/05/health-cares-service-fanatics

[4] James Merlino. *Service Fanatics: How to Build Superior Patient Experience the Cleveland Clinic Way*, 1st ed. (New York: McGraw-Hill Education, 2014).

[5] The Ritz-Carlton Leadership Center. https://ritzcarltonleadershipcenter.com

[6] The Disney Institute. https://www.disneyinstitute.com/

[7] Zappos Insights. https://www.zappos.com/c/zappos-insights

Solving the Climate Crisis (or Other Challenges) REQUIRES Interdisciplinary Perspectives

Environmental Science

Climatology

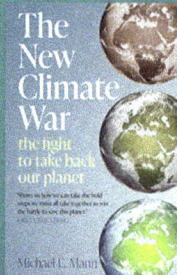

Economics/Policy

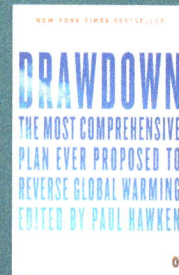

Ecology

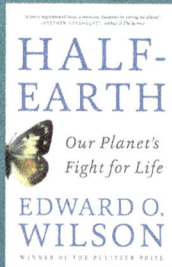

Public Health

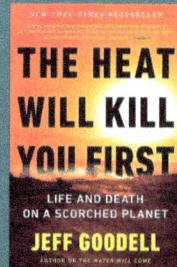

Clean Technology

Renewable Energy

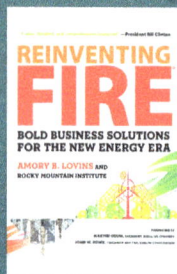

Sociology

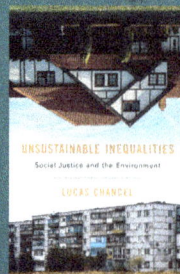

Governance/Activism

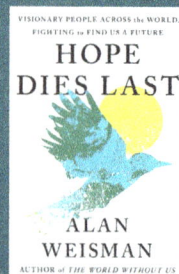

And other disciplines and breakthrough books

Chapter 9
Approach #5: Engage in Interdisciplinary Collaboration

Be open to collaboration. Other people and other people's ideas
are often better than your own.
—Actress Amy Poehler in a Harvard commencement address

Houston, we have a problem.

For years, NASA grappled with a complex challenge that had profound implications for space communications: how to securely exchange encryption keys between nodes in a delayed or disrupted network, a common occurrence in deep space. When internal efforts failed to yield a solution, the agency turned to an unconventional source: the global open innovation community.

In 2014, NASA presented the problem to Topcoder, a global community of 1.5 million software developers, data scientists, and designers, and offered monetary rewards for innovative ideas.[1] Within a few months, the crowd delivered an ingenious solution: applying a variation of the 'Byzantine Generals' approach.[2]

Originally devised to address the challenge of generals coordinating a unified strategy despite the risk of traitors, the method also applies to distributed computing systems where some components may fail or act maliciously.

It worked. NASA used this approach to validate computer inputs, accepting data only from trustworthy sources and disregarding others. But the agency never applied this method to its security network problem in space. "The solution was at NASA, but we didn't see it as a solution for security," said Steve Rader, program manager of NASA's Center of Excellence for Collaborative Innovation and the NASA Tournament Lab. "It required someone outside our community to point that out to us."[3]

This crowdsourced solution saved NASA an estimated 18 months of development time and approximately $1.2 million in research costs compared to their traditional approach, demonstrating the tangible benefits of interdisciplinary problem-solving.

NASA's experience underscores the critical role of interdisciplinary perspectives in driving innovation. A landmark study by InnoCentive revealed that the success of open innovation—or problem-solving through crowdsourcing—often stems from the diverse expertise of the contributors. Notably, the study said, "the further the discipline of the problem solver is from the discipline of the problem, the higher the likelihood of success."

By opening up challenges to outside innovators, organizations can solve problems 4 to 5 times faster and 8 to 10 times cheaper than traditional approaches, according to 1,000 cases studied by Open Assembly, an open talent community founded in a Harvard lab.[4]

This is not surprising since:

- Problem solvers come from all disciplines and regions of the world.
- They may have already solved a similar problem.
- And you pay only for the results.

" By opening up challenges to outside innovators, organizations can solve problems 4 to 5 times faster and 8 to 10 times cheaper than traditional approaches. **"**

When facing a difficult challenge, augmenting your internal talent with open innovation is a strategic and practical approach. A key takeaway from open innovation is the value of building interdisciplinary teams—ideally enriched by contributions from customers and external experts. However, embracing open innovation and open talent requires a shift in the traditional organizational mindset, which often exclusively prioritizes hiring, developing, and retaining employees within rigid internal frameworks.

Recent research by Moreau, Prandelli, and Schreier demonstrates the transformative potential of interdisciplinary collaboration in unexpected contexts. Their study of luxury brand Missoni revealed that bringing together traditional artisans with digital artists and AI specialists produced designs that were rated as more innovative while maintaining the brand's distinctive heritage. This 'unexpected synergy effect' emerged because the contrasting knowledge domains forced explicit articulation of typically tacit expertise, creating opportunities for novel combinations and mutual learning. AI played a dual role in this process—both as a creative contributor and a translation layer between disciplines with different vocabularies and mental models.

Open Innovation: Harnessing Collective Intelligence

NASA's experience reveals a powerful innovation approach that deserves deeper exploration: open innovation. This strategy extends beyond traditional R&D by inviting external contributions, transforming how organizations solve complex problems.

" Open innovation breaks down organizational boundaries. **"**

Open innovation breaks down organizational boundaries. Unlike closed innovation models, where companies rely solely on internal expertise, open innovation taps into global talent pools to accelerate discovery and reduce costs.

LEGO Ideas stands as a prime example of this approach. Since 2008, this platform has invited fans to submit product concepts, with successful ideas earning creators 1% of royalties.[5] The LEGO Saturn V rocket, the Women of NASA set, and the Sesame Street collection emerged from this community-driven process. These customer-created sets consistently rank among LEGO's best-selling products, proving that innovation often comes from your customers who know your products best.[6]

GE's Ecomagination Challenge took a similar path, offering $200 million for innovations addressing clean energy needs. This initiative attracted over 70,000 participants from 150 countries and generated 5,000 ideas. One winning concept—a system to capture waste heat from power plants—has been developed into a commercially viable technology across multiple industries. GE gained innovations, valuable market insights, and potential acquisition targets.[7]

Have you considered how your customers might solve problems you've struggled with internally?

Netflix offers another compelling case. When seeking to improve its recommendation algorithm, the company launched the Netflix Prize in 2006, offering $1 million to anyone who could improve prediction accuracy by 10%. The competition attracted over 40,000 teams from 186 countries. After three years, a combined team of statisticians, computer scientists, and engineers claimed victory with an algorithm that blended 107 different approaches. This crowdsourced solution dramatically improved user experience and helped Netflix build its reputation for personalization.[8]

InnoCentive, founded by pharmaceutical giant Eli Lilly, now operates as an independent platform connecting organizations with over 400,000 problem solvers worldwide. Companies like Roche, NASA, and Procter & Gamble post challenges with rewards ranging from $10,000 to $1 million. The platform boasts a remarkable 80% success rate for problems internal teams couldn't solve.[9]

Think about your most persistent challenges. Could an outside perspective provide the breakthrough you need?

The success of open innovation hinges on specific factors:

• Clearly defined problems with measurable outcomes
• Appropriate incentives that motivate participation
• Transparent processes that build trust with contributors
• Organizational readiness to implement external ideas

The most potent aspect of open innovation is about transforming how you view problems. When you invite diverse perspectives, you often discover that what you thought was the problem wasn't the real challenge. What challenge in your organization might benefit from casting a wider net?

Aligned with the principles of open innovation and interdisciplinary collaboration is the imperative to 'bring the radicals in.' Many organizations struggle to accommodate individuals or challenges that deviate from established norms and conventional thinking. However, if the goal is to foster creativity and drive innovation, embracing these unconventional perspectives is not just beneficial but essential.

While NASA's interdisciplinary innovation demonstrates how diverse expertise can solve technical challenges, Pixar offers a powerful example of creative collaboration that feels more accessible to many organizations. Pixar's groundbreaking animated films emerge from the deliberate integration of multiple disciplines—artists, animators, computer scientists, storytellers, behavioral psychologists, and sound engineers working as unified creative teams. This collaboration is deliberately structured into their development process.

For instance, their 'Braintrust' review sessions bring together diverse perspectives to critique works in progress, with the fundamental understanding that great ideas can come from any discipline. A technical limitation might inspire a narrative solution, or a story need might drive technological innovation. When creating 'Finding Nemo,' the collaboration between artistic vision and computational fluid dynamics achieved the film's revolutionary underwater environments. This interdisciplinary approach has allowed Pixar to consistently produce work that no single discipline could achieve alone, demonstrating that integrating diverse expertise creates possibilities beyond the reach of even the most talented specialist working in isolation.

IDEO, highlighted earlier in Chapter 8, deliberately recruits people they call "T-shaped"—professionals with deep expertise in one area (the vertical bar of the T) and broad interests across many domains (the horizontal bar). This approach has helped them create groundbreaking designs by intentionally bringing together perspectives from fields as diverse as anthropology, engineering, medicine, and fine arts.[10]

When IDEO tackled redesigning a hospital's patient experience, they included a theater director who brought valuable insights about managing emotional journeys and creating meaningful moments—something traditional healthcare consultants might have overlooked.

Another example comes from Procter & Gamble. Its Connect + Develop team scouts, identifies, engages, and collaborates with outside partners such as startups, laboratories, research institutes, and academia to discover key insights, business models, and technologies to enhance P&G's businesses.

Successful products from the program were Swiffer, Mr. Clean Magic Eraser, and Olay Regenerist.[11] Swiffer generated over $500 million in annual sales, a product inspired in part by a similar Japanese mop.[12] Similarly, Mr. Clean Magic Eraser resulted from a partnership with BASF to identify a material originally used for insulation with remarkable cleaning properties.[13] Just a year after its launch in 2003, Mr. Clean Magic Eraser developed a cult following: "This product is AMAZING!!!" one happy customer wrote in her online review. P&G's brand manager, Bob Gilbreath, told a local paper that the enthusiastic response from consumers was "pretty much unbelievable and a lot bigger than our expectations."[14] In 2012, P&G celebrated its one billionth Mr. Clean Magic Erasers production.[15]

Olay Regenerist combined P&G's skincare knowledge with external research on peptide technology to create a popular premium anti-aging line that increased its market share by 20% in the luxury skincare market.[16]

In 2025, P&G asked the community to develop ideas for safe and practical solutions to control insects in and outside the home that are not toxic to people and pets. It had to perform just as well or better than the solutions available at the time.[17]

The Connect + Develop program led to:

- Faster innovation: By tapping into a diverse pool of external talent, P&G accelerated its product development timeline by an average of 60%.
- Cost efficiency: External collaborations reduced the costs associated with in-house R&D.
- Increased creativity: Interdisciplinary and external perspectives brought fresh, unconventional ideas, leading to market successes with over 50% of P&G's product initiatives now involving external innovation partners.[18]

Interdisciplinary teams drive innovation through several key mechanisms that transform how problems are approached. First, they introduce cognitive diversity—different mental models, problem-solving approaches, and knowledge bases that challenge assumptions and reveal blind spots. When engineers, designers, and anthropologists examine the same challenge, they see entirely different aspects of the problem and solution space.

Second, diverse teams disrupt habitual thinking patterns. When forced to explain your approach to someone from another field, you must articulate implicit assumptions that might otherwise go unexamined. Finally, interdisciplinary collaboration creates fertile ground for combinatorial creativity, where elements from different domains merge to create something new. The smartphone emerged from combining telecommunications, computing, photography, and user interface design in ways that would have been unlikely within any single discipline. These advantages explain why the most innovative organizations deliberately cultivate cross-functional teams rather than simply optimizing within specialty silos.

AI's Role in Interdisciplinary Relations

When experts from different fields converge, they can challenge conventional thinking, inspire new ideas, and co-create transformative outcomes that a single discipline might overlook. AI amplifies the potential of such collaboration by bridging knowledge gaps, identifying patterns across domains, and facilitating seamless communication.

> " AI amplifies the potential of collaboration by bridging knowledge gaps and facilitating seamless communication. "

AI systems offer a unique opportunity to simulate interdisciplinary thinking even when diverse team members aren't immediately available. Using prompts like 'Imagine you are an anthropologist examining this customer experience issue' or 'Approach this product design challenge as a biologist would,' tools like ChatGPT can help generate perspectives from disciplines outside your expertise.

While not a replacement for genuine collaboration with experts in those fields, this approach can spark fresh thinking and identify potential disciplinary lenses worth exploring more deeply. This capability allows you to conduct thought experiments across diverse viewpoints, identifying which alternative perspectives might be most valuable for your specific challenge before investing in more extensive collaboration.

Let's see AI in action in the following sample cases:

Project: Designing an energy-efficient smart city

Partners: Urban planners, environmental scientists, engineers, data scientists, and policymakers

Prompt: Design the vision and strategy for a city that wants to create an energy-efficient smart town and rely on all the relevant disciplines.

Use of AI:

1. Data integration and analysis
   AI Tool: Tableau or Google BigQuery
   – Collects and processes city data, such as population density, energy consumption patterns, and environmental metrics, into a unified dashboard.
2. Energy demand forecasting
   AI Tool: IBM Watson Studio or TensorFlow
   – Predicts energy consumption trends based on historical data, weather patterns, and urban activities to plan renewable energy usage.
3. Traffic optimization
   AI Tool: DeepMind (for advanced optimization) or Waze for Cities
   – Analyzes real-time traffic data to propose optimized routes, reducing fuel consumption and emissions.
4. Urban layout simulations
   AI Tool: Autodesk Generative Design or Unity
   – Generates multiple city layout designs optimized for energy efficiency, solar energy capture, and pedestrian flow.
5. Environmental impact analysis
   AI Tool: ESRI ArcGIS or Google Earth Engine
   – Assesses the environmental impact of different urban designs, such as air quality and green space distribution.
6. Citizen engagement
   AI Tool: ChatGPT API or Tidio
   – Provides an AI-powered chatbot to gather public feedback on proposed plans and address community concerns in real-time.

7. Energy systems monitoring
    AI Tool: Microsoft Azure AI or Siemens Mindsphere
    – Monitors and optimizes energy grid performance, ensuring efficient usage
      and minimal waste.

Integrated Smart City Solution Output

When these AI tools work together across disciplines, a comprehensive smart city framework results. Barcelona's 22@District[19] is a real-world example of this approach, where interdisciplinary teams used AI systems to reduce energy consumption by 30%, cut water usage by 25%, and decrease traffic congestion by 17%.

The district combines innovative lighting systems, waste management sensors, mobility optimization, and citizen engagement platforms into a unified urban ecosystem. The project demonstrates how collaborative AI implementation across disciplines creates more sustainable urban environments than would be possible through siloed approaches.

To explore how AI can help develop a comprehensive vision for an energy-efficient smart city, we asked Claude to synthesize insights across disciplines:

Prompt: Design the vision and strategy for a city that wants to create an energy-efficient smart city and, in doing so, rely on all the relevant disciplines.

The AI response outlined a holistic vision integrating urban planning, environmental science, computer science, civil engineering, data science, behavioral economics, and public policy. Key elements included:

*   A digital twin system that creates a virtual replica of the city to test interventions before implementation
*   Microgrids powered by renewable energy with AI-optimized distribution
*   Buildings designed using biomimicry principles with passive heating/cooling
*   A multimodal transportation network prioritizing electric vehicles, cycling, and walking
*   Data-driven resource management using a citywide IoT sensor network
*   Behavioral incentive programs based on nudge theory to encourage sustainable choices
*   Inclusive governance structures ensuring equitable access to technology

For a real example of a smart city, let's consider Singapore, the world's smartest city according to the IMD Smart City Index.[20] Singapore launched its "Smart Nation" initiative in 2014 under Prime Minister Lee Hsien Loong. The government set aside $2.4 billion in 2017 to support this initiative, focusing on enhancing public transport networks, enabling successful aging, and ensuring a secure but open data marketplace.

Singapore stands out because of its extensive sensor network, monitoring everything from traffic to air quality. Advanced water management system recycles wastewater (NEWater), cashless payment systems are placed across public transportation, and even a Virtual Singapore, a digital twin of the entire city used for planning. In October 2024, Prime Minister Lawrence Wong launched Smart Nation 2.0, highlighting the country's achievements over the past decade and setting new goals. The initiative has now widely adopted cashless payments and nearly all government services have been transitioned online.[21]The innovation of this smart city comes from Singapore's integrated approach. Rather than implementing isolated tech solutions, it has a cohesive ecosystem where systems talk to each other.

Similarly, Copenhagen has emerged as a global leader in sustainable smart city development with an intelligent traffic management system reducing congestion by 20%,[22] networked LED street lighting adapting to weather and traffic conditions, a district heating system covering 98% of buildings, and smart waste bins with sensors that optimize collection routes. The city follows a "five-minute" principle, connecting neighborhoods so people can reach essential services quickly, and their harbor baths showcase how smart environmental monitoring transformed polluted waterways into clean swimming areas. Copenhagen has also implemented a revolutionary "green wave" traffic light system that gives cyclists preference in the city during the morning and afternoon rush hours.[23] The city aims to be fully carbon-neutral by late 2025.

Both cities demonstrate how smart technology can transform urban living. Singapore focuses on comprehensive data integration and cutting-edge technology, while Copenhagen emphasizes sustainable mobility and climate solutions. Each offers valuable lessons for cities worldwide looking to become smarter and more livable.

A major contributor to the two cities and numerous others is Carlo Ratti, Professor at the Politecnico di Milano and at MIT, where he directs the Senseable City Lab, founding partner of CRA–Carlo Ratti Associati and, in 2025, Director of the Biennale Architettura in Venice.

Ratti's smart city approach is unique in its human-centric, open-source, and real-time design philosophy. Rather than focusing solely on technology or infrastructure, Ratti emphasizes how people interact with the urban environment. His work blends architecture, data, and digital technology to create cities that are responsive and adaptive to citizens' needs.

Key aspects include:

- Real-time data integration to make cities more efficient and transparent (e.g., MIT Senseable City Lab projects).
- Participatory design, encouraging citizen involvement in shaping urban experiences.
- A focus on temporary, flexible interventions (e.g., the "Living Architecture" or "Copenhagen Wheel") instead of permanent structures.

Ratti's vision is less about control and more about empowering individuals to shape urban life dynamically.

Which elements of either of these smart cities do you think would improve your own city?

Figures 9.1 and 9.2 offer visualization of the Smart City interdisciplinary concepts.

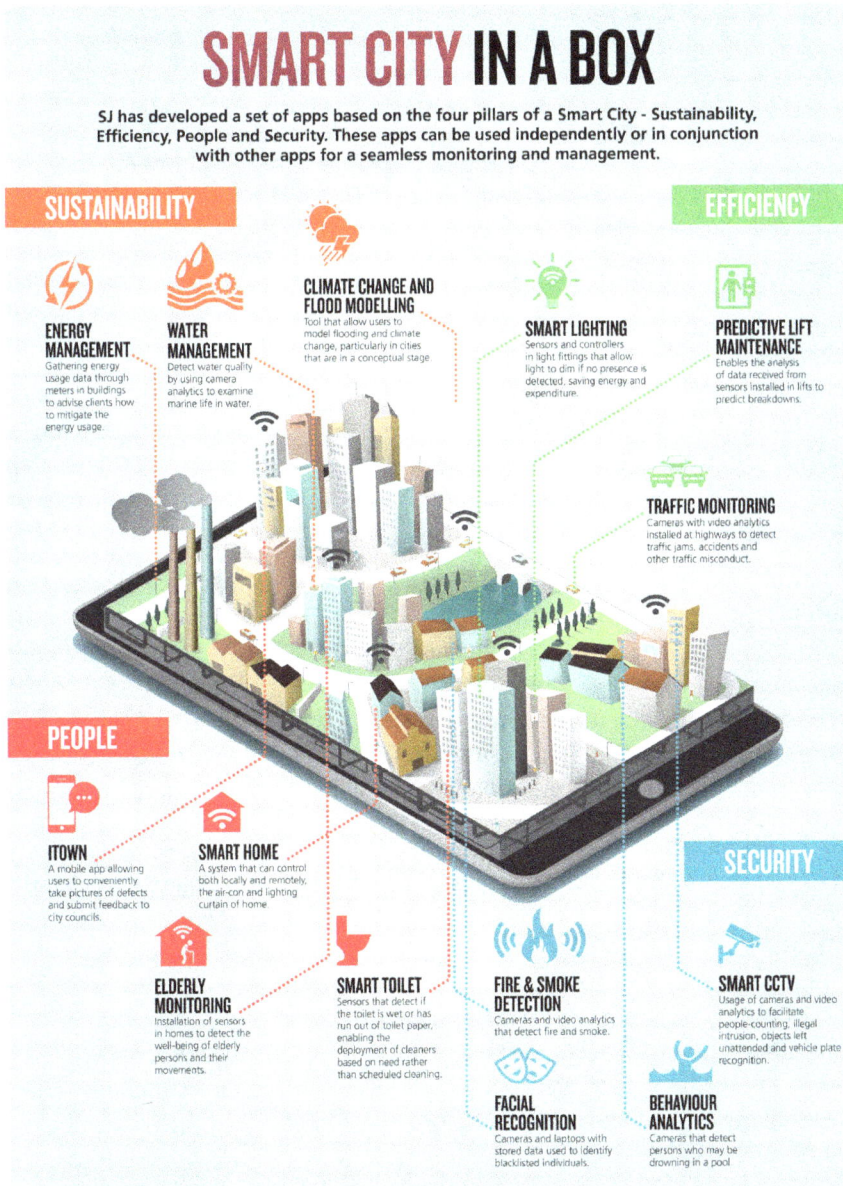

Source: MuchMania, iStock, copyright to use purchased.

Figure 9.1. Smart city in a box

Source: MuchMania, iStock, copyright to use purchased.

Figure 9.2. Smart City by Carlo Ratti and Matthew Claudel[24]

ⓘ Exercise

To expand your disciplinary horizon, list three fields or disciplines entirely outside your own that might view your current challenge from a completely different angle.

For each discipline, identify one concept, method, or perspective from that field that could be applied to your situation. For example, if you're working on improvements in customer service, you might consider:

1. Theatrical performance: How might stage presence and audience engagement concepts transform service interactions?
2. Emergency medicine: What triage principles could help prioritize customer needs more effectively?
3. Architecture: How might designing spaces for emotional experience rather than just function change your approach? After identifying these disciplines, seek resources or experts from each field to further explore these connections.

This interdisciplinary vision demonstrates how AI can synthesize disparate fields into a cohesive strategy that no single discipline could develop independently.

In Summary

1. Break down barriers for breakthrough solutions.

When NASA couldn't solve its space communications challenge internally, it opened it to outside perspectives and saved 18 months of development time and $1.2 million. Your most challenging problems might need fresh eyes from entirely different fields.

What external perspectives could you invite to your most difficult situation that's been developing for months?

In Summary (contd.)

2. **Embrace open innovation as a strategic advantage.**
Organizations solve problems 4–5 times faster and 8–10 times cheaper through open innovation. Companies like LEGO, GE, and Netflix demonstrate that crowdsourcing solutions work because problem solvers from all disciplines and regions may have already solved similar problems, and you pay only for results. How might your customers or a global community help solve challenges you've struggled with internally?

Which specific business challenge could you open to your customers or a broader community that might yield faster, cheaper solutions?

3. **Create "T-shaped" teams.**
Follow IDEO's approach by bringing together people with deep expertise in one area (vertical bar) and broad interests across many domains (horizontal bar). This combination sparks the creative collisions that lead to true innovation.

How might you reorganize your next project team to combine deep specialists with people who have broad interests across multiple domains?

4. **Assemble an interdisciplinary team and invite the radicals.**
The most transformative ideas often come from unconventional thinkers who challenge established norms. Pixar's groundbreaking films emerge from deliberately structured collaboration between artists, scientists, storytellers, and engineers. Think about the disciplines involved in creating a smart city.

Who is the unconventional thinker in your industry whose ideas you've dismissed but might offer the breakthrough perspective you need?

5. **Use AI as your collaboration amplifier.**
AI tools can bridge knowledge gaps between disciplines, simulate interdisciplinary thinking, and help integrate diverse insights into cohesive strategies that no single field could develop alone.

What current project could benefit from using AI to connect insights across different departments or disciplines in your organization?

Our next chapter explores the tools that can cater to different problem-solving contexts and mindsets.

Notes

1   NASA. "DTN Security Key." *NASA*, March 2015. https://www.nasa.gov/wp-content/uploads/2015/03/challenge-summary-dtn-security-key.pdf

2   NASA. *The Power of Crowd-Based Challenges: NASA's Practical Toolkit for Open Innovation.* NASA Technical Reports Server (NTRS), 2017, accessed February 26, 2025. https://ntrs.nasa.gov/api/citations/20170012345/downloads/20170012345.pdf

3   Coursera course titled *Creativity in Business and Other Disciplines.*

4   Getting Smart, "John Winsor on the Open Talent Economy," August 19, 2020, accessed May 16, 2025, https://www.gettingsmart.com/podcast/john-winsor-on-the-open-talent-economy/; John Winsor and Jin H. Paik, *Open Talent: Leveraging the Global Workforce to Solve Your Biggest Challenges*, Harvard Business Review Press, 2024.

5   Lego Ideas. https://en.brickimedia.org/wiki/LEGO_Ideas

6   "The Best LEGO® NASA Sets of the Past and Present." https://www.lego.com/en-us/space/article/lego-nasa-sets-past-present

7   GE, Press Release, February 6, 2011, "GE Rolls Out Second Phase of US$200 Million Ecomagination Challenge Inviting powerful Ideas on Energy savings at Home," accessed May 5, 2025. https://www.ge.com/news/press-releases/ge-rolls-out-second-phase-us200-million-ecomagination-challenge-inviting-powerful-0

8   Wikipedia, "Netflix Prize," accessed May 5, 2025. https://en.wikipedia.org/wiki/Netflix_Prize

9   Michael Fitzgerald. "What Drives Successful Crowdsourcing?" *Harvard Magazine*, December 2016, accessed May 5, 2025. https://www.harvardmagazine.com/2016/12/what-drives-successful-crowdsourcing

10 Morten T. Hansen. "IDEO CEO Tim Brown: T-Shaped Stars: The Backbone of IDEO's Collaborative Culture." *Chief Executive Magazine*, accessed February 26, 2025. https://chiefexecutive.net/ideo-ceo-tim-brown-t-shaped-stars-the-backbone-of-ideoaes-collaborative-culture_trashed/

11 Procter & Gamble. "P&G Names New C+D Leader, Aims Acceleration of Open Innovation Work." News release, July 25, 2012. https://news.pg.com/news-releases/news-details/2012/PG-Names-New-CD-Leader-Aims-Acceleration-of-Open-Innovation-Work/default.aspx

12 Richard Curtis. "New Swiffer Cleans Up for Procter." *Courier*, November 8, 1999. *Cincinnati Business Courier*, accessed February 26, 2025. https://www.bizjournals.com/cincinnati/stories/1999/11/08/story2.html

13 Becki Robins. "The Untold Truth of Magic Eraser." *Grunge*. Last updated February 12, 2022, accessed February 26, 2025. https://www.grunge.com/142701/the-untold-truth-of-magic-eraser/

14 Judy Stark. "A Hand for Mr. Clean," *Tampa Bay Times*, July 24, 2004, updated August 28, 2005, accessed March 8, 2025. https://www.tampabay.com/archive/2004/07/24/a-hand-for-mr-clean/

15 Rebecca Haughey. "Mr. Clean Celebrates Milestone as It Produces Its 1 Billionth Magic Eraser," *Drug Store News*, November 16, 2012, accessed March 8, 2025. https://drugstorenews.com/news/mr-clean-celebrates-milestone-it-produces-its-1-billionth-magic-eraser

16 Olay. "Your Skin on OLAY Peptides." *Olay*, September 2, 2020, accessed February 26, 2025. https://www.olay.com/skin-care-tips-and-articles/your-skin-on-olay-peptides

17 Procter & Gamble. "Non-Toxic Home and Garden." P&G Connect + Develop, accessed November 26, 2024. https://www.pgconnectdevelop.com/current-needs/pest-control

18 Rosie Baker. "P&G to Boost Innovation through Partnerships." *Marketing Week*, November 2, 2010, accessed February 26, 2025. https://www.marketingweek.com/pg-to-boost-innovation-through-partnerships/

19 Barcelona's 22@ District, Wikipedia, accessed May 4, 2025. https://en.wikipedia.org/wiki/22@

20 IMD Smart City Index 2025 Report, "What Makes a City the Most Liveable?" https://www.imd.org/smart-city-observatory/home/

[21] Singapore's Ministry of Digital Development and Information, "Smart Nation 2.0," accessed May 5, 2025. https://file.go.gov.sg/smartnation2-report.pdf

[22] C40 Cities, November 2016, "Cities100: Copenhagen Smart Traffic Signals Boost Cycling," accessed May 4, 2025. https://www.c40.org/case-studies/cities100-copenhagen-smart-traffic-signals-boost-cycling/

[23] Centre for Public Impact. "Green Waves for Bicycles in Copenhagen," April 8, 2016, accessed May 5, 2025. https://centreforpublicimpact.org/public-impact-fundamentals/green-waves-for-bicycles-in-copenhagen/

[24] Smart City by Carlo Ratti and Matthew Claudel. https://www.shelidon.it/carlo-ratti-matthew-claudel-la-citta-di-domani/

Creative Explorer's Map
for Creativity Rules and Tools

Problem Definition Tools –
For Framing Challenges
Challenging Mental Models
Trend Analysis
+4
other approaches

Ideation Tools –
For Generating Ideas
Brainstorming
Six Thinking Hats
+11
other aproaches

Implementation Tools –
For Turning Ideas Into Action
Iteration and Experimentation
Redesign Principles
+6
other approaches

Cross-Category Tools –
That Span Multiple
Categories
Technology Integration
Rules and Structured Methods
+1
other approach

Evaluation Tools –
For Assessing and
Selecting Ideas
Mind Genomics
Conjoint Analysis
+6
other approaches

Chapter 10
Approach #6: Adopt Rules and Tools

Technology is nothing. What's important is that you have a faith in people, that they're basically good and smart, and if you give them tools, they'll do wonderful things with them.
—Steve Jobs

Creativity thrives on diverse approaches and tools catering to problem-solving contexts and mindsets. The creativity tools explored throughout this book and this chapter can be organized into four complementary categories that address different aspects of the creative process.

It is important to note, however, that some of these tools will naturally fit into a number of these categories. For example, De Bono's Six Thinking Hats encourages structured parallel thinking from different perspectives for generating ideas, but it also has strong assessment capabilities for evaluating ideas.

Some of these tools have been discussed throughout the book within the chapter the tool naturally fits into. Therefore, this chapter's purpose is to highlight new tools for you to consider.

Problem Definition Tools—For Framing Challenges

- Challenging Mental Models—questioning existing assumptions and beliefs to reframe problems (see Chapter 5)
- Consumer Insights Analysis—understanding customer needs, behaviors, and journey mapping (including ZMOT) (see Chapter 11)
- Trend Analysis—identifying patterns in consumer behavior, cultural, technological, and business trends (See Chapter 11)
- SWOT Analysis—assessing Strengths, Weaknesses, Opportunities, and Threats to frame strategic challenges (discussed in this chapter)
- Front2Back Transformation—starting with customer needs to define what problems need solving (see Chapter 15)
- Five 'Whys' Technique—drilling down to root causes of assumptions and problems (see Chapter 5)

Ideation Tools—For Generating Ideas

- Brainstorming—which can be used by an individual or in a group (discussed in this chapter)
- Random word/image generators, and mood and inspiration boards (discussed in this chapter)
- Dream chasing/following your vision—pursuing bold, paradigm-shifting aspirations (see Chapter 6)

- Morphological Analysis—breaking down problems into components and recombining elements (see Chapter 7)
- Analogies and Benchmarking—drawing inspiration from other fields, industries, or high performers (see Chapter 8)
- Interdisciplinary Perspectives—bringing together diverse expertise and "radicals" (see Chapter 9)
- SCAMPER (Substitute, Combine, Adapt, Modify, Put to other uses, Eliminate, Rearrange) (discussed in this chapter)
- Six Thinking Hats—structured parallel thinking from different perspectives (discussed in this chapter)
- Blue Ocean Strategy—creating uncontested market spaces (discussed in this chapter)
- Seligman's Five Types of Creativity—Integration, Splitting, Figure/Ground Reversal, Distilled Imagination, Discovery (discussed in this chapter)
- Out-of-the-Box and Inside-the-Box Thinking—unconstrained and constraint-based ideation (discussed in this chapter)
- Curiosity and Imagination Games—creative exercises and playful exploration (see Chapter 13)
- AI-Enhanced Brainstorming—using generative AI tools for idea generation

Evaluation Tools—For Assessing and Selecting Ideas

- 'Yes, and...' techniques to build upon ideas rather than blocking them (discussed in this chapter)
- Question Protocols to establish guidelines for productive inquiry during creative sessions (discussed in this chapter)
- Mind Genomics—systematic testing of idea combinations with target audiences (see Chapter 12)
- RAVES Framework—Relevant, Actionable, Valuable, Exceptional, Shareable criteria (see Chapter 15)
- Conjoint Analysis—testing different combinations of features or approaches (see Chapter 12)
- Six Thinking Hats (Evaluation Phase)—particularly Black Hat (critical assessment) and Yellow Hat (benefits) (discussed in this chapter)
- AI-Powered Critique—using AI to assess pros/cons and feasibility of ideas (see Chapter 14)
- Scenario Planning—Envisioning multiple futures to test idea viability (see Chapter 5)

Implementation Tools—For Turning Ideas Into Action

- Iteration and Experimentation—continuous testing, learning, and refinement cycles (see Chapter 12)
- IDEO Design Thinking Process—Empathize, Define, Ideate, Prototype, Test (see Chapter 15)
- Redesign Principles—eliminate steps/interfaces/inefficiencies, design for quality (discussed in this chapter)
- Customized Creative Process Development—building personalized approaches (see Chapter 15)
- Persistence and Courage Cultivation—developing the mindset to see ideas through (see Chapter 16)
- Technology Leveraging—using emerging technologies (VR/AR, quantum computing, blockchain, etc.) as implementation platforms (see Chapter 14)
- Open Innovation/Crowdsourcing—implementing through external talent networks (see Chapter 9)
- Democratizing Creativity Tools—using accessible platforms (Meta, Google, tools, etc.) for implementation (discussed in this chapter)

Cross-Category Tools—that span multiple categories

- Technology Integration (Generative AI, VR/AR, etc.)—can be used across all phases (see Chapter 14)
- Rules and Structured Methods—various frameworks that can apply to different phases depending on context (see Chapter 15)
- Growth Strategy Frameworks—can help define problems, generate ideas, and guide implementation (see Chapter 15)

Understanding these categories helps you select appropriate tools based on where you are in the creative process. However, these classifications recognize that creativity is not linear. Many tools can be used iteratively across different phases, and the most effective creative processes often cycle between these categories' multiple times.

> " **Experiment with these approaches as we present them, adapting them to your specific challenges and goals.** "

We encourage you to experiment with these approaches as we present them, adapting them to your specific challenges and goals. The power of these tools emerges when you actively apply them to real situations rather than just understanding them conceptually.

PROBLEM DEFINITION TOOLS—FOR FRAMING CHALLENGES

SWOT Analysis

What is it?
SWOT analysis involves assessing the Strengths, Weaknesses, Opportunities, and Threats of a business, project, or situation.

Example of use:
Let's suppose we want to innovate a local bakery business:

Strengths:

- High-quality, freshly baked goods
- Strong local customer base
- Skilled bakers with a passion for creativity

Weaknesses:

- Limited online presence
- Small seating capacity
- Seasonal dips in sales

Opportunities:

- Growing interest in health-conscious and gluten-free products
- Potential for online orders and delivery services
- Collaboration with local coffee shops for cross-promotion

Threats:

- Increasing competition from large chains
- Rising ingredient costs
- Changing consumer habits, like preferring convenience foods

Now that we have analyzed the situation based on SWOT, our business strategy might be as follows:

Leverage strengths: Create a line of signature pastries marketed as artisan products. Highlight freshness and quality in branding.

Address weaknesses: Develop an easy-to-use website and partner with delivery platforms to expand reach and add counter seats.

Capitalize on opportunities: Introduce a health-conscious product line featuring gluten-free, vegan, and sugar-free options.

Mitigate threats: Source ingredients locally to reduce costs and emphasize sustainability, differentiating the bakery from large chains.

How AI can enhance this tool:	AI tools like Semrush[1] for market analysis or HubSpot[2] for customer data analysis can enhance SWOT by providing data-driven insights.

ⓘ Exercise

1. Choose three competitors from completely different industries that solve similar customer pain points. Conduct parallel SWOT analyses and identify strategic blind spots your industry systematically ignores.
2. Use Claude or ChatGPT to project your analysis five years forward by inputting current market trends and asking it to identify how strengths become weaknesses and threats transform into opportunities. Challenge the AI to build scenarios where your biggest strength becomes your fatal flaw.
3. Map how each SWOT element affects seven different stakeholder groups (customers, employees, investors, regulators, suppliers, community, environment). Identify conflicts where one group's opportunity creates another's threat.
4. Assign financial impact ranges to each SWOT element. Calculate the total opportunity cost of not addressing your top three weaknesses and threats within 18 months.
5. Design one integrated strategy that simultaneously leverages your biggest strength while directly addressing your most critical weakness through the same set of actions.

IDEATION TOOLS—FOR GENERATING IDEAS

Brainstorming

What is it?	Brainstorming pushes your mind beyond its first obvious ideas. You can brainstorm alone or as part of a group to generate solutions, explore possibilities, or break through mental barriers. The core principle is simple: produce as many ideas as possible without judging them. Your brain naturally filters and critiques but brainstorming temporarily shuts off that internal editor. This creates space for unexpected connections and wild possibilities that might contain the seeds of breakthrough solutions.
Example of use:	A restaurant owner facing declining sales might brainstorm for 20 minutes, writing down every possible solution without stopping to evaluate. Ideas could range from practical ("add delivery service") to absurd ("turn the dining room into a mini golf course"). The absurd ideas often spark practical ones. That mini golf idea might lead the owner to "create interactive dining experiences" or "host themed nights." A software team stuck on a user interface

problem might gather around a whiteboard and generate 50 different ways users could navigate their app. The quantity creates quality because it forces you past your mental shortcuts.

How AI can enhance this tool: Use AI as your brainstorming partner when working alone. Prompt ChatGPT or Claude to generate 20 wild ideas. Take the most interesting ones and ask the AI to develop them further or combine them with your own ideas. You can also use AI to play devil's advocate. After your brainstorming session, ask it to poke holes in your top ideas or suggest what you might have missed. This creates a back-and-forth that mimics group brainstorming dynamics.

Exercise

1. Set a challenge and add five seemingly impossible constraints (zero budget, 24-hour deadline, no technology, different planet, opposite season). Generate 20 solutions that work within ALL constraints simultaneously. For groups: Have each team member add one impossible constraint, then collectively generate solutions. Rotate constraint-setting responsibility to prevent any individual from dominating the difficulty level.

2. Use different AI tools to simulate 3 expert perspectives: prompt ChatGPT as a strategist, Claude as an anthropologist, Character.ai as a philosopher. Have each AI contribute five unique solutions from their assigned perspective. For groups: Assign different AI tools and perspectives to team members. Have each person advocate for their AI's perspective while the group builds on all AI-generated ideas collectively.

3. Research three failures in your domain from the past decade. Extract the core insight from each failure and reverse-engineer it into a potential breakthrough solution for your challenge. For groups: Divide failure research among team members, then reconvene to share insights. Have the group collectively reverse-engineer the failures into breakthrough solutions, with each person building on others' failure analysis.

4. Combine your three most breakthrough failure-based solutions from Step 3 with your three most practical constraint-based solutions from Step 1. Create hybrid solutions that maintain the boldness of failure-derived insights while keeping the feasibility of constraint-tested approaches. For groups: Pool all failure-based and constraint-based solutions from all members. Use a matrix approach where each person takes responsibility for creating hybrid solutions from different contributors, ensuring cross-pollination between failure insights and constraint creativity.

5. For your top three solutions, map out exactly what would need to be true for them to work. Identify the single most critical assumption for each and design an experiment to test it. For groups: Assign each top solution to a sub-team of two

to three people. Have sub-teams present their stress tests to the full group for collective refinement and assumption-challenging before finalizing experiments.

Random Word/Image Generator

What is it?	Your brain loves patterns—it's hardwired this way to help you understand the world around you, create shortcuts to learning, and not have to approach each experience as new. But this is both a strength and a limitation, as we can become rigid in our thinking. Random word and image generators break this rigidity by creating random, unexpected content on demand to help you develop new patterns for fresh, novel ideas. They pull from databases to produce words, phrases, or visuals without human input. Most use algorithms to ensure true randomness, or you can set them to follow specific parameters.
Example of use:	A writer, for example, might set a word generator to generate words they must write about without stopping for ten minutes. Writers often say that writing without stopping to edit helps their mind form unexpected paths, overcoming writer's block. A designer might use an image generator to generate random, abstract shapes, helping them break free from their typical, familiar design forms. But you don't have to limit the use of these tools when you are stuck. Teachers use generators to spark storytelling or number problems. Similarly, making them a regular part of your creative practice will strengthen your creative muscles by building new neural pathways. You will soon notice yourself making unusual connections in everyday life that perhaps others miss.
How AI can enhance this tool:	Use other AI-powered assistants alongside random word[3] and image[4] generators to enhance your results. For example, feed your random words to ChatGPT or Claude, and ask the AI to draft an outline for a story, poem, or concept around them for you to work on. Alternatively, use a mind-mapping tool like Ayoa.[5] Drop random words into different branches and let the AI suggest connections and related concepts.

⚡ Exercise

1. Start with a clear intent: Know your purpose before you generate. Are you trying to overcome creative blocks, brainstorm ideas, or find unexpected connections? Use a dedicated random word generator to create four random words, or a random image generator for three random images. Prompt Claude or ChatGPT to identify any hidden thematic connections or archetypal patterns that might not be immediately obvious.

2. Take your random elements and use AYOA Mind Map tool to create a visual web of all possible connections between them. Map both obvious and non-obvious relationships, creating branches that show how elements could relate across different conceptual domains (emotional, functional, structural, symbolic). Let AYOA's AI suggest additional connection pathways you missed.

3. Using your connection map from Step 2, design three distinct solutions to your challenge incorporating elements from the connection pathways you have mapped. Build solutions that leverage the strongest connection clusters while incorporating the most isolated elements as creative constraints.

4. Take your solutions from Step 3 and test how they would function in radically different contexts: 1900s technology/society, current day, and a speculative future. Adapt each solution to work within each era's constraints while maintaining its core random-element DNA. Prompt Claude or ChatGPT to analyze how your random elements would be interpreted differently across these time periods and suggest era-appropriate adaptations.

5. For your strongest solution from Step 4, deliberately reverse or contradict some of the connection relationships you established with your mind mapping tool. Force your solution to work with these contradictory connections, creating a final refined solution that succeeds by embracing paradox rather than avoiding it. Use AI to enhance your refined solution even further, asking it to help you find higher-order principles that make the contradictions simultaneously true and useful.

Mood board

What is it?	Mood boards offer another path to fresh thinking. You can combine images, colors, textures, and words into visual collections to spark new ideas. Designers use them to plan spaces, writers to visualize stories, and marketers to build brand identity. However, anyone can create one to clarify their vision or break through creative blocks.
Example of use:	If you want to redesign your living room, simply grab some magazines, cut out images of spaces you love, and add fabric swatches and photos of objects that inspire you. Arrange them on some cardboard, a scrapbook, or a digital platform. You will have a visual map showing patterns in your taste, such as your attraction to a specific type of material or color combination, that you might not have noticed by simply thinking about it.
How AI can enhance this tool:	Pinterest[6] is a digital platform that allows you to create a digital scrapbook for personal or professional projects. Canva[7] includes mood board templates with an impressive library of design tools. You can create and customize boards with built-in graphics and

fonts. For teams, Miro[8] offers collaborative whiteboarding with mood board templates. Teams can work together in real-time, including complex visual brainstorming. Adobe Firefly Boards has various tools for advanced designers to create stunning digital mood boards.

ⓘ Exercise

1. Define your vision: Create a comprehensive vision framework with four layers: emotional atmosphere (how should people feel?), functional purpose (what should it accomplish?), cultural context (what values does it embody?), and temporal positioning (past/present/future influences). Write two to three specific descriptors for each layer that will guide your entire visual collection process.
2. Generate 50 initial images using AI tools like DALL-E or Midjourney based on your four-layer framework, varying prompts to explore each dimension. From these 50, select 15 that create unexpected tensions or reveal contradictions between your different layers. These tension points will become the most valuable elements of your mood board.
3. Organize your 15 selected images into three distinct visual clusters, each telling a different aspect of your story. Each cluster must contain four to five images that create a mini-narrative when viewed together. The three clusters should represent: your core vision, your aspirational evolution, and your shadow elements (what you're deliberately avoiding or transforming).
4. Use an accompanying AI tool (such as Canva, Adobe Firefly Boards, or Miro), upload your clustered mood board and ask the AI to identify missing visual elements that would strengthen your narrative.
5. Arrange and curate: Upload your AI-generated images to a digital mood board platform like Pinterest. Arrange them by importance and visual flow. Remove images that don't serve your original vision. Aim for final images that tell a cohesive story.

SCAMPER

What is it?   SCAMPER is a creative thinking technique that helps you generate new ideas by asking seven specific questions about an existing product, service, or problem. Each letter stands for a different approach: **S**ubstitute, **C**ombine, **A**dapt (or Augment or Adjust), **M**odify (or Magnify), **P**ut to other use, **E**liminate, and **R**emove (or Rearrange). You systematically work through each letter/question to spark fresh perspectives and find breakthrough solutions.

Example of use: Suppose a designer wanted to create a more innovative and appealing water bottle design. To generate ideas using SCAMPER:

- *Substitute*: Replace plastic with biodegradable materials like bamboo or plant-based polymers to create an eco-friendly bottle.
- *Combine*: Merge the bottle with additional functionality, such as a built-in filter for purifying water or a compartment for fruit infusers.
- *Adapt*: Borrow features from other products, like a collapsible design inspired by telescopes, to make the bottle portable and space-saving.
- *Modify*: Enhance the shape or features by redesigning the cap to double as a small cup or adding an ergonomic grip for comfort.
- *Put to other uses*: Repurpose the water bottle as a multifunctional tool, including a hidden storage compartment for keys or cash during workouts.
- *Eliminate*: Remove unnecessary components, such as reducing complex logos or external packaging, to make the product more minimalist and sustainable.
- *Rearrange*: Change the placement of features, like moving the handle to the base or side for better balance and portability.
- Result: A unique, customer-focused water bottle that is eco-friendly, collapsible, with a built-in filter and hidden storage, appealing to sustainability-conscious and active users.

| How AI can enhance this tool: | Use Midjourney[9] or DALL-E[10] to visualize different design iterations based on SCAMPER modifications to accelerate the prototyping process rapidly. |

⚡ Exercise

1. Choose a specific product, service, or process you want to improve. Apply each SCAMPER element systematically: Substitute (what materials/components could be replaced?), Combine (what could be merged?), Adapt (what could be adjusted from other contexts?), Modify (what could be magnified/minimized?), Put to other uses (how else could this be used?), Eliminate (what's unnecessary?), Rearrange (what could be reordered?). Generate at least three ideas for each SCAMPER element, creating 21 potential modifications.

2. Take your most promising modification from Step 1 and apply SCAMPER again to three different levels: the business model that supports your modified solution, the industry structure that contains that business model, and the societal need that drives the entire system. Each level must fundamentally transform the level below it, creating a cascading series of interconnected changes.

3. For your modifications from Step 2, prompt ChatGPT or Claude to identify contradictions where SCAMPER elements oppose each other (e.g., where

"substitute" conflicts with "combine," or "eliminate" contradicts "modify"). Ask the AI to help design solutions that simultaneously implement opposing SCAMPER elements, creating coherent paradoxical innovations that shouldn't work but do.

4. Apply your paradoxical solutions through the lens of different stakeholders: your harshest critic, your biggest competitor, your end user's most vulnerable advocate. Each stakeholder perspective must modify your solution to serve their agenda while maintaining your core paradoxical innovation.

5. Combine all stakeholder modifications from Step 4 into one comprehensive system that redesigns the entire value chain from raw materials to end-of-life disposal. Your final solution must incorporate the foundational SCAMPER modifications, the cascading transformations, the paradoxical innovations, and all stakeholder requirements while creating new economic relationships between previously unconnected players in the ecosystem.

De Bono's Six Thinking Hats

What is it?	A close adjunct to analogies is lateral thinking, created by Edward De Bono, a Maltese doctor educated at Oxford and Cambridge. He understood that the mind works as a self-organizing pattern recognition system.[11] This mindset helps people develop routines to interact with a complex world, but it also locks in views and makes it hard to change perceptions at will. Lateral thinking is a structured process to counter the natural tendency of the mind to seek out and use familiar patterns.[12]
	De Bono's Six Thinking Hats is a method for structured parallel thinking in individuals or groups. Each "hat" represents a different perspective or mode of thinking. When working in a group, everyone must wear the same hat simultaneously to avoid personal preferences and conflicts about ideas.
Example of use:	Once ideas are created, De Bono's 'Six Thinking Hats' methodology lets individuals and teams explore, develop, implement, and evaluate them.[13] Each 'hat' represents a viewpoint the wearer must take, whether positive or negative. Through this method, participants weed out conflicting thinking styles to work together constructively to explore and implement these ideas, rather than fight over who is right or wrong.[14] Too often, team collaboration meetings typically result in one or two of the loudest voices or ideas dominating the conversation. The result is that a better idea could have been stifled because people use their intelligence and experience to argue for the concept they favor and reject the alternatives.[15]

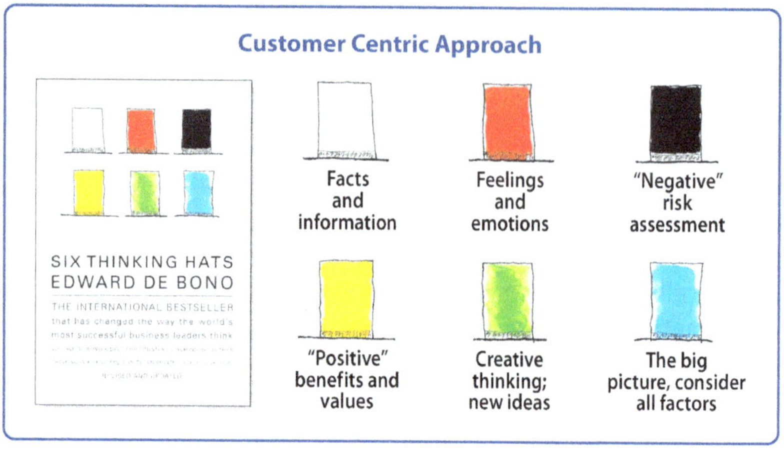

Figure 10.1. De Bono's Six Thinking Hats

Here's how it works, along with specific steps for implementation:

The Six Hats

1. White Hat: Neutral and objective, focused on facts and information

2. Red Hat: Emotional and intuitive, expressing feelings without justification

3. Black Hat: Cautious and critical, pointing out potential risks and problems

4. Yellow Hat: Optimistic, identifying benefits and opportunities

5. Green Hat: Creative and growth-oriented, generating new ideas and possibilities

6. Blue Hat: Process control, organizing the thinking process, and maintaining focus.

How AI can enhance this tool:

White Hat: AI can provide relevant facts, statistics, and research on the topic. It can analyze data and identify patterns or gaps that need addressing and generate insights into best practices or competitor approaches.

Example: For a product design challenge, Claude or ChatGPT can offer market research trends, consumer behavior data, and case studies to ground the discussion in reality.

Red Hat: AI can help articulate emotional reactions to ideas or scenarios, suggest user personas and explore how they might feel about potential innovations, and simulate responses based on different emotional drivers, such as excitement or skepticism.

Example: Use Character.ai[16] to create different characters with certain personality traits, and brainstorm how a new app design might make users feel more connected or frustrated and why.

Black Hat: AI can play the role of a constructive skeptic, identifying flaws, risks, or potential barriers. It can highlight regulatory, technical, or ethical challenges. It can offer solutions to mitigate identified risks or make the idea more robust.

Example: If someone suggests using a new generative AI tool, use Claude, ChatGPT, or DeepSeek[17] to flag concerns about data privacy or bias while proposing alternative approaches to address them.

Yellow Hat: AI can expand on the positive aspects of ideas, exploring potential breakthroughs or large-scale impact. It can suggest additional opportunities for growth or synergies with other projects. It can help identify long-term benefits and marketable strengths.

Example: For a sustainable packaging innovation, Jasper,[18] particularly suited for marketing angles, can brainstorm how it could improve brand image, attract eco-conscious consumers, and open new markets.

Green Hat: AI can generate novel and unconventional ideas using prompts, scenarios, or metaphorical thinking. It can apply creative tools like lateral thinking, random word associations, or analogy generation to spark new perspectives. It can combine existing ideas into hybrid solutions.

Example: If someone is stuck on creating a new fundraising campaign, AI might propose gamification, AI-powered storytelling, or AR/VR donor experiences. Try using Copy.ai[19] for marketing copy, or Sudowrite[20] to test metaphorical ideas.

Blue Hat: Pi.ai[21] can act as a meeting facilitator. With the right prompts and information about the meeting's agenda and participants, Pi can help structure discussions, encourage balanced contributions, summarize key points, identify action items, and outline next steps. However, it's important to remember that as an AI, Pi cannot fully understand the nuances of human communication, such as tone, body language, or subtle cues. So, it's crucial for meeting participants to provide clear and concise prompts to communicate openly and effectively with Pi throughout the meeting.

ℹ️ Exercise

1. Choose a complex decision you're facing. Apply each of the six thinking hats systematically: White Hat (facts, data, information needs), Red Hat (emotions, feelings, intuition), Black Hat (caution, critical assessment, risks), Yellow Hat (optimism, benefits, opportunities), Green Hat (creativity, alternatives, new ideas), Blue Hat (process control, thinking about thinking). With each hat, document insights and generate at least five specific points for each hat perspective.

2. Take your analyses apply each hat's perspective across three time horizons: immediate consequences (next 6 months), medium-term impacts (2–3 years), and long-term effects (generational/10+ years). Create a 6×3 matrix showing how each hat's insights change across time periods, identifying where current hat perspectives might become irrelevant or contradictory over time.

3. Using your temporal matrix, employ different AI tools to roleplay four key stakeholders for each hat perspective. Prompt ChatGPT as customers using White Hat facts, Claude as competitors applying Black Hat criticism, Character. ai as future generations wearing Green Hat creativity, and Perplexity as regulators with Yellow Hat optimism. Generate distinct stakeholder-hat combinations and identify the most surprising insights that challenge your original hat analysis.

4. From your stakeholder-hat insights, identify the six most significant contradictions where different hat-stakeholder combinations reach opposing conclusions. Work through each one to find higher-order principles that make both opposing perspectives simultaneously true and strategically useful for your decision.

5. Synthesize previous steps into a weighted decision framework. Create a scoring matrix where each of your resolved paradoxes from Step 4 is weighted by: relevance to your core decision (1–10), temporal urgency from Step 2 (1–10), stakeholder impact intensity from Step 3 (1–10), and implementation complexity from your original Step 1 analysis (1–10). Your final decision must integrate all hat perspectives while explicitly acknowledging which paradoxes carry the most strategic weight.

Blue Ocean Strategy

What is it?   This framework for innovation encourages businesses to move away from intense competition in existing markets (or red oceans) and instead create new, uncontested markets (or blue oceans). This approach focuses on offering unique value by redefining what a product or service can be, often appealing to untapped customer needs or removing industry-standard pain points. The goal is to render competitors irrelevant by breaking away from traditional competitive strategies.

Example of use: This approach can be operationalized by analyzing consumers' perceptions and preference data using several multidimensional scaling programs to establish the brand's positioning by segment. The resulting maps, especially the 3rd dimension, can help identify potential blue oceans.[22] For example, a fitness company applying this strategy might create a hybrid wellness subscription that combines VR workouts, personalized nutrition planning, and mental health coaching. Instead of competing with traditional gyms or streaming fitness classes, this new offering targets tech-savvy individuals who want a holistic, immersive wellness experience without leaving their homes. By blending fitness, technology, and wellness, the company establishes a new category that doesn't exist in conventional markets, capturing untapped demand. Real-world success: Peloton successfully implemented the blue ocean strategy by combining high-end exercise equipment with subscription-based interactive classes, creating a new market category that blended home fitness, technology, and community. At the height of the pandemic in 2021, it achieved a peak market valuation of nearly $50 billion and fundamentally changed how consumers think about home workouts.[23]

How AI can enhance this tool: BlueOcean[24] can help identify potential blue ocean opportunities by analyzing vast amounts of market data to find underserved customer segments and value propositions. Netflix used the blue ocean strategy to transition to online streaming from DVD rentals, creating a new, uncontested market space.[25]

ⓘ Exercise

1. Map the unspoken beliefs that define your entire industry. List eight to 10 fundamental assumptions that ALL major players accept as gospel truth. Go beyond surface features to core beliefs about customer behavior, delivery methods, pricing models, and value propositions. Example: "Customers must physically visit stores to buy cars" or "Fitness requires expensive equipment and memberships."

2. Identify customer segments your industry systematically ignores or underserves due to a perceived belief that they don't fit the standard business model. Research why these groups are excluded. What specific pain points do they experience that your industry dismisses as "not our problem"? Focus on groups with genuine needs rather than inventing artificial segments.

3. Select your industry's most entrenched assumption from Step 1. Use AI to systematically challenge this belief. AI Prompt: "Act as a contrarian strategist. Here's a core assumption in [your industry]: [insert assumption]. Generate 10 ways this assumption could be completely wrong. What evidence would disprove it? How would successful companies in other industries approach this differently?" Document the most compelling counter-arguments and alternative approaches.

4. Design a solution that serves your neglected segment by completely rejecting the sacred rule you challenged in Step 3. Create a value curve comparing your proposed solution against industry standards across six to eight key factors. Where will you eliminate, reduce, raise, or create value compared to existing players? Your solution should make traditional competitors irrelevant rather than slightly better.

5. Create a detailed prototype or detailed service blueprint of your Blue Ocean concept. Test it with 15 to 20 people from your target neglected segment. Ask: "Would you pay $X for this approach instead of current alternatives? What would convince you to abandon traditional solutions entirely?" Document responses and refine your concept based on patterns that emerge. Your goal is creating something people didn't know they wanted but can't live without once they see it.

Marty Seligman's Five Kinds of Creativity

What is it?   This framework was developed by Prof. Marty Seligman,[26] founder of the Positive Psychology Discipline. It categorizes the diverse ways creativity can manifest in scientific discovery and problem-solving. It highlights that scientific innovation is not confined to brainstorming or divergent thinking but encompasses a spectrum of approaches that reshape how we perceive and engage with challenges.

Example of use: Each approach reflects a unique cognitive strategy or perspective:

- Integration: focuses on synthesizing seemingly unrelated concepts, discovering previously unnoticed connections. This might involve unifying ideas across disciplines to create holistic solutions.

  Example: Dr. Frances Arnold's work integrating evolutionary biology with enzyme engineering led to the development of directed evolution of enzymes, earning her the 2018 Nobel Prize in Chemistry. Her approach has revolutionized pharmaceutical manufacturing and biofuel production.[27]

- Splitting: involves breaking down what seems homogeneous into distinct components, revealing nuances and new possibilities by challenging assumptions of uniformity.

  Example: The periodic table of elements is an example of splitting what was once considered homogenous (earth, air, fire, and water) into distinct components (118 chemical elements). This process revealed new possibilities in understanding matter, challenging previous assumptions of uniformity.[28]

- Figure/Ground reversal: reimagines the focus of scientific inquiry, suggesting that shifting attention from the prominent (foreground) to the less apparent (background) can uncover novel insights or answers.

  Example: The most obvious example is the earth going around the sun.

- Distilled Imagination: emphasizes the ability to mentally project beyond immediate realities—envisioning alternate times, spaces, or social settings to generate fresh ideas or theories.

  Example: Einstein's thought experiments about riding on light beams led to his special theory of relativity, demonstrating how imagination can lead to groundbreaking theoretical advances.[29]

- Discovery is the creative process of generating something entirely new and distinguishing between accidental and intentional discovery.

  Example: Although initially accidental, Alexander Fleming's discovery of penicillin was recognized as significant because of his prepared mind and scientific creativity in pursuing its implications.[30]

How AI can enhance this tool:
AI Application: Tools like Semantic Scholar[31] and Elicit[32] use AI to help researchers identify connections across disciplines, supporting integration-style creativity by revealing patterns in scientific literature that might remain hidden.

🅘 Exercise

1. Choose a multi-layered problem that has resisted conventional solutions for at least six months. This should be something where obvious approaches have failed. Define the challenge in one sentence, then identify why traditional thinking keeps failing. What makes this problem particularly stubborn? Focus on challenges where breakthrough thinking—not just harder work—is required.

2. Identify three to five completely unrelated fields that solve analogous prob-
    lems. Research how each field approaches similar challenges using different
    principles, technologies, or philosophies. Map the core mechanisms each
    field uses. Look for underlying patterns that transcend surface differences.
    Example: If tackling team communication, study how ant colonies coordinate,
    how jazz musicians improvise together, how emergency rooms handle chaos,
    and how video game guilds organize.

3. Take your challenge and use AI to systematically break it into distinct, hidden
    components. AI Prompt: "Act as a research scientist analyzing this problem:
    [your challenge]. Apply splitting analysis: What separate sub-problems are
    hiding within this larger issue? What elements am I treating as one thing
    that are actually multiple distinct challenges? Break this down like a scientist
    discovering new elements within what seemed like a single compound."
    Document each distinct component the AI identifies.

4. Apply three different reversal strategies to your challenge: Focus Reversal:
    What if the "background" elements you're ignoring are actually the key? List
    what you consider peripheral and investigate if they're central. Temporal
    Reversal: What if the solution comes from a completely different time period?
    How would someone from 100 years ago or 100 years in the future approach
    this? Stakeholder Reversal: What if you optimized for the people who seem
    least important to this problem?

5. Combine insights from all previous steps into three radical solution
    prototypes. Each prototype should integrate elements from your mapping
    (Step 2), address distinct components (Step 3), and incorporate at least one
    reversal insight (Step 4). Test these prototypes through mental simulation:
    Project each solution five years into the future. What unexpected
    consequences emerge? What new possibilities open up? Select your most
    promising prototype and identify the first experiment you could run this
    week to test its core assumption.

Inside-the-Box Thinking

What is it?   Inside the box thinking works within established rules, systems,
                 and boundaries. You solve problems using existing methods,
                 proven strategies, and conventional approaches relying on logic,
                 experience, and tested frameworks.

                 Inside-the-Box Thinking reflects the practical realities of life: We
                 often face constraints of one sort or another, whether it's on our
                 budget, time, capabilities, social obligations, or other factors. These
                 limitations don't mean we cannot innovate; we just need to find a
                 more creative way to work around them.

Example of use:	Toyota's lean manufacturing system demonstrates Inside-the-Box Thinking at its finest. Facing severe resource constraints in post-war Japan, Toyota developed the just-in-time production system that minimized waste, reduced inventory costs, and maximized efficiency. Born from limitations, this approach became a global standard that revolutionized manufacturing.[33]

Similarly, LEGO's sustainability initiative demonstrates Inside-the-Box Thinking at its best. When challenged to replace petroleum-based plastics with sustainable materials, LEGO faced extremely tight constraints: new materials had to match existing bricks' precise dimensional tolerance, durability, and color consistency while remaining compatible with pieces manufactured decades earlier. Rather than abandoning these constraints, LEGO innovated within them, ultimately developing plant-based polyethylene that maintains perfect compatibility with their existing system. This exemplifies how creativity often flourishes by not ignoring constraints and embracing them as creative catalysts.

As an individual, you might use Inside-the-Box Thinking for your monthly household budget. Suppose you earn $4,000 monthly and struggle to save money while covering your expenses. Inside-the-Box Thinking means working with that $4,000. You might, for example, discover that you spend $200 monthly on takeaways, but you could reduce it by cutting back to $50. You also find that you've been paying $50 each month on a long-forgotten gym membership, which, if you temporarily freeze or cancel the membership altogether, could provide yet another saving. Similarly, you realize that cutting back on impulse purchases, streaming services, or paid Apps that you rarely use, coffees, and all manner of other unnecessary purchases, yields an impressive monthly saving that you can either put away in savings or towards your credit card bill to pay it off faster. You haven't changed your income or borrowed money. You have simply moved existing resources from less valuable uses to more valuable ones. Your $4,000 budget constraints forced you to become more strategic with your creative thinking.

How AI can enhance this tool:	For businesses: AI can identify the most efficient resource allocation within existing constraints. The fashion brand Zara, for example, uses AI-driven demand forecasting to manage its inventory management processes, AI-driven recommendation engines to personalize the shopping experience for each customer, and predictive demand modeling to enhance its supply chain

forecasting to respond to trends quickly while working within logistical constraints.[34]

For individuals, AI tools such as YNAB (You Need A Budget) can be used for financial planning to recognize patterns in your spending habits. LinkedIn Premium[35] can be used for career development to analyze your existing skills and suggest internal career moves or skill combinations that boost your value without changing companies. Coursera's AI recommends courses that build on skills you already possess. (See Appendix III for our own Coursera offer.) MyFitnessPal[36] uses AI to create meal plans from foods you already eat, just in better combinations. This is just a small selection of the AI tools you could utilize for your benefit. We encourage you to conduct your research to discover more.

⚡ Exercise

1. Choose a significant goal you've been unable to achieve due to perceived limitations. Map every available resource across five categories: time, skills, relationships, tools/assets, and knowledge. Be forensically detailed. Include underutilized assets, dormant skills, forgotten connections, and time currently allocated to low-value activities. Go beyond obvious resources—include your reputation, past experiences, digital assets, and indirect access through your network.

2. Identify and categorize your constraints into three types: Hard constraints (truly unchangeable laws, physics, regulations), Soft constraints (assumed limitations you've never tested), False constraints (mental barriers disguised as real limitations). Map how each constraint currently blocks your progress. Challenge yourself: Which "impossible" limitations have you never tested?

3. Use AI to discover hidden resource combinations and identify constraint-breaking strategies. AI Prompt: "Act as a resource optimization strategist analyzing this challenge: [your goal] with these available resources: [list from Step 1] and these constraints: [list from Step 2]. Find unexpected ways to combine existing resources that I haven't considered. How would Toyota's lean manufacturing principles or LEGO's compatibility constraints apply here? What resource combinations could turn my biggest constraint into my competitive advantage?" Document the most promising resource recombination strategies.

4. Create a detailed reallocation plan that moves resources from current uses to high-impact applications. Focus on: Time arbitrage: Shift hours from low-impact to breakthrough activities. Skill stacking: Combine existing abilities in novel ways. Relationship leveraging: Transform social connections into strategic assets. Asset repurposing: Use tools/resources for unintended applications. Quantify the impact: What measurable improvement will each reallocation generate?

5. Implement your reallocation blueprint for 30 days. Track three key metrics: Resource velocity: How much faster are you progressing toward your goal? Innovation quotient: How many creative solutions emerged from working within constraints? Efficiency gains: What percentage improvement in results per resource unit invested? Document breakthrough moments when constraints forced you to discover solutions you would never have found with unlimited resources. Identify which constraint-driven innovations you'll permanently adopt even if resources become unlimited.

Out-of-the-Box Thinking

What is it?   A companion of Inside-the-Box Thinking is Out-of-the-Box Thinking, a commonly used method of thinking from a new perspective. One way to illustrate this is with the following example: Imagine three rows of three dots arranged in a square.

Figure 10.2. How to connect the 9 points with 4 straight lines

Now try connecting them using four straight lines without lifting the pencil off the page. This can only be done if you think outside the box.

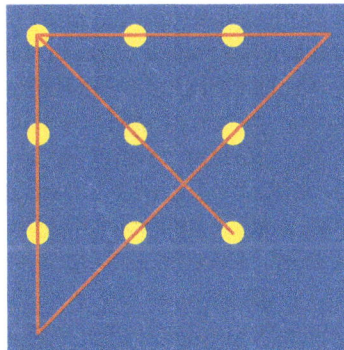

Figure 10.3. The only way to connect the 9 points with 4 straight lines is going outside the box

Stretching your thinking to expand beyond the obvious is a worthy exercise to unlock creativity and innovation.

Example of use:

Dollar Shave Club attacked Gillette's $13 billion empire with a $1 razor and a viral video.[37] Instead of competing on blade technology or shaving science, the company focused on convenience and humor, using the shared customer frustration with high prices and the hassle of buying razors in store. Co-founder and CEO Michael Dubin created the company's first promotional (profanity-laced) video that cost $4,500 to make. The video crashed the company's servers within the first hour and generated 12,000 orders within 48 hours.[38] Dubin's unconventional approach to creating promotional videos probably stemmed from his background in improv comedy at Upright Citizens Brigade, helping him use humorous, authentic content that cuts through traditional advertising noise. Unilever acquired the company for $1 billion in 2016.[39]

How might an individual use out-of-the-box thinking to overcome a challenge? Let's suppose Blake, a marketing graduate, is looking for a job but can't get hired because they don't have two to three years' marketing experience. The conventional thinking would be to apply for level-entry jobs and hope someone gives them a chance. However, out-of-the-box thinking might be to create the work experience themselves by solving a real problem for someone else. Suppose Blake identified 10 local restaurants struggling with empty tables during lunch hours. Blake could contact them and offer to create detailed marketing plans for each restaurant, complete with social media strategies, promotional ideas, and customer retention programs.

Blake could spend two weeks implementing the ideas and documenting the results per restaurant. Imagine if three restaurants saw profitable results and hired Blake as a consultant? The result is that Blake has solved a real problem for businesses in the community, turned a weakness (unable to find work) into a strength with a fresh perspective, and created their work in the meantime. Taking this step further to prevent restaurants from benefiting from Blake's hard work without actually offering the consultant role, Blake could create a platform, document everything publicly with blog posts, case studies, before/after photos, and revenue numbers (with permission). In this way, Blake is simultaneously building a personal consulting brand, demonstrating their expertise publicly, and providing real value to their local restaurants. Out-of-the-box thinking has enabled Blake to create real value for themselves and others.

How AI can enhance this tool: Use an AI assistant like ChatGPT or Claude to challenge your assumptions and generate alternative perspectives. You could, for example, ask ChatGPT to play devil's advocate with the prompt, "Reframe this in a way that challenges the way I see this problem." Alternatively, try this prompt courtesy of Professor Ethan Mollick: "Pretend to be an innovative entrepreneur who always pitches good ideas."[40]

Exercise

1. Identify a challenge where you feel completely stuck despite multiple attempts. Write down every "realistic" solution you've considered and why each won't work. List all the rules, assumptions, and boundaries you're accepting as unchangeable. Include industry norms, social expectations, resource limitations, and timing constraints. Focus on challenges where you keep cycling through the same ineffective approaches despite knowing they won't work.

2. Take your three strongest "unchangeable" assumptions from Step 1. For each assumption, research examples of people or organizations that succeeded by completely violating this rule. Study how Dollar Shave Club ignored razor technology assumptions, or how Blake created work experience by solving real problems instead of waiting for job offers. Document the specific mindset shifts that enabled these rule-breakers to see opportunities others missed.

3. Use AI to systematically challenge your mental constraints and generate radical alternatives. AI Prompt: "Act as a contrarian entrepreneur who always finds unconventional solutions. Here's my challenge: [your situation] and here are the assumptions I'm making: [list from Step 1]. Pretend constraints don't exist and generate 10 absurd solutions that completely ignore these assumptions. Then, for each absurd idea, identify what kernel of breakthrough thinking it contains that I could actually implement." Extract the most promising unconventional approaches from AI responses.

4. Apply three radical thinking strategies to your challenge: Complete Problem Reversal: Instead of solving your problem, design how to make it dramatically worse. Then reverse each "worse" strategy into a potential solution. Infinite Resource Thinking: If you had unlimited time, money, and influence, what would you do? Then identify which elements of this "impossible" solution you could actually implement on a smaller scale. Context Destruction: What if your challenge existed in a completely different context (different country, time period, or industry)? How would the solution change?

5. Select your most promising unconventional approach from Steps 3 to 4. Create a small-scale prototype or pilot test that requires minimal resources but tests the core breakthrough assumption. Design this test to run for exactly 2 weeks.

Define clear success metrics that prove your unconventional approach works better than traditional methods. Execute the test, document what happens, and identify which "impossible" barriers were actually mental constructs versus real obstacles. Use results to refine your approach and scale the elements that generated genuine breakthroughs.

EVALUATION TOOLS—FOR ASSESSING AND SELECTING IDEAS

"Yes and..." Techniques

What is it?	'Yes, and...' techniques are designed to build upon ideas rather than blocking them.
Example of use:	These tools thrive in modern creative environments. Google and IDEO have incorporated the improvisational theater principle of 'Yes, and...' into their brainstorming protocols, requiring participants to build upon ideas before critiquing them. This simple rule transforms meeting dynamics from competitive idea evaluation to collaborative idea development, often generating solutions that no individual would have conceived alone.
How AI can enhance this tool:	Each of the following tools has different strengths for collaborative thinking. Claude excels at idea expansion and creative building. Input a concept, and Claude generates multiple variations while maintaining your original direction. ChatGPT works well for rapid-fire brainstorming sessions. It responds quickly to build on ideas. Perplexity carries out deep research. It finds real-world examples and data to support emerging concepts. Notion AI[41] integrates directly into your workspace. You can capture ideas and have AI expand them within your existing documents. Copy.ai specializes in marketing and business applications. It transforms basic concepts into compelling narratives and campaigns.

i Exercise

1. Write down a simple problem. Generate three potential solutions without editing yourself. Start each response with "Yes, and we could also..."
2. Partner building (10 minutes): Share your problem with someone else. Person A presents their first solution. Person B responds: "Yes, and what if we..." Continue for five rounds, building on each other's ideas.
3. Group amplification (15 minutes): Gather three to four people around one challenge. Each person adds one element using "Yes, and..." Go around the circle three times. Record every contribution without evaluation.
4. AI Collaboration (10 minutes): Take your best group idea to an AI assistant. Prompt the assistant, "Here's our concept: [idea]. Yes, and we could also..." Let

AI expand in directions you hadn't considered. Build on AI suggestions with more "Yes, and…" responses.

5. Reality integration (10 minutes): Review all generated ideas. Ask: "Which elements could we implement?" Combine practical pieces into one actionable plan, and schedule the first concrete step.

IMPLEMENTATION TOOLS—FOR TURNING IDEAS INTO ACTION

Redesign Principles

What is it?   Redesign principles offer specific pathways for improvement. This approach focuses on taking an existing product, system, or concept and reimagining it to improve functionality, aesthetics, efficiency, or user experience. It doesn't aim to invent something entirely new but instead transforms or refines what already exists to meet current or emerging needs better. This principle emphasizes iterative improvement and the application of creative thinking to adapt to new contexts or challenges. A popular set of rules that provide redesign principles is the following:

- Eliminate steps
- Eliminate interfaces
- Eliminate inefficiencies
- Eliminate bottlenecks
- Design for quality

Example of use: **Electric toothbrushes:** Eliminated the manual brushing motion (eliminating steps) while incorporating precision timers to improve brushing technique (designing for quality). Oral-B's smart toothbrushes with AI-powered brushing recognition increased effectiveness by 25% compared to manual brushing.[42]

Robot vacuums: Eliminated the manual labor of vacuuming (eliminating steps) and incorporated sensors to navigate efficiently around obstacles (eliminating inefficiencies). iRobot's Roomba series decreased household cleaning time weekly; the time saved depends on the room size.

Interactive whiteboards: Eliminated the need for traditional chalk or markers (eliminating interfaces) while adding digital capabilities for saving and sharing content (eliminating inefficiencies). According to education research, SMART Board installations in educational settings improved student engagement by 40%.[43]

Biodegradable packaging: Redesigned conventional packaging to eliminate environmental waste (eliminating inefficiencies) while maintaining or improving protective qualities (designing for quality). Companies like Ecovative Design created mushroom-based packaging that decomposed within 45 days while matching the protective properties of Styrofoam.[44]

Infrared non-contact thermometers: Eliminated physical contact required for temperature measurement (eliminating interfaces) while providing faster readings (eliminating bottlenecks). During the COVID-19 pandemic, these devices reduced screening time in public spaces compared to traditional methods.[45]

How AI can enhance this tool:	Autodesk Fusion 360[46] uses AI-powered generative design to redesign products for improved efficiency and reduced material use. When General Motors used this approach to redesign vehicle components, they achieved 40% weight reduction while maintaining performance standards.

i Exercise

1. Map your current process: Choose something you use daily—your morning routine, a work task, or a digital tool. Write down every single step involved. Be specific. Example: Making coffee might include 15 steps from finding the filters to cleaning up.
2. Hunt for elimination targets: Go through your mapped process and mark:
   • Unnecessary steps you could remove
   • Multiple interfaces you could combine
   • Time-wasting inefficiencies
   • Points where things slow down or stop.
   Ask yourself: "What if I didn't do this step?"
3. Redesign one element: Pick the most significant pain point from Step 2. Sketch or describe how you'd eliminate it. Don't just improve it—remove it or combine it with something else.
4. Test your redesign: Try your new approach for one whole day or cycle. Track what happens. Does it work better What breaks? What improves?
5. Iterate based on results: Take your test results and refine further. Can you eliminate one more step? Can you combine the two remaining interfaces?

Democratizing creativity

What is it?	Creativity gets assistance from platforms like Meta (Facebook, Instagram, WhatsApp, Meta Quest) that offer free digital tools to help you or your organization blossom. For instance, Meta's AI Studio enables creators to develop AI-powered chatbots that can

interact with followers, offering personalized experiences and fostering deeper connections.

Meta has also introduced features like the Creator Marketplace,[47] facilitating collaborations between brands and creators, and expanded monetization options like subscriptions and digital collectibles on Instagram. These innovations empower creators to produce diverse content, engage more effectively with their communities, and explore new revenue streams, amplifying their creative potential.

Example of use:	Using Facebook's professional mode, Edith Galvez, a Latina food lover, gained over 400,000 followers in less than six months. She praises the Reels Open program and Reels Bonuses for allowing creators to monetize their work. Galvez particularly values the analytics tools that help her track her Reels' reach and audience engagement.[48] Lauren Magenta, founder of Own Your Brand, has successfully leveraged Google Workspace[49] and Gemini to transform her business operations. She uses Google Workspace to run her entire business, demonstrating the versatility of Google's tools for creators and entrepreneurs. Gemini for Google Workspace has revolutionized how she manages client enrollment, a critical aspect of her business. Magenta uses Gemini to quickly draft personalized emails to potential clients in her voice, improving communication efficiency.[50]
How AI can enhance this tool:	Google offers a variety of tools to assist creators in producing and managing content across different media. Here are some notable options:

1. Google for Creators:[51] A comprehensive platform providing resources, guidance, and inspiration for content creators. It includes tools like Google Trends[52] for exploring the trend of popular search topics and Site Kit[53] for integrating Google services into your website.

2. Google Web Designer:[54] A free, professional-grade HTML5 authoring tool that enables the creation of interactive and animated web content, including advertisements and web pages. It offers a visual interface with design tools and integrates with other Google products.

3. Google Sites:[55] A user-friendly website creation tool that allows you to build websites without requiring coding skills. It's part of the Google Docs Editors[56] suite and integrates seamlessly with other Google services.

4. Google Forms:[57] A tool for creating online forms and surveys with various question types. It enables real-time response analysis and is accessible from any device.

5. YouTube Create:[58] An editing and production tool within YouTube that provides easy-to-use features like filters, effects, transitions, and a library of royalty-free music to enhance your videos.

6. Google Vids:[59] An online video creator and editor that allows users to create and edit videos directly within Google Workspace[60], offering features like scene trimming and integration with Google Drive.

7. Google My Maps:[61] A tool that lets you create and share custom maps, useful for visual storytelling and embedding maps into websites.

⚡ Exercise

Choose one of the many Google tools mentioned above, and use one to address a challenge or start a new project that piques your interest. Use an additional AI assistant like Claude, ChatGPT, or, depending on the challenge/project, one of the many other specialist AI assistants to enhance and refine your results.

Question Protocols

What is it? | One of the most powerful yet underutilized creative thinking tools is asking, 'What's missing?' This question shifts perspective from analyzing what exists to identifying gaps, oversights, and opportunities.

Example of use: | When evaluating a strategy, product design, or solution, deliberately pause to consider:

- What element has been overlooked?
- Which stakeholder perspective hasn't been considered?
- What assumption remains untested?
- What constraint have we accepted without questioning?

This practice helps overcome the human tendency to focus on what's present rather than what's absent, often revealing critical insights that transform the approach. The most innovative organizations institutionalize this question, making it a standard part of their review processes to ensure more comprehensive thinking and reduce the risk of significant oversights.

How AI can enhance this tool:	AI assistants excel at pattern recognition and can identify blind spots we miss. They quickly process vast amounts of information and offer diverse perspectives. AI can, for example, spot recurring themes across industries. When you describe a marketing challenge, it might reference solutions from healthcare, education, or manufacturing that share similar structures. A retail company struggling with customer retention could benefit from strategies AI identifies in subscription software or fitness clubs. AI can instantly review thousands of case studies. It identifies what worked, what failed, and why. This speed reveals gaps in your research that would take weeks to uncover manually. Ask Claude about the unintended effects of your decisions. Use ChatGPT for brainstorming sessions when you need volume and variety. Perplexity excels at deep research and can find recent developments that change your context.

ℹ️ Exercise

1. Choose a current project, decision, or problem you're working on. Write it down in one clear sentence.
2. Ask your AI assistant: "What might I be missing about [your challenge]? What perspectives haven't I considered?" Document the responses.
3. List all stakeholders you've identified. Then ask AI: "Who else might be affected by this that I haven't mentioned?" Add these new voices to your analysis.
4. Challenge your assumptions: Tell AI your key assumptions about the situation. Ask: "Which of these assumptions should I question? What evidence would disprove each one?"
5. Share your perceived limitations with AI. Ask: "Which constraints are real versus imagined? What would happen if each constraint didn't exist?" Before finalizing your approach, have AI play devil's advocate: "What could go wrong with this plan? What have similar efforts missed in the past?"
   Document insights immediately and review patterns across all six steps to identify your biggest blind spots.

OTHER TOOLS FOR CREATORS

- Canva:[62] A versatile design platform that provides free or paid access to a wide range of templates, graphics, and fonts, enabling users to create social media posts, presentations, and more. Canva's Magic Studio suite includes AI-powered tools like Magic Design, Magic Edit, and Magic Write to enhance creativity and design.

Success story: Small business owner Sarah Johnson used Canva to create professional marketing materials for her local bakery, increasing her social media engagement by 200% and growing her customer base by 35% without hiring an experienced designer.

- Adobe Photoshop[63]: A paid, leading graphics editor that has become the industry standard for digital image editing and graphic design. Photoshop offers a comprehensive suite of tools for tasks such as photo retouching, compositing, and creating complex digital artwork.
  Success story: Photographer Brandon Woelfel developed his distinctive neon-lit portrait style using Photoshop's color grading tools, building a following of over 3 million on Instagram and securing brand partnerships with major companies.

- Adobe Express[64]: A free or paid, user-friendly tool that allows creators to design graphics, videos, and web pages. It offers AI-powered features such as Animate All, One-Click Apply, and Text-to-Image, which help users efficiently produce high-quality content.
  Success story: Teacher Monica Garcia used Adobe Express to create engaging educational materials during remote learning, increasing student participation by 45% and was recognized for innovation in digital education.

- H5P:[65] An open-source content collaboration framework that enables the creation, sharing, and reuse of interactive HTML5 content directly within web browsers, including interactive videos, presentations, quizzes, and timelines.
  Success story: University professor James Chen used H5P to transform traditional lectures into interactive learning experiences, resulting in a 30% improvement in student test scores and significantly higher course satisfaction ratings.

- Photopea:[66] A free, web-based photo and graphics editor that supports various file formats, including PSD, JPEG, and PNG. It offers features similar to Adobe Photoshop, making it a valuable tool for image editing and graphic design.
  Success story: Freelance designer Miguel Santos used Photopea exclusively to build his portfolio while unable to afford Photoshop, eventually securing clients including local businesses and nonprofit organizations.

- Audacity: A free, open-source, cross-platform audio software for multi-track recording and editing. It's widely used for podcasting, music production, and sound editing.
  Success story: The popular true crime podcast "Criminal" initially used Audacity for audio production, growing to over 20 million downloads before upgrading to professional studio equipment.

Many more creator tools are beyond the scope of this book to list. Explore on your own to find the best tools for your needs.

ⓘ Exercise

1. Select your goal or challenge.
2. Identify your current approach to address this goal or challenge.
3. Choose one of the approaches that has piqued your interest or any of the other approaches you discover.
4. Design and implement an experiment that applies this new approach to your challenge using one of the exercises in the tools described.
5. Measure the results of your experiment and compare them to the outcome of your old approach.
6. Use AI to enhance, challenge, and expand your results.

Reflect on the differences in the results. What have you learned? How has the new approach opened your mind to consider new possibilities you haven't considered? How can you apply these lessons to other challenges? How has AI improved either the process or the results? How will you continue to use AI with this type of challenge in the future?

In Summary

1. Creativity thrives on structure.

We presented tools that fall into categories depending on where you are in the creative process. However, this is not a rigid rule about which categories the tools fall into. Rather, the tools will often span more than one category as they guide your thinking and amplify your creative output.

Which creative challenges in your life would benefit from more structure rather than hoping inspiration strikes?

2. Multiple approaches break different mental blocks.

From SWOT analysis to random word generators to De Bono's Six Thinking Hats, whichever tool appeals to you will help to attack creative obstacles from different angles. SCAMPER systematically explores modifications while Blue Ocean Strategy creates entirely new markets by ignoring industry assumptions.

Which of your thinking patterns feels most stuck in familiar loops that need disruption?

In Summary (contd.)

3. AI amplifies every creative technique.

Modern AI assistants enhance each tool presented. Generative AI like ChatGPT expands brainstorming sessions, visual AI creates mood board elements, and specialist AI like Character.ai simulates different perspectives. The key is using AI as a creative partner that challenges assumptions and generates perspectives you would never consider alone.

How could AI push your thinking beyond the obvious solutions you always reach for?

4. "Yes, and..." builds better ideas than blocking them.

Evaluation tools focus on developing ideas collaboratively rather than shutting them down immediately. Implementation tools like redesign principles offer specific pathways: eliminate steps, interfaces, and inefficiencies while designing for quality.

How often do you kill promising ideas too early instead of building them into something better?

5. A powerful creative question is "what's missing?".

"What's missing?" shifts focus from analyzing what exists to identifying gaps and opportunities. This question reveals critical insights that transform approaches. Combined with accessible tools like Canva and Google Workspace, anyone can now access professional-grade creative capabilities.

What crucial element might everyone in your field be overlooking that represents your biggest opportunity and what do you do to assure that you will be aware of newer approaches to enhance creativity?

In the next chapter, we will discuss how you can glean insights from trends. Given that in this book we present a range of illustrative approaches, and that new approaches to enhance creativity are being developed all the time, our question of "What's missing?" applies also to the range of approaches we present.

Notes

1 Semrush. https://www.semrush.com/
2 HubSpot. https://www.hubspot.com/
3 Random Word Generator. https://randomwordgenerator.com/
4 Random Image Generator. https://www.fotor.com/features/random-image-generator/
5 Ayoa Mind Mapping Tool. https://www.ayoa.com/
6 Pinterest is a digital pinboard, used for digital mood boards and inspirational ideals. https://www.pinterest.com/
7 Canva. https://www.canva.com/
8 Miro. https://miro.com/
9 Midjourney.ai. https://www.midjourney.com/
10 DALL-E. https://openai.com/index/dall-e-3/
11 De Bono organization website, accessed August 16, 2024. https://www.debono.com/
12 Lateral Thinking website, accessed August 16, 2024. https://www.lateralthinking.com/what-is-lateralthinking
13 De Bono organization website, accessed August 16, 2024, https://www.debono.com/
14 Ibid.
15 "Six Thinking Hats," The de Bono Group website, accessed August 19, 2024. https://www.debonogroup.com/services/core-programs/six-thinking-hats/
16 Character.ai. https://character.ai/
17 Deepseek.ai. https://www.deepseek.com/en
18 Jasper.ai. https://www.jasper.ai/
19 Copy.ai. https://www.copy.ai/
20 Sudowrite. https://sudowrite.com/
21 Pi.ai. https://pi.ai/talk
22 Yoram Wind. *Positioning Analysis Strategy*, Legends in Marketing (Vol. 7, p. 94). Sage Publishing LLC, 2014, accessed March 3, 2025.
23 Emil Tabakov. "7 Key Blue Ocean Strategy Examples You Should Know About." *Icanpreneur*, November 1, 2024, accessed February 26, 2025. https://www.icanpreneur.com/blog/7-key-blue-ocean-strategy-examples
24 BlueOcean.ai. https://www.blueocean.ai/
25 Suvodip Sen. "An Empirical Study on How a Late Comer Firm NETFLIX Deploys 'Blue Ocean Strategy' and Created Value for Shareholders." *SSRN Scholarly Paper*, January 10, 2023, accessed February 26, 2025. https://papers.ssrn.com/sol3/papers.cfm?abstract_id=4311597
26 Gabriella Rosen Kellerman and Martin E.P. Seligman. "Cultivating the Four Kinds of Creativity." *Harvard Business Review*, January-February 2023, accessed May 22, 2025. https://hbr.org/2023/01/cultivating-the-four-kinds-of-creativity
27 Gretchen Vogel. "'Revolution Based on Evolution' Honored with Chemistry Nobel." *Science*, October 3, 2018, accessed February 26, 2025. https://www.science.org/content/article/revolution-based-evolution-honored-chemistry-nobel
28 Gabriella Rosen Kellerman. and Martin E.P. Seligman. "Cultivating the Four Kinds of Creativity." *Harvard Business Review*, January-February 2023, accessed February 26, 2025. https://hbr.org/2023/01/cultivating-the-four-kinds-of-creativity
29 Gary S. Berger. "Imagination Is More Important Than Knowledge." *Einstein: The Man and His Mind*, May 26, 2024, accessed February 26, 2025. https://einstein-themanandhismind.net/imagination-is-more-important-than-knowledge/
30 Robert Gaynes. "The Discovery of Penicillin—New Insights After More Than 75 Years of Clinical Use." *Emerging Infectious Diseases* 23, no. 5 (May 2017), accessed February 26, 2025. https://pmc.ncbi.nlm.nih.gov/articles/PMC5403050/

31 Semantic Scholar. https://www.semanticscholar.org/

32 Elicit, https://elicit.com/

33 Toyota Management System. "How Toyota's Just-In-Time (JIT) System Revolutionized Manufacturing." *INEAK*, September 10, 2023, accessed February 26, 2025. https://www.ineak.com/how-toyotas-just-in-time-jit-system-revolutionized-manufacturing/

34 Digital Defynd. "5 Ways Zara Is Using AI." *Digital Defynd*, accessed February 26, 2025. https://digitaldefynd.com/IQ/ways-zara-using-ai/

35 LinkedIn. Premium https://premium.linkedin.com/

36 MyFitnessPal. https://www.myfitnesspal.com/en/

37 Wikipedia, Dollar Shave Club. https://en.wikipedia.org/wiki/Dollar_Shave_Club#History

38 INC Magazine, Kris Frieswick, "The Serious Guy Behind Dollar Shave Club's Crazy Viral Videos," April 2016, accessed May 21, 2025. https://www.inc.com/magazine/201604/kris-frieswick/dollar-shave-club-michael-dubin.html

39 Lindsey Blakely. "How a $4,500 YouTube Video Turned Into a $1 Billion Company," Inc Magazine, July/August 2017, accessed May 21, 2025. https://www.inc.com/magazine/201707/lindsay-blakely/how-i-did-it-michael-dubin-dollar-shave-club.html

40 Ethan Mollick. Wharton School on Instagram, accessed May 21, 2025. https://www.instagram.com/reel/CouqouUNc4N/?igsh=d2syOTFhc2InNWVt

41 Notion.ai. https://www.notion.com/product/ai

42 Dental Product Shopper. "Research and Experience Tell the Oral-B iO Story." *Dental Product Shopper*, October 19, 2022, accessed February 26, 2025. https://www.dentalproductshopper.com/article/research-and-experience-tell-the-oral-b-io-story

43 Christine Siegel. *Integration of Smart Board Technology and Effective Teaching.* Fairfield University, 2011, accessed February 26, 2025. https://digitalcommons.fairfield.edu/cgi/viewcontent.cgi?article=1054&context=education-facultypubs

44 Ecovative. "Mushroom Packaging." *Ecovative Design*, accessed February 26, 2025. https://mushroom-packaging.com/pages/about

45 BPL Medical Technologies. "Infrared Thermometers—Why They Are Crucial in Times of COVID-19." *BPL Medical Technologies Blog*, accessed February 26, 2025. https://www.bplmedicaltechnologies.com/blog/infrared-thermometers--why-they-are-crucial-in-times-of-covid-19-24549/

46 Autodesk Fusion 360. https://www.autodesk.com/products/fusion-360/overview?term=1-YEAR&tab=subscription&plc=FSN

47 Meta Creator Marketplace. https://about.fb.com/news/2024/02/creator-marketplace-for-brands-and-creators-to-collaborate-on-instagram/

48 Facebook Creators. "Inspiring the Aspiring: Creators Share Their Successes with Professional Mode for Facebook Profiles." *Facebook Creators*, November 7, 2022, accessed February 26, 2025. https://creators.facebook.com/professional-mode-success-stories/?locale=en_US

49 Google Workspace. https://workspace.google.com/

50 Google Cloud. "321 Real-World Gen AI Use Cases from the World's Leading Organizations." *Google Cloud*, December 19, 2024, accessed February 26, 2025. https://cloud.google.com/transform/101-real-world-generative-ai-use-cases-from-industry-leaders

51 Google for Creators. https://creators.google/en-us/

52 Google Trends. https://trends.google.com/trends/

53 Google Site Kit. https://sitekit.withgoogle.com/

54 Google Web Designer. https://webdesigner.withgoogle.com/

55 Google Sites. https://sites.google.com/u/0/?pli=1&authuser=0

56 Google Docs Editors. https://workspace.google.com/products/docs/

57 Google Forms. https://workspace.google.com/products/forms/

58 YouTube Create. https://www.youtube.com/creators/youtube-create/

59 Google Vids. https://workspace.google.com/products/vids/

[60] Google Workspace. https://workspace.google.com/

[61] Google My Maps. https://www.google.com/maps/d/u/0/

[62] Canva. https://www.canva.com/

[63] Adobe Photoshop. https://www.adobe.com/uk/products/photoshop.html

[64] Adobe Express. https://www.adobe.com/express/

[65] H5P. https://h5p.org

[66] Photopea. https://photopea.com

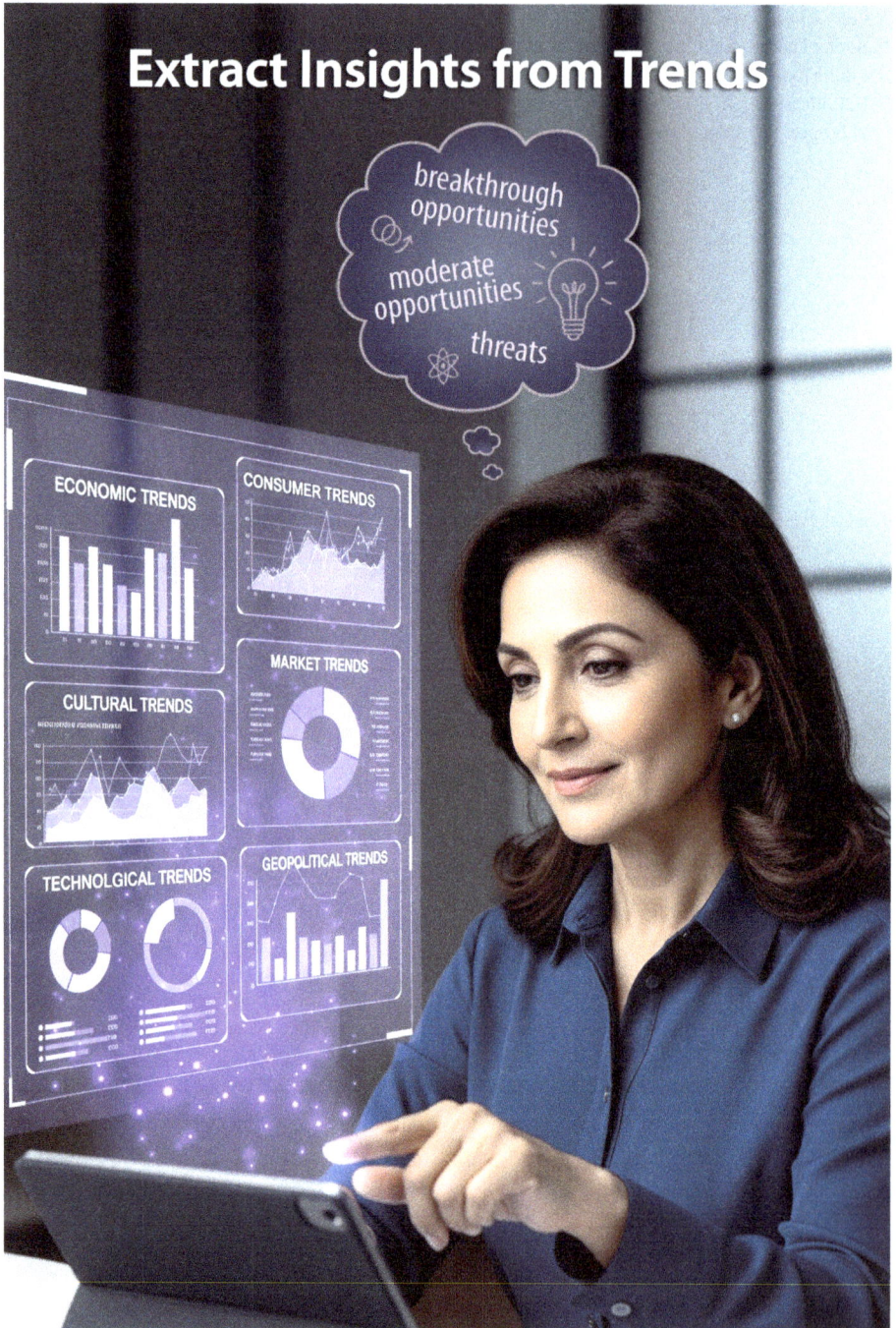

Chapter 11
Approach #7: Extract Insights from Trends

Nothing happens quite by chance. It's a question of accretion of information and experience.
—Jonas Salk, Founder of the Salk Institute for Biological Studies

In an era where consumer preferences, cultural norms, technological advancements, and business dynamics constantly shift, staying ahead requires more than passive observation—it demands active engagement with trends. This chapter explores how to identify emerging trends that shape industries, the way we live, work, and play, to help you unlock fresh ideas, adapt to change, and create meaningful products, services, or experiences.

Consider how Netflix transformed from a DVD rental service to a streaming giant by closely analyzing consumer behavior trends. By observing shifts toward digital consumption and on-demand entertainment, Netflix recognized an opportunity to pioneer streaming services, successfully disrupting the entertainment industry and establishing a new paradigm for media consumption.

To illustrate how trend analysis drives innovation, consider how Warby Parker transformed the eyewear industry by identifying and acting on converging trends. The founders recognized several key patterns:

- Rising healthcare costs making traditional eyewear increasingly expensive; increasing importance of socially responsible business practices;
- and the emerging direct-to-consumer business model disrupting traditional retail.

Rather than focusing on any single trend, they designed a business that responded to all of them simultaneously, creating stylish, affordable eyewear sold directly to consumers online, with a buy-one-give-one social impact model. Their trend analysis went beyond spotting obvious patterns to understanding the interconnections between consumer values, distribution channels, pricing models, and social responsibility.

This comprehensive approach to trend analysis helped them not merely participate in existing trends but create an entirely new category that anticipated where the market was heading before it arrived.

While identifying enabling trends is essential, recognizing constraining trends that may limit opportunities or create new challenges is equally important. Factors such as political polarization, regulatory uncertainty, economic inequality, privacy concerns, and supply chain vulnerabilities can significantly impact the viability of new initiatives.

> **By methodically assessing both trends, organizations can develop more resilient strategies that account for potential headwinds**

A balanced trend analysis examines both accelerators and inhibitors to innovation. For example, a company developing new consumer finance products must consider not only enabling trends like increased smartphone adoption and demand for financial wellness tools but also constraining trends like growing data privacy regulations and economic volatility.

By methodically assessing both trends, organizations can develop more resilient strategies that account for potential headwinds rather than assuming an unobstructed path to success.

Consumer Behavior Trends

Over the years, consumer behavior has undergone significant transformation influenced by technological advances, economic shifts, and evolving societal values. For example, e-commerce and digital platforms have revolutionized shopping habits, with consumers increasingly favoring online purchases for convenience and broader selection. According to eMarketer, e-commerce sales grew from $5.81 trillion in 2023 to $6.33 trillion in 2024,[1] demonstrating the scale of this shift. This trend has been further accelerated by the COVID-19 pandemic, which compelled many to adopt online shopping out of necessity.

Additionally, there is a growing demand for personalized and convenient experiences, leading to the proliferation of on-demand services and social commerce, where consumers expect seamless purchasing opportunities across all touchpoints. Today, 73% of shoppers use multiple channels during their journey, moving effortlessly between online and offline environments—researching on phones, comparing prices online, and picking up purchases in physical locations. Economic factors, such as inflation's impact on household budgets, have also played a role, prompting consumers to become more budget-conscious and seek value-driven purchases.

This omnichannel approach delivers impressive results for businesses that adapt. Companies implementing strong omnichannel strategies see 89% customer retention rates compared to just 33% for companies with weak approaches,[2] and experience 494% higher order rates when using three or more channels.[3] Successful retailers offer flexible fulfillment options like Buy Online Pick-up In-Store, they personalize interactions, and shift the focus from targeting individual channels to following customers across their entire shopping journey.[4]

Environmental concerns have also led to a rise in eco-conscious shopping behaviors, with many consumers prioritizing sustainable and ethically produced goods. Moreover, the influence of social media and digital connectivity has fostered a culture of immediacy and trend responsiveness, with consumers rapidly shifting preferences based on online trends and influencer endorsements.

Technological forces have dramatically reshaped how consumers discover, evaluate, and purchase products. The proliferation of smartphones has created an 'always connected' consumer who can shop anytime and anywhere. AI-powered recommendations and voice assistants are changing search behaviors, while AR allows virtual 'try before you buy' experiences. Meanwhile, political forces influence consumer confidence and spending patterns, with policy changes around tariffs, privacy regulations, and economic stimulus directly impacting purchasing decisions.

Insights from Consumer Behavior Trends

1. *Consumers engage in dynamic and changing journeys.* Realizing there isn't a simplistic linear path in decision-making can yield new marketing ideas. Consider the purchase journey, as illustrated in Figure 11.1, "Illustrative Consumer Journeys." This visual model demonstrates the complex, non-linear nature of the modern consumer journey, with multiple touchpoints and decision loops.

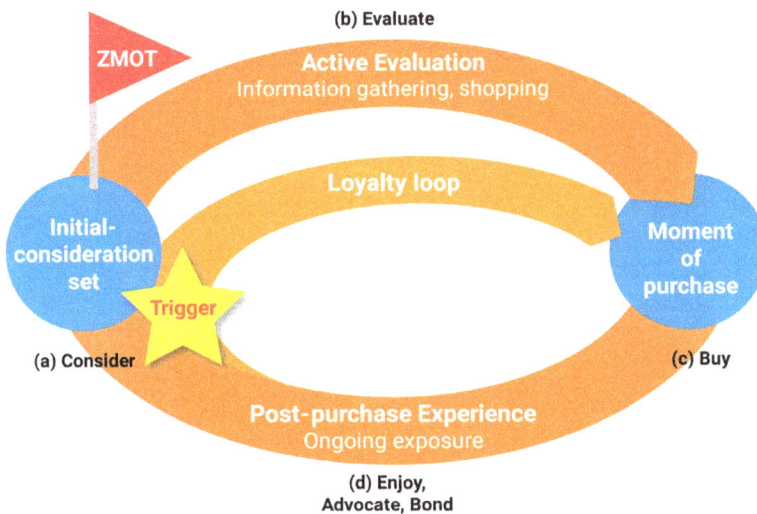

Figure 11.1. Illustrative consumer journeys[5]

The diagram shows many paths consumers can take when making a purchase. Moreover, the same consumers will have different journeys for different situations, contexts, and purposes. Understanding these varied routes provides opportunities to engage consumers at critical touchpoints with tailored messaging and experiences.

2. *The Zero Moment of Truth (ZMOT).* It is a concept introduced by Google in 2011 to describe the critical point in consumer decision-making when individuals research products or services online before purchasing. During ZMOT, consumers actively seek information through various digital channels, including search engines, product reviews, social media, and comparison websites, to inform their choices.[6] Recognizing and engaging consumers at this stage

is crucial for businesses aiming to influence purchasing decisions and build brand trust.

Significantly, ZMOT updates the First Moment of Truth (FMOT) concept in marketing, established by Procter & Gamble, that refers to the first few seconds a consumer sees and considers a product in a store.

For example, Sephora successfully leverages ZMOT by providing detailed product information, customer reviews, tutorial videos, and virtual try-on tools on their website and app. This comprehensive approach ensures that when consumers research beauty products, Sephora effectively influences their decision process before visiting a physical store.

3. *Increased preference for real-time, personalized experiences.* While not applicable for every situation, there is a strong trend towards faster, more relevant, customized customer experiences, especially as the marketplace has become more competitive. Research by McKinsey shows that when executed well, such experiences enable businesses to differentiate themselves and drive customer loyalty and revenues.[7] For example, Nike lets customers configure their shoes through a 3D sneaker-customization platform, providing real-time, shareable snapshots of finished footwear to enhance personalization.[8] Consider how you might apply personalization to your creative solutions. What aspects of your product or service could be customized to individual preferences? How might you leverage data to create more relevant experiences?

4. *Difference between high- and low-involvement purchase decisions.* High-involvement decisions are personally significant to the consumer, whether financially or socially. This includes buying a car, a house, or an insurance policy. Low-involvement purchases are the opposite: Inexpensive purchases with low risk, such as buying candy.

The level of involvement depends on the individual consumer and their specific context. A high-involvement purchase for one person (e.g., a premium coffee machine for an enthusiast) might be low-involvement for another. Understanding where your offering falls on this spectrum for different customer segments is crucial for developing appropriate marketing strategies, product features, and customer experiences. Consumers typically conduct extensive research and require detailed information for high-involvement products, while convenience, habit, or minor differentiating features may drive low-involvement purchases.

5. *Most buying decisions, whether B2B or B2C, involve a 'buying center'—a group of people involved in or influencing the decision.* Key roles include the following:[9]

   • Initiators: Individuals who first recognize the need for a product or service and initiate purchasing.
   • Users: Those who will directly use the product or service. Their feedback and requirements are crucial in the decision-making process.

- Influencers: People who, due to their expertise or position, influence the buying decision by providing information and criteria for evaluating options.
- Deciders: Individuals with the authority to make the final purchasing decision.
- Buyers: Personnel responsible for the formal aspects of the purchase, such as negotiating terms and processing orders.
- Gatekeepers: Those who control information flow to other buying center members, such as administrative assistants or technical personnel.

Consider a family purchasing a new TV: the child might be the initiator who requests it, the parents are the deciders and buyers, while older siblings might serve as influencers recommending certain features or brands. Understanding these dynamics allows marketers to create targeted messages for each decision-maker role.

Understanding the structure and dynamics of the buying center is essential for marketers aiming to effectively target and communicate with all stakeholders involved in the purchasing process. By identifying and addressing each role's specific concerns and motivations, marketers can tailor their strategies to better meet the buying center's needs and facilitate a successful sale.

6. *Most buying decisions result from many factors; the simplistic stimulus-response model, where you see an ad and buy the product, is a myth.* It's important to identify the reasons for buying, the determinants of the buying decision, and the relative importance of each. Research is regularly conducted to identify the key determinants of consumer behavior. Try to map out the various influences on purchasing decisions in your target market. How do social, psychological, personal, and cultural factors influence consumer choices? This understanding can lead to more nuanced and effective creative solutions.

7. *Importance of emotional appeals.* Emotions are very powerful motivators. Neuroscientific research has shown that emotions play a critical role in decision-making, often overriding logic and at times in a subconscious way.[10] It's always important to try incorporating this dimension in any message to consumers.

> **“** **Emotions are powerful motivators—try to incorporate this in your message to your audiences.** **”**

Research by the Institute of Practitioners in Advertising (IPA) has conclusively demonstrated that emotional advertising campaigns significantly outperform rational ones. Their analysis of over 880 case studies found that emotional campaigns outperformed rational ones in increasing penetration, sales, and market share in the long term. The lone exception is for direct response.[11]

Similarly, Nielsen's research has shown that ads with above-average emotional response generate 23% more sales than those with average emotional response.[12]

For example, Dove soap's 'Real Beauty' campaign 2004 struck a chord by featuring women of diverse body types, ages, and ethnicities.[13] By promoting messages of self-acceptance and confidence, Dove touched on a deeply moving issue and fostered a sense of authenticity and trust. This campaign enhanced brand loyalty and sparked a conversation about beauty and self-esteem. In 2019, it was selected by the Global Effie Awards as one of the five most effective brands of the last 50 years.[14]

8. *Significant differences in complexity of the buying process and the length of the journey in three types of buying situations*:

   - First-time purchase: This involves an extensive search, comparison of alternatives, and information gathering. Consumers lack experience with the product category and face higher perceived risk.
   - Repeat buying: These routine purchases may become habitual or automated, requiring minimal decision-making effort.
   - Modified repurchase: When some conditions have changed (new market entrants, product modifications, evolving needs), consumers engage in limited problem-solving, revisiting some aspects of the original decision process.

   Consider how your creative solutions can address each of these situations differently. First-time buyers may need educational content and reassurance, repeat buyers might benefit from loyalty programs or subscription services, while modified repurchase situations present opportunities to highlight improvements or new features.

9. *Increased preference for omnichannel services that seamlessly integrate online and offline experiences, with 24/7 availability.* Many consumers want a seamless experience between the physical and digital channels. According to *Harvard Business Review* research, 73% of shoppers use multiple channels during their shopping journey, and these omnichannel customers spend 4% more in-store and 10% more online than single-channel customers.[15] How might your creative solutions bridge the gap between digital and physical experiences? Consider how information, services, and experiences can flow smoothly across different touchpoints.

10. *All markets are heterogeneous, and a one-size-fits-all approach is rarely optimal.* Identify and understand the key segments and select your target group. The trend toward hyper-personalization is pushing segmentation toward a "segment of one" approach, where offerings can be tailored to individual preferences and needs. When developing creative solutions, consider how they might be adapted or customized for different market segments. What features or messaging might resonate more strongly with specific segments?

11. *Increased desire for authenticity and global altruism from brands.* This drives not only consumer behavior, but human behavior in general. People want to

work for companies that are changing the world and with a strong sense of purpose. How can your creative solutions incorporate authentic values and meaningful purpose? Consider not just the functional benefits of your offering, but also its broader impact on society and the environment.

12. *Consumers are 'always on.'* Many consumers are reachable at any time since they almost always have their smartphones. This unprecedented access and opportunity should give rise to meaningful, innovative ideas about connecting with them. Think about how your creative solutions can leverage this constant connectivity without becoming intrusive. How might you create value through timely, relevant interactions that respect consumer boundaries and preferences?

Cultural Trends

Consumer behavior reflects cultural trends in society and, at the same time, also helps shape them. Understanding current and emerging trends is a significant source of ideas for creative new products, services, and experiences. It is also a requirement when evaluating any idea to ensure relevancy. While there is no exhaustive or agreed-upon list of cultural trends, it is helpful to be alert to identify them and start with your list.

We asked ChatGPT to identify major cultural trends shaping society at the time of writing, and it highlighted several significant movements:

- Digital minimalism and tech-life balance: A growing movement rejecting constant connectivity in favor of intentional technology use, manifested through digital detoxes, 'dumb phones,' and screen time management apps.
- Sustainability and eco-consciousness: Beyond recycling, this encompasses low-waste lifestyles, secondhand fashion, repair culture, and plant-based diets.
- Mental health awareness: Destigmatization of mental health issues, with therapy becoming normalized and mental wellness practices like meditation entering the mainstream.
- Multigenerational living: Economic factors and cultural shifts drive more families to live together, creating new dynamics in home design, consumption patterns, and social structures.
- Creator economy: The democratization of content creation has empowered individuals to monetize their skills and interests through platforms like YouTube, TikTok, and Instagram.

These illustrative trends offer rich inspiration for creative innovation across industries. Consider how they affect your life as a consumer, employer, employee, family member, and other roles you play in society. Also, how do these trends affect your solution to the challenges you face? Feel free to add to and modify them.

One example is how the environmental emphasis has created the sustainable fashion movement. There is ongoing development of eco-friendly materials such as organic cotton and recycled fabrics; implementation of ethical production practices such as fair labor practices; introduction of 'circular fashion' business models, including clothing rental services; and marketing strategies where brands highlight their sustainability pledges.[16]

When using AI tools for trend analysis, be mindful that these systems may exhibit bias toward optimistic or technology-centric trends based on their training data.

To counterbalance this tendency, deliberately craft prompts that encourage comprehensive analysis. Instead of simply asking 'What are the key trends in [industry]?', try more nuanced queries like: 'What are the enabling AND constraining trends affecting [industry]?' or 'What trends might negatively impact our assumptions about [market]?' You might also specify diversity in your request: 'Identify technological, social, economic, regulatory, and environmental trends affecting [domain].'

These more structured prompts help ensure your AI-assisted trend analysis captures a fuller spectrum of factors that might influence your creative direction, rather than focusing only on the most visible or positive patterns.

Trend analysis naturally complements the SWOT framework we explored earlier. While SWOT provides a snapshot of current strengths, weaknesses, opportunities, and threats, trend analysis adds a crucial temporal dimension—revealing how these factors are likely to evolve over time.

For example, a capability that represents a strength today might become less relevant as trends shift market demands. Similarly, what appears as a threat in the current environment might transform into an opportunity as trends reshape industry dynamics.

By combining SWOT's structural analysis with the dynamic perspective of trend monitoring, you create a more robust foundation for creative strategy development. Consider conducting a 'Future SWOT' exercise where you project how each quadrant might change based on the trends you've identified, revealing potential pivot points and innovation opportunities that might otherwise remain hidden.

Science and Technology Trends

Advances in science and technology are also fertile grounds for innovation. Think about how your use of technology has changed over the years, from computers to tablets and smartphones. These gave rise to things like mobile apps, which can spark new solutions in you, as well as cloud computing, AR/VR/MR, AI and machine learning, quantum computing, blockchain, genomics, robotics, new energy solutions, among many others.

One good source of tech trends is MIT Technology Review, which comes out with its annual list of trends. Here is the MIT Breakthrough Technologies List for 2024 and 2025:[17]

Table 11.1: MIT Breakthrough Technologies, 2024 and 2025

2024	2025
1. AI for everything	1. Vera C. Rubin Observatory
2. Super-efficient solar cells	2. Generative AI Search
3. Apple Vision Pro (MR headset)	3. Small Language Models
4. Weight-loss drugs	4. Robotaxis
5. Enhanced geothermal systems (clean energy)	5. Fast-Learning Robots
6. Chiplets (small chips linked to perform like a regular-sized chip)	6. Long-Acting HIV Prevention Medication
7. First gene-editing treatment	7. Green Steel
8. Exascale computers	8. Methane-Reducing Feed Supplements for Cows
9. Heat pumps that use electricity to both heat and cool	9. Wheat Disease Surveillance System
10. Twitter killers such as Bluesky, Threads, and others	10. Sustainable Aviation Fuel (SAF)

Source: MIT Technology Review

Another valuable resource for understanding emerging technologies is the annual Consumer Electronics Show (CES). The 2025 CES highlighted several significant trends that are shaping the future of technology and consumer products:

- AI-Powered everything: From smart home devices to healthcare solutions, artificial intelligence is integrated into every product category, offering unprecedented personalization and automation.
- Sustainable tech: Eco-friendly innovations dominated the show, including solar-powered devices, biodegradable electronics, and solutions for reducing energy consumption.
- Health tech revolution: Advanced home diagnostics, remote patient monitoring systems, and AI health assistants are transforming personal healthcare and wellness management.
- Immersive reality: Next-generation VR and AR devices are creating more seamless blends between digital and physical worlds, with applications extending beyond gaming to education, workplace collaboration, and retail.
- Autonomous systems: Beyond self-driving cars, autonomous robots for delivery, household tasks, and industrial applications demonstrated significant advances in capability and accessibility.
- Connectivity everywhere: With 5G firmly established and 6G on the horizon, ultra-connected devices enable new experiences and services requiring minimal latency[18] and maximum bandwidth.

Business Trends

Business trends can arise from the consumer, cultural, scientific, and technological trends in your field and even non-adjacent sectors. They include being digital- or mobile-first, using data and analytics, shifting to omnichannel, focusing on stakeholders instead of shareholders, developing a purpose-driven organization, new business and revenue models, global M&A, strategic alliances, and others.

Consider developing your list of business trends by researching industry reports, following business publications, and observing successful companies in your field and adjacent sectors. Which companies or organizations can you think of that successfully leveraged these trends? And what new products, services, and experiences did so as well?

When looking at trends, imagine not just following them but creating a trend or movement. For example, consider Pop Art, Minimal Art, Conceptual Art, Abstract Expressionism, and Impressionism movements. In politics, consider the Separatist movements in Spain and Canada.

Shelley Zalis, CEO of The Female Quotient, founded one such movement in 2015. Her organization exists to advance gender equality in the workplace by nurturing a community of women in business and partnering with influential organizations. "There was such a scarcity of women at the top, which was such a shame, because, for me, I know we're better together," Zalis said.[19] One of her signature initiatives is the Equality Lounge, a space co-located at conferences and events dedicated to discussions about equality. They were invited to host the Lounge at the World Economic Forum in Switzerland.

> **Companies that successfully adapted to the evolving political environment leveraged data-driven insights, strategic forecasting, and cross-industry collaboration to stay ahead.**

The 2024 presidential election in the United States demonstrated the profound impact political shifts can have on business trends and operations. Within the first 100 days, the administration's policies reshaped trade relationships, immigration policies, regulatory environments, and labor markets.

Consider, for example, the dramatic shift from promoting DEI in the previous administration to erasing any reference to it, from accepting LGBTQ+ to attacking transgender individuals participating in sports. From punishing the January 6, 2021, rioters to pardoning them and hailing them as patriots, calls to overtly recognise and revive Columbus Day while simultaneously ignoring recognition of Indigenous Peoples' Day.[20] These changes highlight the importance of scenario planning and building flexible business models that can adapt to shifting political landscapes. Organizations that anticipated these potential changes were better positioned to navigate the transition while minimizing disruption to their operations and stakeholder relationships. Understanding the complex interdependencies between various forces of change is essential for identifying new business opportunities and mitigating potential risks.

Companies that successfully adapted to the evolving political environment leveraged data-driven insights, strategic forecasting, and cross-industry collaboration to stay ahead. For instance, businesses in manufacturing and technology closely monitored shifts in trade policies to assess potential supply chain disruptions, while firms in finance and health care prepared for regulatory changes that could affect investment strategies and compliance requirements.

At the time of writing, businesses must now also contend with: higher tariffs for companies importing materials and components, regulatory rollbacks of climate, pollution and renewable energy initiatives creating market uncertainty and slowing down investment in renewable technology; the installation of crypto-friendly policies, yet introducing concerns about financial stability, the value of the dollar and consumer protection. The rise of AI-driven analytics plays a crucial role in navigating these issues, helping organizations model various policy scenarios and adjust their strategies in real time. By integrating political risk assessments into their long-term planning, businesses can protect their core operations and identify new growth opportunities.

Advertising and Media Trends

A recent McKinsey & Company article provides a concise and insightful summary of the evolution of the advertising and media industries. "Brands once reached people primarily through mass media like TV, print and radio, gaining precious few consumer insights. The internet changed all that with targeted and interactive campaigns online. More recently, retail media networks (RMNs) helped retailers enter the media business. Leveraging shopper and transaction data, RMNs help brands reach prospective customers through their websites, apps and even off site channels. Commerce media networks (CMNs) are the latest shift poised for tremendous growth. CMNs are advertising ecosystems that have expanded beyond retail. For industries as varied as financial services, travel and even healthcare, CMNs integrate ads directly into the customer experience across multiple online and offline channels. Many CMNs use first party data from transactions, customer behavior and loyalty programs to deliver targeted ads, boosting relevance and sales.

The McKinsey market forecast has projected that by 2027 the US commerce media market will reach more than $100 billion with a growth rate outpacing display connected TV and even search.[21]

AI and Trend Analysis

AI fundamentally transforms trend analysis through several key capabilities. First, natural language processing can continuously monitor millions of social media posts, news articles, and online discussions to identify emerging patterns before they become apparent in traditional trend reports. Second, machine learning algorithms can detect subtle correlations between seemingly unrelated trends, revealing compound effects that might escape human analysts. Finally, predictive modeling can project trend trajectories, helping organizations distinguish between fleeting fads and genuine shifts in consumer behavior or market dynamics.

In Summary

1. Embrace the power of trend analysis to unlock breakthrough innovations.
Your ability to identify shifts in consumer behavior, culture, technology, and business will position you to create solutions that resonate in a dynamic marketplace before others catch on.

What emerging trends in your industry, and other related and unrelated industries, are you ignoring that could become tomorrow's breakthrough opportunities?

2. Look for interconnected patterns, not isolated trends.
Warby Parker didn't just spot online shopping growth, the founders recognized how rising healthcare costs, consumer comfort with e-commerce, and social responsibility converged. Your most powerful ideas will come from seeing these intersections that others miss.

Which seemingly unrelated trends might combine to create a new market opportunity in your field?

3. Balance enabling and constraining trends in your analysis.
Don't focus solely on positive patterns. Political shifts, regulatory changes, and economic factors all create boundaries that shape opportunity. Your most resilient strategies will acknowledge both headwinds and tailwinds in the market.

How might current constraints in your industry reveal hidden opportunities?

4. Understand the nuances and complexities of the consumer journey.
The linear purchase path is dead. Consumers engage in dynamic, multi/omni-channel experiences influenced by emotional connections and buying centers with multiple decision-makers. Your creative solutions must account for this rich complexity.

How can you redesign your approach to match the complexity of your customers' Journey and decision process?

5. Stay vigilant about emerging technologies that can transform your industry.
From AI infiltrating every product category to sustainability innovations, from health tech to immersive reality, and from current media to Commerce Media Networks, your future success depends on spotting these shifts early and acting on them with purpose and authenticity.

Which emerging technology seems peripheral to your business today but could completely reshape your competitive landscape within five years?

You have a unique opportunity to develop solutions that don't just follow change but actively shape it, establishing new paradigms that others will eventually follow. Our next chapter focuses on experimentation and iteration to adapt and refine your novel ideas.

Notes

[1] eMarketer. Worldwide Retail Ecommerce Forecast 2024, accessed April 7 2025. https://www.emarketer.com/content/worldwide-retail-ecommerce-forecast-2024

[2] Magenest. "The Ultimate Guide to Omnichannel Retail Statistics: Current State, Trends, and Future Insights," June 25, 2024, acessed May 5, 2025. https://magenest.com/en/omnichannel-retail-statistics/

[3] WebFX Digital Marketing. "70+ Retail Statistics Marketers Should Know in 2025," accessed May 7, 2025. https://www.webfx.com/industries/retail-ecommerce/retail/statistics/

[4] McKinsey & Company. "The Value of Getting Personalization Right—or Wrong—is Multiplying," November 12, 2021, accessed May 7, 2025. https://www.mckinsey.com/capabilities/growth-marketing-and-sales/our-insights/the-value-of-getting-personalization-right-or-wrong-is-multiplying

[5] D. Court, D. Elzinga, S. Mulder and O.J. Vetvik. *The Consumer Decision Journey*. McKinsey & Company, 2009. https://www.mckinsey.com/capabilities/growth-marketing-and-sales/our-insights/the-consumer-decision-journey

[6] Jim Lecinski. *Winning the Zero Moment of Truth*. eBook. Google, accessed December 9, 2024. file:///C:/Users/debis/OneDrive/Documents/Downloads/2011-winning-zmot-ebook_research-studies.pdf

[7] Erik Lindecrantz, Madeleine Tjon Pian Gi, and Stefano Zerbi. "Personalizing the Customer Experience: Driving Differentiation in Retail." McKinsey & Company, April 28, accessed December 9, 2024. https://www.mckinsey.com/industries/retail/our-insights/personalizing-the-customer-experience-driving-differentiation-in-retail?utm_source=chatgpt.com

[8] Ibid.

[9] Open Text WSU. *Core Principles of Marketing*. Washington State University, accessed December 9, 2024. https://open.lib.umn.edu/principlesmarketing/chapter/4-3-buying-centers/

[10] NeuroLaunch Editorial Team. "Emotional Appeal in Advertising: Harnessing the Power of Feelings to Connect with Consumers." *NeuroLaunch*, October 18, 2024, accessed December 9, 2024. https://neurolaunch.com/emotional-appeal/

[11] Mindi Chahal. "Getting Emotional About Advertising," *Marketing Week*, October 31, 2013, accessed March 8, 2025. https://www.marketingweek.com/getting-emotional-about-advertising/

[12] Bethany Shocki. "Not All Podcasts Are Created Equal: The Value of Advertising to an Emotionally-Connected Audience," *Soundrise*, April 11, 2024, accessed March 8, 2025. https://www.wearesoundrise.com/perspectives/the-value-of-advertising-to-an-emotionally-connected-audience

[13] Dove. "Real Beauty Pledge." *Dove Campaigns*, accessed January 25, 2025. https://www.dove.com/us/en/campaigns/purpose/real-beauty-pledge.html

[14] "2019 Global Effie Awards and '5 for 50' Effies Announced at the 50th Annual Effie Awards Gala," Effie Awards, May 31, 2019, accessed. March 8, 2025. https://www.effie.org/news/2019-global-effie-awards-and-5-for-50-effies-announced-at-the-50th-annual-effie-awards-gala/

[15] Emma Sopadjieva, Utpal M. Dholakia, and Beth Benjamin. "A Study of 46,000 Shoppers Shows That Omnichannel Retailing Works," *Harvard Business Review*, January 3, 2017, accessed March 8, 2025. https://hbr.org/2017/01/a-study-of-46000-shoppers-shows-that-omnichannel-retailing-works

[16] Faster Capital. "Cultural Influences: How Cultural Influences Shape Customer Preferences." *Faster Capital*, June 13, 2024, accessed December 9, 2024. https://fastercapital.com/content/Cultural-Influences--How-Cultural-Influences-Shape-Customer-Preferences.html

[17] *MIT Technology Review*. "10 Breakthrough Technologies 2024." January 8, 2024, accessed December 9, 2024. https://www.technologyreview.com/2024/01/08/1085094/10-breakthrough-technologies-2024/

[18] Latency refers to the delay or "lag" experienced when data travels across a network, measured in milliseconds. Low latency significantly improves the speed and responsiveness of online activities such as gaming, browsing or videoconferencing.

[19] Coursera course titled *Creativity in Business and Other disciplines*.

[20] CBS News, "Trump Says He's "Bringing Back Columbus Day from the Ashes," April 27, 2025, accessed May 7, 2025. https://www.cbsnews.com/news/trump-columbus-day-indigenous-peoples-day/

[21] J. Trotte, M. Brodherson and Q. George. The Evolution of Commerce Media: Navigating a New Era in Advertising. https://www.Mckinsey.com/capabilities/growth-marketing and sale/our-insights/the-evolution-of-commerce-media-navigating-a-new-era- in-advertising

Experimentation Is a Must

09-21-2016 | HOW TO BE A SUCCESS AT EVERYTHING **FAST C@MPANY**

Why These Tech Companies Keep Running Thousands Of Failed Experiments

The most innovative businesses are finding ways to experiment quickly and ~~~~~ knowing full well that most tests will be duds.

December 4, 2023

FDA U.S. FOOD & DRUG ADMINISTRATION

The Importance of Clinical Trial Transparency and FDA Oversight

By: Robert M. Califf, M.D., Commissioner of Food and Drug~

STATSIG

WHITEPAPER

The rise of experimentation as the industry standard

Fri Apr 18 2025

PUBLICATION

amazon | science

Top challenges from the first practical online controlled experiments summit

By Brent Smith, James McQueen, et al.
2019

HARVARD BUSINESS REVIEW

Experimentation

Want Your Company to Get Better at Experimentation?

Learn fast by democratizing testing. by Iavor Bojinov, David Holtz, Ramesh Johari, Sven Schmit and Martin Tingley

~~January-February 2025~~

THE SCIENCE OF SUCCESS

The Power of Experiments: How To Drive Innovation and Opportunity During Times of Uncertainty with Stefan Thomke

MARCH 12, 2020 IN DECISION MAKING, FOCUS & PRODUCTIVITY

+

Chapter 12
Approach #8: Embrace Experimentation and Iteration

*Our success at Amazon is a function of how many experiments we do
per year, per month, per week, per day.*
—Amazon founder Jeff Bezos

Creativity thrives in refining, reshaping, and adapting concepts through continuous feedback and real-world testing. By embracing iteration, innovators gain knowledge from each attempt, while experimentation turns assumptions into data-driven insights, reducing uncertainty while fostering bold thinking. This testing, learning, and improving cycle leads to innovative and resilient outcomes.

Experimentation is fundamental to the creative process and a core concept throughout this book. Rather than committing to a single approach or solution, experimentation encourages exploring multiple possibilities, gathering data about their effectiveness, and making informed refinements. This scientific mindset transforms abstract, creative concepts into concrete, validated innovations.

Psychophysicist and market researcher Howard Moskowitz has developed an experimental methodology called mind genomics. This method systematically explores how people respond to various combinations of ideas or messages to reveal subconscious thinking patterns. Based on their mindsets, they are segmented into groups. Mind genomics can be applied to product development or any solution in which gauging sentiment is critical.[1]

The methodology consists of five steps:

Step 1: Identify the problem.

Step 2: Ask four questions.

Step 3: Supply four answers.

Step 4: Design an experiment

Step 5: Analyze the data

The most complex parts are to ask the right questions and choose the correct answers; it typically takes some iteration to get the proper sets.

Applying mind genomics to the case of a hospital seeing 17% of congestive health failure patients return because they do not practice a healthy lifestyle, Moskowitz did the following:

Step 1: Identify the problem. Patients are not caring for themselves well enough because 17% are returning to the hospital.

Step 2: Ask four questions. "What do we think about our condition?" "What life changes do we need to make in our diet?" "What kind of changes do we need to make in our exercises?" "What do we hope for in the end?"

Step 3: Supply four answers to the last question. "I want to live to see my grandkids graduate from high school." "I want to travel." "I'd like to play golf again." "I'd like to have dinner with my wife and friends without having to watch every calorie."

Step 4: Combine the answers in groups of two, three, or four in an experimental design and send them to 100 people. Each person received 24 different combinations.

Step 5: Through statistical regression, Moskowitz linked the presence or absence of the 24 elements to people's responses. They were then segmented into groups based on their mindsets. These three groups emerged:

Group 1: They wanted to see their grandchildren. *Group 2*: They wanted to be in control of their lives. *Group 3*: Their doctor could do no wrong.

Moskowitz put new patients into one of the three groups based on their mindsets. After they were discharged, the hospital gave them a refrigerator button with encouraging words related to their mindset to motivate the practice of a healthy lifestyle. The result was reduced patient return rates from 17% to less than 5%.

Moskowitz said most people think of solving a problem in terms of a marathon, in which the runner is pumped, prepped, and positioned in the right direction. But that's not the correct posture to take. Instead, they should act more like a 2-year-old toddler. He walks one direction, tumbles, giggles, gets up, and walks in a different direction. This openness is key to proper iteration. Start the process without preconceived ideas. Do one iteration, take a break, and do a second. By the third and fourth, you'll crack it.

At the core of Moskowitz's method is conjoint analysis. This statistical technique determines how people value different product or service attributes by analyzing how they make trade-offs among various combinations of features. By systematically presenting different combinations and measuring responses, researchers can understand which elements impact preferences and decisions most.

Conjoint Analysis is one of the most powerful and commonly used approaches for assessing consumer preferences for products and services' features/benefits. See for example, the rich literature on it by Green, Krieger, Wind, titled "Thirty Years of Conjoint Analysis."[2]

Successful and Unsuccessful Experiments

History is filled with bold experiments that transformed industries or failed spectacularly. Learning from both outcomes provides valuable insights for your creative journey.

> " **History is filled with bold experiments that transformed industries or failed.** "

Successful experiments

1. Tesla's Direct-to-Consumer Model: Breaking from the traditional dealership model, Tesla pioneered selling cars directly to consumers. Despite regulatory challenges and industry skepticism, this experiment successfully reduced costs, created a seamless customer experience, and built stronger customer relationships. The approach has since influenced other automakers' strategies.
2. The Apollo Program: NASA's moonshot initiative represents one of history's greatest experimental endeavors. Facing technological limitations and immense uncertainty, the program embraced a culture of rapid prototyping, learning from failures, and systematic problem-solving. This experimental mindset achieved the moon landing and generated countless innovations with widespread applications beyond space exploration.
3. FarmBot: This open-source precision farming robot began as an experiment to automate small-scale food production. Through continuous iteration and community feedback, the project evolved into a sophisticated system that plants, waters, and weeds with minimal human intervention. Its success demonstrates how experimental approaches can democratize advanced technology.
4. Figma has transformed design through its web-based art and design platform and pioneering development philosophy.[3] Instead of perfecting features before release, Figma launches minimum viable products (MVPs) and evolves them based on real usage, as seen with Auto Layout, where initial simplicity revealed unexpected use cases that shaped subsequent iterations. This approach has driven Figma's rapid growth from a startup in 2016 to a $12.5 billion industry essential with impressive 90% profit margins. The platform now encompasses four core products (Figma Design, Dev Mode, FigJam, and Figma Slides) and continues expanding with new offerings like Figma Draw, Figma Buzz, and AI capabilities announced at Config 2025. Major firms, including Microsoft Teams and Zoom, use it to redesign their user experience. Despite Adobe's failed $20 billion acquisition attempt in 2023 (which ended with a $1 billion termination fee),[4] Figma maintains its independence and growth trajectory, proving that the company is creating solutions that genuinely serve users' needs.

Unsuccessful experiments

1. Humane's AI Pin, an AI-powered device designed to wear like a brooch on one's shirt or coat, launched with great anticipation in 2024 by its founders: two former Apple executives. The AI Pin projected text onto your palm, negating the need for a screen. But poor user experience, a $699 price tag plus $24 a month for connectivity, overheating, and other issues felled the device. It went bust in less than a year. HP bought Humane's assets for $116 million, far less than the $230 million it raised as a startup from investors such as Microsoft, SoftBank, LG, and Volvo.

2. Google Glass: Despite significant technological innovation, Google's early con-
    sumer version of AR glasses failed to gain traction. The experiment stumbled
    due to privacy concerns, unclear use cases, high price points, and social stigma
    around wearing the device. However, Google learned from this failure and suc-
    cessfully repositioned the technology for enterprise applications.

3. Segway: Hyped as a revolutionary transportation device that would transform
    cities, the Segway ultimately failed to meet expectations. The experiment faced
    regulatory hurdles, high costs, and practical limitations that prevented main-
    stream adoption. Despite its commercial disappointment, the technology pio-
    neered self-balancing mechanics that influenced later successful products like
    hoverboards and electric scooters.

4. New Coke: Coca-Cola's 1985 reformulation of its flagship product stands as a
    classic case of experimental failure. Despite extensive taste tests suggesting
    preference for the new formula, the company underestimated consumers'
    emotional attachment to the original product. The backlash forced a quick
    return to the classic formula, demonstrating the importance of considering
    psychological factors in experiments.

The risk of not experimenting can be even greater than the risk of failed
experiments. Companies that resist experimentation often face gradual decline
as competitors innovate and market conditions change. Kodak's reluctance to
fully embrace digital photography (despite having invented it), Blockbuster's
hesitation to adapt its business model to streaming, and Nokia's slow response
to the smartphone revolution demonstrate how the failure to experiment can
lead to market irrelevance.

There is a rich amount of literature on product and business failures that
can offer insights into the reasons behind their failure and how to avoid them.
These ideas can be at the core of new experiments to test whether they will
work for you and your idiosyncratic conditions. For more information, check
out *Why Smart Executives Fail* by Sydney Finkelstein,[5] *Billion Dollar Lessons* by
Paul Carroll and Chunka Mui,[6] and CB Insights' "The Top 20 Reasons Startups
Fail" report.[7] *Harvard Business Review* regularly publishes case studies on
innovation failures,[8] while the Museum of Failure (both physical and online)
showcases products that missed the mark but advanced our understanding.[9]
What failed experiment will inspire your next breakthrough?

Practice Makes Perfect

Don't stop with your first solution; continue to
explore other iterations. Experimentation is a
key concept that can yield surprising benefits.

> **"**
> **Experimentation is a
> key concept that can
> yield surprising
> benefits. "**

Consider your initial option one of many possibilities, then test it against other potential solutions and your current approach (as controls).

To appreciate the power of iteration in design, consider Barbara Eberlein's creation of a modern kitchen in a 19th-century townhouse. She faced a classic problem: a historic townhouse designed for 19th-century living with no kitchen on the main floor, typical of that era when kitchens were in basements and used only by household staff. To create a 21st century family kitchen, she explored hundreds of iterations including: annexing an adjacent butler's pantry and coat closet; eliminating the rear staircase to the ground floor kitchen and relocating it underneath the stairs to upper floors; moving the coat closet to the front entrance for better access; opening the new kitchen door into a hallway instead of directly into the dining room creating a buffer zone between cooking and dining spaces; adding a pocket window to borrow natural light from the dining room interior into the kitchen; and creating an eat-in area for casual family dining within the kitchen itself.

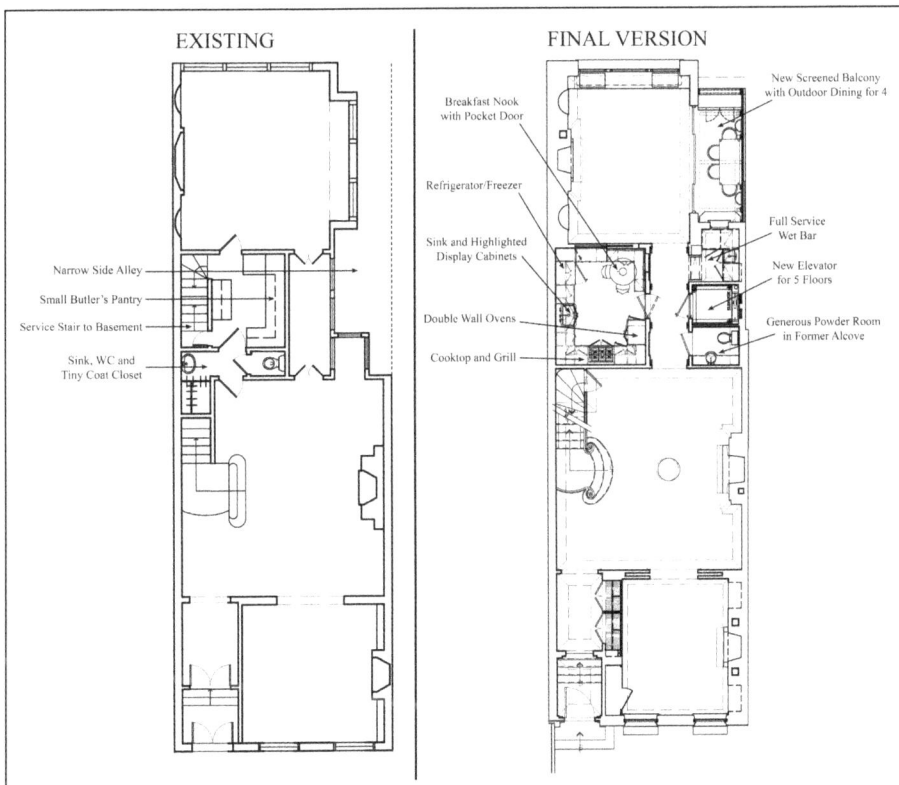

Figure 12.1. The creation of a kitchen for a 19th century home

The Lesson for You

Eberlein's approach is valuable because each iteration builds upon the previous one, creating more value with each pass. Rather than settling for the first workable solution, she kept asking: "What could be better?"

This process shows that:

- Creative solutions often come from embracing constraints
- Small changes can have outsized impacts
- Each iteration reveals new possibilities invisible in earlier solutions
- The final design is demonstrably better in functionality, comfort, and value

When you're tackling your own projects, remember Barbara's approach. Don't stop at your first good idea. Keep exploring, keep refining, and keep asking "what could be better?" That's how ordinary solutions become extraordinary ones.

The Benefits of Experimentation

1. Experimentation is the only way to establish a causal link between your selected strategy and the results. The FDA, for example, only approves a new drug after testing the results against a placebo. Also, tech giants like Amazon and Google conduct thousands of experiments while running their businesses.

    > " **Experimentation is the only way to establish a causal link between your selected strategy and the results.** "

2. Experiments encourage the generation of innovative, bold initiatives. There is little value in experimenting with minor variations of a strategy. Bold experiments create opportunities for breakthrough innovations and significant competitive advantages.

3. Experimentation requires measurement, which ensures that the test and control results are measured and compared. This data-driven approach reduces reliance on opinions and assumptions, leading to fact-based decision-making.

4. When using sophisticated experiments beyond simple A/B testing, you can confuse competitors who do not know your experimental design and therefore cannot read the results. You will end up gaining a substantial competitive advantage.

5. Continuous experimentation is key to creating a culture of innovation that challenges the status quo. As a result, the organization is more likely to attract, hire, and retain more creative people.

Experiments and AI

A critical aspect of using AI in experimentation is how dramatically it compresses the experimentation timeline by enabling 'digital twins'—virtual simulations of products, services, or entire business models that can be tested thousands of times under varying conditions before physical implementation. This approach has revolutionized industries from pharmaceuticals to automotive design, where AI-powered simulations can predict real-world performance with increasing accuracy, reducing both cost and time to market for innovative concepts.

Consider a marketing team developing campaign concepts. Previously, creating mock-ups for multiple approaches might require days of designer time, making comprehensive exploration prohibitively expensive. With generative AI, the same team can visualize dozens of concept directions in an afternoon, evaluate them with stakeholders, and rapidly iterate on the most promising options.

This capability doesn't replace human judgment. The team still decides which concepts align with brand strategy and warrant further development, but it dramatically expands how many possibilities can be explored before committing resources.

This transformation addresses one of the most significant barriers to experimentation: the fear that exploring multiple paths will consume too much time and budget. With AI accelerating the process, organizations can embrace more thorough exploration without sacrificing efficiency.

Funding Concerns

To address any concerns about funding experimentation, consider starting with 'zero-budget innovation'—approaches that require minimal investment beyond existing resources.

Begin with paper prototypes or digital mockups rather than functional builds. Use AI tools to generate concept visualizations without designer time. Conduct small-scale tests with existing customers rather than expensive market research. As writer Eric Ries notes in 'The Lean Startup,' early experimentation aims not to build scalable solutions but to answer critical uncertainties with the minimum required investment.

Once small experiments demonstrate promise, their results often make securing resources for more substantial testing much easier. Many successful innovations began with bootstrapped experiments that generated enough evidence to justify greater investment. Start small, focus on learning, and let initial results build the case for expanded experimentation.

i Exercise

Identify a challenge you're currently facing and design a simple experiment to test a potential solution. Define your hypothesis, design your methodology, the test and control groups, measurement criteria, and timeline. After running the experiment, reflect on what you learned and how you might refine your approach in the next iteration.

By now, you've learned that innovation is rarely a linear journey—it's a dynamic process fueled by insights from your iterative experimentation. You can generate transformative ideas by staying alert to shifts in consumer behavior, cultural values, technological breakthroughs, and business models. Pairing these insights with a culture of iteration and experimentation ensures that your ideas evolve, improve, and stay relevant.

In Summary

1. Experimentation is the only way to determine if innovation works.
The FDA requires rigorous trials before approving new drugs. Amazon and Google run thousands of experiments while operating their businesses. Without controlled testing, you're gambling with resources and relying on guesswork rather than evidence. Smart experimentation reveals the causal link between your strategy and results, separating correlation from causation. When you skip testing, you risk scaling failed concepts or missing breakthrough opportunities hidden in unexpected results.

What assumption about your current approach are you treating as fact without having tested it?

2. Treat innovation like a toddler's approach.
Walk, tumble, giggle, and try again instead of a perfectly planned marathon. Your best ideas emerge from multiple attempts, not a single flash of brilliance. Howard Moskowitz demonstrated this with his mind genomics methodology, reducing hospital readmission rates from 17% to under 5% by testing different motivational messages for patients.

How might you approach your next challenge with a toddler's openness rather than a marathoner's fixed path?

3. Run bold experiments with minimal resources.
Tesla's direct sales model and Figma's release-and-refine approach prove that testing actual concepts beats endless planning. Start with paper prototypes or digital mockups. Use AI tools to generate concept visualizations. Let small successes build the case for bigger investments.

What small experiment could you launch this week that challenges an assumption in your field?

In Summary (contd.)

---

4. Learn equally from failures and successes.

Google Glass flopped with consumers but thrived in enterprise applications. New Coke taught Coca-Cola about emotional attachment to products. The Humane AI Pin's quick demise shows what happens when technology doesn't solve real problems. Each failure offers valuable insights that can fuel your next breakthrough.

Which of your past "failures" contains valuable insights you haven't yet extracted?

5. Use AI to compress your experimentation timeline.

Generate dozens of concepts in an afternoon instead of weeks, expanding possibilities without exhausting resources. AI-powered "digital twins" let you simulate products, services, and business models thousands of times before physical implementation, dramatically reducing costs and accelerating innovation cycles.

How could you use AI tools to expand your range of possible solutions without sacrificing efficiency?

6. Iterate, Iterate, Iterate.

Barbara Eberlein created a kitchen in a 19th-century townhouse by making hundreds of iterations. Each iteration revealed new possibilities, proving how repeated refinements turn ordinary solutions into extraordinary ones.

What current project could benefit from another round of refinement rather than being considered "done"?

We encourage you to put the approaches we discuss in the book into practice by designing experiments to test the value of the various approaches. Remember that creativity flourishes when you combine structured observation with systematic testing and refinement.

As you explore the following chapters, consider how these approaches amplify your creativity and spark groundbreaking innovations.

Notes

[1] H.R. Moskowitz. "Mind Genomics: The Experimental, Inductive Science of the Ordinary, and its Application to Aspects of Food and Feeding." *Physiological Behavior*, 107(4), 606-613. DOI: 10.1016/j.physbeh.2012.04.009, https://pubmed.ncbi.nlm.nih.gov/22542473/

[2] Paul E. Green, Abba M. Krieger, and Yoram Wind. "Thirty Years of Conjoint Analysis: Reflections and Prospects," Publication: *Interfaces*, Volume 31, Issue 3 (supplement), June 2001, accessed May 7, 2025. https://pubsonline.informs.org/doi/10.1287/inte.31.3s.56.9676

[3] Figma Learn. "What Is Figma?" https://help.figma.com/hc/en-us/articles/14563969806359-What-is-Figma

[4] Adobe. "Adobe and Figma Mutually Agree to Terminate Merger Agreement," December 18, 2023, accessed May 7, 2025. https://news.adobe.com/news/news-details/2023/adobe-and-figma-mutually-agree-to-terminate-merger-agreement

[5] Sydney Finkelstein. *Why Smart Executives Fail: And What You Can Learn from Their Mistakes,* Paperback, May 25, 2004.

[6] Paul B. Carroll and Chunka Mui. *Billion Dollar Lessons: What You Can Learn from the Most Inexcusable Business Failures of the Last 25 Years,* Paperback, August 25, 2009.

[7] CB Insights. "The Top 12 Reasons Startups Fail." https://www.cbinsights.com/research/report/startup-failure-reasons-top/

[8] *Harvard Business Review*, "Innovation." https://hbr.org/topic/subject/innovation

[9] MOX, Museum of Failure. https://museumoffailure.com/

The Reward of Curiosity

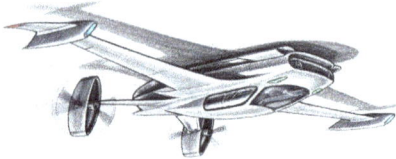

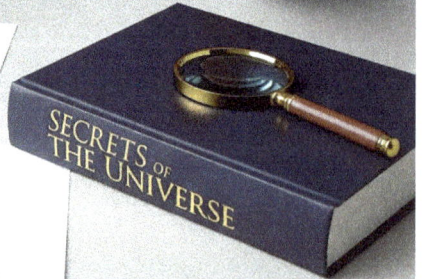

Chapter 13
Approach #9: Foster Curiosity and Imagination

Imagination is more important than knowledge. For knowledge is limited, whereas imagination embraces the entire world, stimulating progress, giving birth to evolution.
—Albert Einstein

Curiosity drives us to question the status quo, while imagination allows us to envision what doesn't yet exist. Together, they form the bedrock of innovation.

On an individual level, curiosity sparks personal growth and professional development. It pushes you beyond your comfort zone, potentially into new territory where breakthrough ideas emerge. Curious professionals stay relevant in rapidly changing environments, continuously adding fresh perspectives and skills to their repertoire.

Imagination gives your curiosity direction and purpose. It transforms questions into possibilities and concepts into tangible solutions. When you exercise your imagination, you develop the ability to mentally prototype ideas before investing resources, visualize outcomes before they materialize, and connect seemingly unrelated concepts into novel approaches.

These individual capabilities create ripple effects. Organizations don't innovate; people do. When organizational CEOs and leaders foster a culture of curiosity and imagination, individuals can contribute unique insights that collectively drive organizational innovation. A company filled with curious, imaginative people will naturally become more adaptable, creative, and forward-thinking.

In this chapter, we'll explore practical methods to strengthen your curiosity and imagination. You'll learn structured approaches to ask better questions, techniques to expand your creative thinking, and frameworks for applying imaginative solutions to real-world challenges.

> " **The quality of your questions determines the quality of your creative process.** "

Developing Curiosity

Are you naturally curious? Do you frequently daydream? If you are such a person, it means your mind is already trying to burst free of its boundaries. But whether you are one or not, there are numerous ways to develop and enhance your curiosity and imagination.

Curiosity—the desire to know or learn—can be systematically cultivated through various practices:

1. Ask questions constantly: Make it a habit to ask "why," "how," and "what if" questions about everyday phenomena. When you encounter something new, instead of making assumptions, inquire about its purpose, function, or origin. The quality of your questions determines the quality of your creative process. Consider how the following questions shifts your thinking from surface-level to deeply generative:

Table 13.1: Organizational Questions

Default Question	Better Question	Why It's Better
"How can we improve this?"	"What part of this process do people secretly hate but never talk about?"	Targets hidden pain points that often reveal the most valuable opportunities for innovation
"What do customers want?"	"When do people turn to us, and what are they hoping we'll help them improve or become?"	Shifts focus from features to transformative outcomes and emotional needs
"Why isn't this working?"	"What assumptions are we making that might not be true anymore?"	Examines foundational beliefs that may be outdated rather than just addressing symptoms
"How can we reduce costs?"	"If we had to deliver twice the value at half the cost, what would we do differently?"	Creates a constructive constraint that forces innovative thinking rather than incremental cuts
"What's our competition doing?"	"Who's solving similar problems in completely different industries, and what can we learn from them?"	Expands reference points beyond obvious competitors to find novel approaches

Notice how the better questions create positive tension: they stimulate fresh thinking and are specific enough to generate helpful responses. They often make people slightly uncomfortable because they probe areas of complacency or challenge implicit assumptions.

The most valuable questions often feel uncomfortable precisely because they challenge our mental comfort zones. You've likely hit on something important when you ask a question that produces immediate awkward silence or nervous laughter. These reactions signal that the question has penetrated below surface-level discussion to touch on unexamined assumptions or uncomfortable truths. Rather than retreating from this tension, recognize it as a sign that your inquiry has the potential to generate genuine insights.

Organizations that cultivate psychological safety around uncomfortable questions—where people feel secure exploring challenging topics without fear of judgment—develop significantly greater creative capacity. They can discuss what others won't, enabling them to see opportunities others miss and address problems others avoid.

While curiosity represents the deliberate pursuit of new knowledge, serendipity—discovering valuable insights while searching for something else—often yields the most transformative creative breakthroughs. What appears to be 'wasted time' in efficiency-oriented environments can be fertile ground for unexpected connections and novel ideas.

> " **What appears to be 'wasted time' in efficiency-oriented environments can be fertile ground for unexpected connections and novel ideas.** "

Organizations seeking to foster creativity should, therefore, create space for both directed curiosity (focused exploration of specific questions) and wandering curiosity (open-ended exploration without immediate objectives).

The focus on questions should not be limited only to organizations and should be expanded to individuals. Consider, for example, the following individual questions:

Table 13.2: Individual Questions

Default Question	Better Question	Why It's Better
"What should I learn next?"	"What problems do I repeatedly encounter that I lack the skills to solve effectively?"	Targets specific knowledge gaps that directly impact personal effectiveness rather than arbitrary learning
"How can I be more creative?"	"What activities make me lose track of time, and what patterns do they share?"	Identifies your natural flow states where creativity already thrives, revealing your intrinsic creative strengths
"Why am I stuck in my career?"	"What assumptions am I making about success that I've never questioned?"	Examines personal beliefs that may be limiting rather than external factors, opening new possibilities
"How can I manage stress better?"	"What would my day look like if designed around my peak energy periods?"	Creates a constructive constraint that forces thinking about structural changes rather than just coping mechanisms
"What do successful people do?"	"Who solves problems similar to mine but in completely different fields, and what can I learn from them?"	Expands reference points beyond obvious role models to discover novel approaches more suited to your unique situation

Source: Claude.ai[1]

Notice how each question shifts from general, passive inquiry to specific, actionable exploration focused on individual growth and personal innovation. When you ask yourself better questions, you bypass surface-level thinking and dig into the rich soil where novel ideas grow. By regularly practicing this kind of purposeful questioning, you train your brain to spot hidden connections and opportunities you might have missed. The most innovative people aren't necessarily those with the most answers, but those who have mastered the art of asking the right questions and followed their questions into active discovery.

2. Read widely: Expose yourself to diverse topics and perspectives by reading books, articles, and research from outside your expertise. This cross-disciplinary knowledge often sparks unexpected connections and insights.

3. Practice mindful observation: Take time to notice details you typically overlook in your environment. This heightened awareness can reveal patterns, problems, and possibilities that may inspire creative solutions. Take a course in art appreciation that could result in a new way of seeing.

4. Embrace the unfamiliar: Deliberately seek out new experiences, whether trying different cuisines, visiting unfamiliar places, or engaging with people whose backgrounds differ from yours. Novelty stimulates curiosity.

5. Follow your interests down rabbit holes: When something captures your attention, allow yourself to explore it deeply. These journeys of discovery often lead to unexpected insights and creative breakthroughs.

Enhancing imagination—Individually

Imagination—the ability to form new ideas or concepts not present to the senses— can be strengthened through the following:

1. Visualization exercises: Practice mentally creating detailed scenarios, whether realistic or fantastical. Try envisioning products that don't exist or how existing products could be transformed.

2. Storytelling: Create narratives around everyday objects or scenarios. This practice helps develop the ability to connect disparate elements into coherent wholes—a key aspect of creative thinking.

3. Role-playing: Mentally put yourself in different positions or perspectives. How would a child, an engineer, or an artist approach your current challenge? This shift in viewpoint can generate fresh insights.

4. Constraint removal: Identify the assumptions or limitations in a situation, then imagine what would be possible if these constraints didn't exist. This technique often reveals innovative possibilities.

5. Dream journaling: Record your dreams upon waking and look for unusual juxtapositions or scenarios that might inspire creative solutions to real-world problems.

Enhancing imagination—Organizationally

1. Organizations can encourage imagination by building in time to allow employees to explore new ways of doing things. Schedule "What If" or "How Might We" days, where employees are encouraged to generate ideas that regular, routine workdays might otherwise suppress.

2. Foster a culture where the question itself is rewarded, not just the answers, and inspire teams by being genuinely interested in diverse perspectives. Leaders must actively show employees that they value their employees' ability to figure things out for themselves, and that this directly impacts business performance. Two examples of organizations that foster a spirit of imagination among employees are:

   i. W.L. Gore & Associates: The "No Bosses" Approach: W.L. Gore & Associates (makers of Gore-Tex fabrics, medical devices, and innovative electronics products) has built an extraordinary culture around what the company calls a "lattice" organizational structure instead of a traditional hierarchy. At Gore, employees are called "associates" and create their roles. What makes Gore's approach remarkable is its commitment to small, autonomous teams. The company deliberately limits the size of its teams to 150 to 200 people. Teams of this size allow people to know each other's skills and interests. This environment nurtures natural curiosity with several core principles: the belief in the individual, freedom in commitments, and a culture where mistakes are viewed as part of the creative process.[2]

   ii. 3M Corporation: The 15% Rule: 3M has maintained a reputation for innovation through its legendary "15% rule"—a policy that encourages employees to dedicate 15% of their work time to exploring projects of their choosing.[3] This structured freedom has led to some of 3M's most iconic products, including Post-it Notes. What makes 3M's approach powerful is how it integrates curiosity into the company's operational DNA. 3M doesn't just allow curiosity—it requires it. The company has created a system where innovation is rewarded by spinning successful new product teams into new divisions led by the original team. 3M's innovative approach speaks for itself, as it generates approximately a quarter of its revenue from products that are less than five years old.[4]

3. Both examples show how well-designed organizational architecture can transform individual curiosity and imagination into collective innovation. They prove that curiosity can be systematically cultivated through thoughtful leadership and appropriate structures.

Creative Games and Activities

Playing games specifically designed to boost creativity can significantly enhance your innovative thinking. Here are several practical examples:

1. Random word association: Select a random word (use a dictionary or online generator) and challenge yourself to connect it to your problem or project. For example, if you're designing a new coffee maker and get the word "butterfly," you might explore folding mechanisms inspired by butterfly wings for a compact design.

2. 30 circles challenge: Draw 30 circles on a page and transform each into a distinct object in three minutes. This exercise, popularized by IDEO, trains your brain to generate multiple solutions rather than perfecting a single idea quickly.
3. Reversed assumptions: List all the assumptions about a product or service, then reverse them to spark new possibilities. For instance, "Restaurants must have menus" becomes "Restaurants have no menus," perhaps leading to a concept where chefs create personalized dishes based on customer preferences.
4. Alternative uses: Take an everyday object and list as many alternative uses as possible. This classic creativity test (mentioned in Chapter 2) strengthens your ability to see beyond an object's intended purpose.
5. Oblique Strategies: Created by Brian Eno and Peter Schmidt, this deck of cards contains cryptic directives like "Use an old idea" or "What would your closest friend do?" that push creative thinking in unexpected directions when you're stuck.

These and other creativity games help develop what creativity researchers call "divergent thinking"—the ability to generate multiple solutions to open-ended problems, a cornerstone of innovation.

Science Fiction, Futuristic Art, and Fantasy as Creativity Catalysts

Many of today's innovations were first imagined in science fiction. For example, Star Trek's communicators preceded flip phones, while the gesture-based interfaces in Minority Report inspired real-world touchless technology. Science fiction author Arthur C. Clarke predicted geostationary satellites decades before they became a reality.

Science fiction doesn't just predict technological developments; it actively inspires them. The engineers who created the first cell phones at Motorola explicitly cited Star Trek as their inspiration. Similarly, many NASA scientists and engineers cite science fiction influencing their career choices and technical approaches.

> **Fantasy narratives and futuristic art can expand your creative horizons.**

Disney Imagineering: Applied Imagination. Fantasy narratives and futuristic art can expand your creative horizons by presenting worlds with different rules, technologies, and social structures, inspiring innovative approaches to real-world challenges.

To see a living example of creativity in action, consider *The Imagineering Story*, available in book form or 6-part documentary. It dives into the history and creative processes of Walt Disney Imagineering, the division that oversees the design and building of its theme parks and attractions.

Disney's 'Imagineers' build on a foundation of storytelling they call "The Art of the Show" to engage theme park visitors.[5] They practice 'Blue Sky Speculation'—

or coming up with ideas without constraints. With refinement, these ideas could become a reality.

A concrete example of Blue Sky Speculation in action is the development of Disney's 'Flight of Passage' attraction in Animal Kingdom. Imagineers began with a seemingly impossible idea: allowing guests to feel what flying on a banshee (a creature from the film Avatar) is like. Rather than immediately focusing on technical limitations, they first explored the pure experience they wanted to create—the sensation of flight, the bond with a living creature, and the wonder of Pandora's alien landscape.

This unconstrained thinking led them to develop a groundbreaking ride system that combines 3D projection, physical effects, and a unique vehicle design that creates the sensation of a breathing animal beneath the rider—something that might never have emerged if they had started with technical constraints.

Imagineers also place great attention to detail for complete guest immersion. For example, bakery scents infuse the theme parks' Main Street, U.S.A. section to evoke small-town America. Imagineers also practice "plussing," or continually seeking to improve attractions. When designing Star Wars: Galaxy's Edge, Imagineers continuously added details like worn pathways and aged building facades to create a more authentic, lived-in environment. Finally, they work across disciplines to tap diverse ideas, bringing together architects, engineers, artists, writers, and technologists.

Disney describes its Imagineering division: "Walt Disney Imagineering is the creative engine that designs and builds all Disney theme parks, resorts, attractions, and cruise ships worldwide, and oversees the creative aspects of Disney games, merchandise, product development, and publishing businesses."[6] The film reinforces some approaches we've been discussing, such as the importance of exploration and experimentation.

Igniting Curiosity and Imagination at a Societal Level

What if we lived in a world where curiosity was our most valuable natural resource? A society that cultivated imagination as intentionally as we build infrastructure? The evidence suggests this may be more than just a pleasant fantasy. It's a competitive advantage waiting to be seized.

1. Reimagine Educational Systems
    Finland has boldly rejected memorization and standardized testing and has built an education system where creativity thrives alongside academic rigor. The result is that their students consistently outperform those from nations obsessed with tests.[7] What if your organization or community became the Finland of your industry?

2. Transform Spaces into Wonder Labs

   Picture a city where every library, museum, and public space becomes a labo-ratory for the imagination. Where community centers host intergenerational curiosity circles and storefront windows showcase citizen experiments. The physical spaces we build shape our thinking, and the most innovative organizations deliberately design for both. How might your environment, if you can change it, be optimized for efficient execution or imaginative exploration?

3. Create Sanctuaries for Deep Thought

   In our notification-saturated world, uninterrupted thinking has become a rare luxury. Yet the most valuable insights often emerge during reflection when we "consider what it all means."[8] Which leader will have the courage to create sacred spaces for contemplation—physical rooms and protected time—where imagination can breathe?

4. Redefine Success Beyond Test Scores

   We'll optimize for standardized thinking as long as we measure success by standardized metrics alone. The visionary leaders are already expanding their definition of success beyond conventional metrics. The societies and organizations that flourish in the coming decades will be the ones that nurture human capacities that algorithms alone can't replicate, the ability to wonder, dream, imagine, and ask "What if?" The question isn't if we can afford to prioritize curiosity. The question might be, can we afford not to?

The Role of AI in Fostering Curiosity and Imagination

One final thought on fostering curiosity and imagination is the role of AI. It revolutionizes curiosity and imagination by revealing hidden patterns and pushing our thinking beyond boundaries. As we have expressed throughout this book, AI does not and will not replace human creativity, but can amplify it. The partnership between human imagination and AI opens up possibilities that neither can achieve alone across individual, organizational, and societal contexts. Let's examine these in more detail:

> " AI does not and will not replace human creativity but can amplify it. "

1. *On an individual level,* AI can transform your personal curiosity journey by providing random, unexpected ideas that break your predictable thinking pattern. This, in turn, will encourage you to dig deeper to explore ideas further. Try ChatGPT's "surprise me" feature[9] to discover adjacent concepts you might not have thought of. For visual thinking, Midjourney helps you see concepts from multiple perspectives. Prompt it with "show me five different interpretations of resilience."[10] Readwise is an online platform with a supporting

mobile app that reveals connections between research papers or books you've read, spotting patterns across seemingly unrelated topics.[11] For an even more powerful approach, ask Claude to review a past project and find hidden themes or suggest three new questions about the project that might help you approach it from an entirely different angle. AI can help you step out of your comfort zone and expand your horizons.

2. *AI can create unprecedented imagination spaces with a measurable impact for organizations.* Teams at IBM use their Enterprise Design Thinking platform with AI-enhanced collaboration tools that capture and connect ideas across departments, generating 2.5x more viable concepts during innovation sprints.[12] Financial services firm Capital One has embraced AI throughout its organization, developing its virtual assistant Eno and other AI technologies to help transform customer experiences and financial services.[13] Productivity gains are equally impressive when AI is effectively incorporated into organizational culture. Autodesk's AI and generative design tools significantly streamline design processes by automating repetitive tasks, enabling designers to focus on the creative aspects of their work rather than routine analysis and documentation.[14] Companies embracing AI as a collaboration partner rather than just a productivity tool unlock a competitive advantage that transforms not just what they make but also how their people think.

3. *Socially,* AI can democratize curiosity and imagination across communities through collaborative learning environments. For example, a Harvard Graduate School of Education study found that students in AI-enhanced classrooms ask more questions and engage in deeper critical thinking.[15] AI-powered interactive installations like "Intention" by French artist Louk Amidou create multi-sensory experiences that respond to human gestures in public spaces. These foster cross-generational curiosity exchanges that bridge divides between tech-savvy youth and not-so-tech-savvy yet experience-rich elders.[16] AI translation tools from companies like Worldly support over 60 languages for live two-way translation, breaking down language barriers that may have previously limited creative collaboration across cultures.[17] Moving forward into the near future, the next wave of social innovation could be using AI to transform public spaces to attract residents of all ages and backgrounds.[18] As AI continues to evolve, and humans continue to harness its power, we believe that humankind will continue to witness the transformation of passive consumers into active co-creators for a more inclusive, expressive, and collectively intelligent society.

The champions of tomorrow won't necessarily be those who are more intelligent from a classical viewpoint, but those who dare to partner with AI to wonder, dream, and ask "what if?" AI-enhanced curiosity and imagination are rapidly becoming a competitive necessity for personal growth, career prospects, businesses, and communities. The sooner we embrace AI to foster our curiosity and creativity, the better equipped we will be to shape the exciting future.

i Exercise

Cultivate curiosity and imagination:

1. **Curiosity journal:** Spend five minutes daily writing down questions about things you encounter. At the end of each week, research answers to your three most intriguing questions.
2. **Media diet expansion:** Each month, consume content from a field entirely outside your expertise—a scientific journal, a fantasy novel, or a documentary on an unfamiliar culture.
3. **Curiosity walk:** Take a 20-minute walk to find five interesting things you've never noticed before in your familiar environment.
4. **What-if scenarios:** Regularly practice asking 'What if?' questions about everyday situations, products, or services. For example, "What if refrigerators could communicate with grocery stores?"
5. **Cross-industry inspiration:** Choose a random industry different from your own and research its innovations. Imagine how these innovations might apply to your field.

In Summary

1. Curiosity and imagination form the bedrock of innovation.
When you ask better questions like "What assumptions might not be true anymore?" instead of "Why isn't this working?" you break through mental comfort zones and unlock creative breakthroughs.

What unquestioned assumption in your work or life might be limiting your creative potential right now?

2. Organizations that thrive on innovation, like W.L. Gore with its "no bosses" approach or 3M with its "15% rule," have built curiosity into their DNA.

How might you redesign your team's structure or schedule to make curiosity a requirement rather than just a permission?

3. Creative games shake up your thinking.
Try the 30 circles challenge, reversed assumptions, or random word association to train your brain to generate multiple solutions rather than perfecting a single idea.

Which creative exercise could you commit to practicing for just 10 minutes tomorrow to break your routine thinking patterns?

In Summary (contd.)

---

4. Science fiction and fantasy expand your creative horizons.

Disney's Imagineers practice "Blue Sky Speculation"—imagining without constraints—before considering technical limitations, leading to groundbreaking innovations like the Flight of Passage attraction.

What would your next project look like if you removed all practical constraints and focused purely on the ideal experience?

5. AI amplifies creativity.

Use AI tools to discover unexpected connections, visualize concepts from multiple angles, and collaborate across disciplines, giving you a competitive edge in today's innovation landscape.

How could you partner with AI to explore one challenging problem you're facing from five completely different perspectives?

Our next chapter examines leveraging emerging technology to transform creative concepts into reality.

Notes

[1] Claude.ai, prompt: "Analyze "Organizational Questions" provided by Mukul Pandya. Provide a similar set of questions an individual can ask that can transform their thinking from surface-level to deeply generative.

[2] Al Gore, "Our Story". https://www.gore.com/about/the-gore-story#our-culture

[3] 3M, "3M's 15% Culture," accessed May 8, 2025. https://www.3m.co.uk/3M/en_GB/careers/culture/15-percent-culture/

[4] Science Direct, Pedro Conceição, Dennis Hamill, and Pedro Pinheiro. "Innovative Science and Technology Commercialization Strategies at 3M: A Case Study," *Journal of Engineering and Technology Management*, Vol. 19, Issue 1, March 2002, Pages 25–38, accessed May 9, 2025. https://www.sciencedirect.com/science/article/abs/pii/S0923474801000443

[5] Wikipedia, s.v. "Walt Disney Imagineering," accessed December 10, 2024. https://en.wikipedia.org/wiki/Walt_Disney_Imagineering

[6] Walt Disney Imagineering. "About Imagineering," *Disney Imaginations*, accessed March 1, 2025. https://disneyimaginations.com/about-imaginations/about-imagineering/

[7] Examples Of, "Successful Examples of Education Reform Driving Change." https://examples-of.net/education-reform/

[8] Walden University. "Teaching Strategies: Sparking Curiosity in Learning." https://www.waldenu.edu/online-masters-programs/ms-in-education/resource/teaching-strategies-sparking-curiosity-in-learning

[9] ChatGPT Surprise Me. https://chatgpt.com/g/g-t3yVXR3AA-surprise-me

[10] Midjourney. https://www.midjourney.com/explore?tab=top

[11] Readwise. https://read.readwise.io/new

[12] IBM. "The Intersection of AI and Design Thinking." https://www.ibm.com/think/topics/AI-and-enterprise-design-thinking

[13] Harvard Digital Innovation and Transformation. "Capital One: Transforming traditional banking to an AI-first experience," accessed May 9, 2025, https://d3.harvard.edu/platform-digit/submission/capital-one-transforming-traditional-banking-to-an-ai-first-experience/

[14] Autodesk. "The Future of Making Will be Powered by Generative Design and Generative AI," accessed May 9, 2025. https://www.autodesk.com/design-make/articles/generative-design-and-generative-ai

[15] Harvard Graduate School of Education, Elizabeth M. Ross. "Embracing Artificial Intelligence in the Classroom," July 20, 2023, accessed May 9, 2025. https://www.gse.harvard.edu/ideas/usable-knowledge/23/07/embracing-artificial-intelligence-classroom

[16] The Conversation, Burcu Olgen, and Carmela Cucuzzella. "Artificial Intelligence Can be Used to Design Engaging and Interactive Public Art," accessed May 9, 2025. https://theconversation.com/artificial-intelligence-can-be-used-to-design-engaging-and-interactive-public-art-209104

[17] Science News Today, Muhammad Tuhin, March 29, 2025, "AI-Powered Language Translation: Breaking Down Global Barriers." https://www.sciencenewstoday.org/ai-powered-language-translation-breaking-down-global-barriers

[18] Jose A. Guridi et al., "Image Generative AI to Design Public Spaces: A Reflection of How AI Could Improve Co-Design of Public Parks," ACM Journals, *Digital Government: Research and Practice*, Vol. 6, No. 1, February 12, 2025, Accessed May 9, 2025. https://dl.acm.org/doi/full/10.1145/3656588

2025
Top 10
MIT Technology
Breakthroughs

Vera C. Rubin Observatory

AI Agents

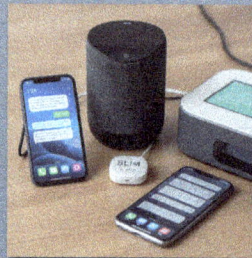
Small Language Models (SLMs)

Robotaxi

Fast-Learning Robots

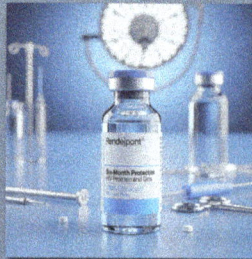
Long-Acting HIV Prevention Medication

Green Steel

Cattle Burping Remedies

Wheat Disease Surveillance System

Cleaner Jet Fuel

Chapter 14
Approach #10: Leverage Emerging Technologies

We use one stage of technology to create the next stage, which is why technology accelerates and grows in power.
—Ray Kurzweil, computer scientist, author, entrepreneur, futurist and inventor

Emerging technologies have become catalysts for creativity and imagination, transforming once-futuristic concepts into everyday realities. They break traditional barriers and create new possibilities for creative expression, opening doors we never knew existed. Consider how virtual reality lets architects walk through buildings before they're built, or how 3D printing turns digital dreams into physical objects overnight. Today, AI generates original art and music, redefining artistic boundaries. VR transports designers into immersive worlds where they can build architectural marvels in real time. Blockchain fuels creative economies by enabling digital artists to sell unique works as NFTs, and even biotechnology is reshaping fashion, with lab-grown fabrics inspiring eco-conscious couture.

While Chapter 3 dives into the practicalities of harnessing AI tools to enhance your creativity, we will broaden the arena to include VR/AR/MR, NFT/blockchain, quantum computing, and precision (personalized) medicine, as illustrative emerging technologies that can inspire creativity in us. Each of these and other new technologies represents a new platform for your experimentation.

Generative AI: By now, most of us are aware of generative AI's many capabilities. It can write poems, compose music, paint, code, and tackle nearly any cognitive and creative challenge. But the bigger question is this: Does it enhance your creativity? Or does it lull you into a sense of dependency on the AI model such that your creativity becomes dull?

The research by Pagani and Wind examined more than 1,000 examples of AI models in action and narrowed them down to 85 to use in highly creative tasks.[1] They found that 78% of these uses demonstrated enhanced human creativity when AI was integrated into the creative process. They discovered that generative AI can be used to enhance human creativity. It not only transforms the creative process, but it also challenges society's understanding of creative thinking and the creative process.

The authors classified them into three primary levels of AI's creative characteristics:

- **Mimicking the human condition:** The AI models' algorithms are trained to recognize patterns in data and make a probabilistic decision. For example, British musician Reeps One began training a deep learning AI model on his voice, enabling it to replicate his beatboxing style and come up with new rhythms. This collaboration resulted in the groundbreaking 'Second Self' project, where Reeps performed duets with his AI twin, creating vocal compositions impossible for a single human to produce.[2]

- **Combining concepts:** AI models may combine different ideas, such as styles of music and paintings, to generate new alternatives. The AI model learns from vast amounts of data and mixes them to create artistic work that stimulates human creativity. Artists will now have various creative ideas—instead of just one—to compare against each other and promote their creative process. An example is MuseNet, a deep neural network from OpenAI that can generate four minutes of musical compositions from 10 instruments by combining their styles. The AI model finds patterns of music harmony, rhythms, and styles and learns to predict what follows next.

- **Building novelty:** AI models may compose new music, create works of art, design objects, write a poem, among other creative endeavors. These experiments in computational creativity are enabled by significant advances in deep learning to make AI models flexible, so they can take on a task to discover patterns and generate them. This is accidental creativity, and the inner element of randomness in deep learning algorithms leads to variability in the model's output, leading to novel, creative applications. A striking example is the collaboration between artist Sougwen Chung and her AI system DOUG (Drawing Operations Unit Generation). Chung trains the AI in her drawing style and then paints alongside it in real-time performances.[3] The system doesn't merely imitate her work but develops its variations, creating a genuine artistic dialogue that pushes Chung's work in unexpected directions. Her installations have been featured at the Victoria and Albert Museum in London[4] and the Museum of Contemporary Art in Geneva.[5]

> **AI serves as a catalyst to inspire the human capacity for creativity.**

Based on the available research, one can conclude that AI is not only a tool but also a means that inspires the human capacity for creativity.

Metaverse

The metaverse is an immersive virtual space shared by many users, like a virtual world with character avatars interacting with each other and the digital world around them. This concept integrates technologies such as virtual reality (VR), which creates a fully immersive virtual world for users to experience in a computer-generated world augmented reality (AR), which overlays digital elements of the virtual world

> **The metaverse turns audiences into participants, transforming art from observation into experience.**

onto the real, physical world, and mixed reality (MR) which is a blend of the two, allowing users to interact with digital objects in their physical environment.

The metaverse trend peaked in 2021 when Facebook CEO and co-founder Mark Zuckerberg famously renamed his social media empire to Meta after the company pivoted to the metaverse as the next big thing in computing. But it didn't gain much traction for many reasons: People did not want to wear bulky VR helmets for extended periods; the virtual worlds did not broaden their appeal beyond a gaming audience; among others. The industrial metaverse, however, gained more traction as an environment for experimenting, modeling, and testing in, for example, virtual factory floors.

In 2022, generative AI in the form of ChatGPT took the limelight. Zuckerberg pivoted as well, redirecting the company's main efforts towards developing large language models and AI applications for Facebook, WhatsApp, Instagram, and Messenger—while keeping a foot in the metaverse with his virtual reality/augmented reality/MR headset Meta Quest and 'Orion' AR glasses that look like regular spectacles.

In 2023, Meta partnered with Ray-Ban to release smart glasses that look and feel like traditional sunglasses while incorporating AI, cameras, and speakers. Priced at around $300, these glasses have made wearable tech more accessible and stylish than previous attempts like Google Glass.

However, the metaverse sparked creativity by giving people and organizations another environment to develop their avatars and other assets. They could create stories, hold concerts and exhibitions, and build their fantastical mini-worlds fueled by their imagination. For example, the fashion brand Coach launched its Spring 2024 collection on virtual platforms Roblox and Zepeto, where users can style their avatars with its products.[6]

The metaverse also has a significant role to play in the industry. For instance, AR/VR glasses transform industries by providing immersive, interactive, and efficient tools that redefine workflows and customer experiences. In manufacturing and industrial settings, AR glasses let workers visualize assembly instructions, maintenance steps, or real-time data directly within their field of view, improving efficiency and reducing errors.[7]

Companies like Boeing and Siemens have integrated AR into their operations to streamline complex processes, saving time and resources. VR glasses, on the other hand, are revolutionizing training by creating realistic simulations for employees to practice skills in risk-free environments, such as piloting aircraft or performing surgery. This leads to higher proficiency and safer operations in industries where mistakes can be costly or dangerous.

Musicians and artists are embracing the metaverse to connect with their fans. For example, music producer Alex Karlsson (who has worked with Korean-pop acts like BTS and SuperM) held a collaborative songwriting session with hundreds of fans in the metaverse during a demo event.[8] Artists are also using the metaverse as a new canvas of expression. They can create works of art where fans can see the display in multiple virtual locations, or build immersive installations that visitors can interact with virtually in responsive environments. The metaverse also makes it far easier for artists to collaborate simultaneously in various locations. Essentially, the metaverse has changed artistic creation by blurring the line between creator and audience. When visitors can step inside a painting or become part of a musical composition, art transforms from a passive experience into an interactive journey.[9]

The impact of AR/VR glasses is also significant in customer-facing industries such as retail, real estate, and entertainment. In retail, brands use AR glasses to offer personalized shopping experiences, allowing customers to virtually try clothing or visualize furniture in their homes before purchasing.[10] The real estate sector benefits by enabling clients to tour properties remotely through VR glasses, saving time while expanding market reach.[11] Entertainment and gaming industries are leveraging the immersive capabilities of AR/VR glasses to create next-level interactive experiences, as seen in VR games and augmented sports events.[12] As these technologies become more accessible and affordable, their integration across industries will continue to drive innovation, enhance efficiency, and create new business models.

How AI can enhance the metaverse: AI enables intelligent, adaptive, and personalized virtual experiences. It powers realistic avatars, allowing lifelike interactions and expressions. AI-driven algorithms also enhance world-building by automating the creation of immersive environments, making them dynamic and responsive to user actions.

Additionally, AI personalizes experiences by analyzing user behavior to tailor content, recommend activities, or customize virtual settings. For example, AI can generate non-player characters (NPCs) with advanced conversational abilities, enriching engagement and realism. By optimizing interactions, automating content creation, and enhancing personalization, AI serves as a key driver of innovation and scalability within the metaverse.

How VR, AR, and MR can Enhance Your Creativity

Headsets and glasses have become more affordable, allowing you to use VR, AR, and MR to boost your creativity. For example:

- Writers or anyone who needs to use a computer from their desk can use Immersed, a VR app that enables you to work in a distraction-free space.[13]
- Teachers or presenters can use Microsoft Mesh, an MR platform that enables teams to support educational collaboration around 3D immersive objects or experiences. This is particularly useful for STEM educators, as it allows students to engage with complex concepts.[14]
- Artists can use a VR headset combined with the Sketchar app to fully immerse themselves in the creative process of creating art in a virtual space.[15]

- Designers can use Adobe Medium, a VR App that enables you to sculpt virtual, 3D objects, characters, or abstract art. These items can be manipulated, tweaked, perfected, and shared with anyone online before building them offline in the real world.[16]
- Musicians can use Virtuoso-VR to play virtual musical instruments and perform in an immersive environment.[17]

These are merely a small sample of the many emerging VR, AR, and MR technologies that can boost your creativity, and we actively encourage you to search for more in your respective field that may increase and enhance your creativity.

NFTs and Blockchain

Using blockchain technology, NFTs (Non-Fungible Tokens) are unique digital assets that represent ownership or proof of authenticity for items such as art, music, videos, collectibles, and more. Unlike cryptocurrencies, NFTs are not fungible, or interchangeable. They are one-of-a-kind or limited-edition items with unique identifying codes that make them distinct. Examples of NFTs are digital art, trading cards, and in-game assets. NFTs peaked in 2021, with total sales volume reaching $17.6 billion.[18] But the hype died down, with trading volumes plunging a year later.

While in its heyday, NFTs sparked a wave of creativity when they first debuted, especially as their prices escalated. The most expensive NFT ever sold was "Everydays: the First 5,000 Days" by digital artist Beeple (Mike Winkelmann) at a Christie's auction for $69.3 million on March 11, 2021. It is a collage of 5,000 individual images created daily over 13-plus years. The buyer was a Singaporean crypto investor named Vignesh Sundaresan.[19]

Beyond high-profile sales, NFTs have enabled creative experimentation in unexpected ways. For instance, musician Imogen Heap used NFTs to create a new model for music distribution, allowing fans to purchase shares in songs and receive royalties. The Kings of Leon band released their album "When You See Yourself" as an NFT, including special editions with unique artwork and front-row concert seats, creating a new relationship between artists and fans.

Blockchain is a decentralized digital ledger technology that securely records transactions across a network of computers. Each transaction is stored in a "block," linked chronologically to form a "chain," ensuring that once data is recorded, it cannot be altered retroactively without altering all subsequent blocks. This design provides transparency, security, and immutability. All parties can see the ledger.

Blockchain's immutable nature has sparked innovative new products, such as smart contracts that automatically enforce the terms of an agreement when predefined conditions are met. For example, if someone is behind on car payments, the smart contract could automatically turn off the car's ignition system by interfacing with a starter interrupter device. Blockchain also gave rise to trading of asset tokens, like a fraction of ownership in a piece of property, on its immutable network.

Blockchain technology has been instrumental in enhancing product traceability and safety within the food industry. A notable example is Walmart's implementation of a blockchain-based system to track the origin of its produce. Traditionally, tracing the source of a food product could take days or even weeks, hindering the ability to respond swiftly to contamination issues. By adopting a blockchain solution, Walmart reduced the time required to trace produce origins to just 2.2 seconds. This rapid traceability ensures faster response times during food safety incidents and enhances transparency throughout the supply chain, thereby improving product quality and consumer trust.[20]

In the luxury goods sector, blockchain has been used to fight counterfeiting and verify product authenticity. For instance, Louis Vuitton has explored blockchain solutions to provide customers with verifiable proof of authenticity for their products. By embedding unique identifiers within products and recording them on a blockchain ledger, customers can easily verify the legitimacy of their purchases. This application protects brand integrity and enhances the overall customer experience by ensuring that consumers receive genuine products.[21]

AI enhances NFTs and blockchain by enabling dynamic, intelligent, and personalized digital assets—it can create unique, high-quality designs at scale for NFTs. Dynamic NFTs, powered by AI, can evolve based on external data or user interactions, adding layers of interactivity and long-term value. AI also strengthens blockchain security by detecting fraud, monitoring transactions, and identifying real-time anomalies.

How NFT and Blockchain Technology can Enhance Your Creativity

NFTs and blockchain technology allow creators to unlock value and spark innovation. For example:

- As NFTs are created with a unique address published on the blockchain, you can create NFT art that cannot be copied or forged. This opens up possibilities of creating unique collectibles with scarcity, which can potentially be highly profitable.
- Web 3, which incorporates NFTs and blockchain technology, makes it easier for creators to develop a following and nurture their audience with exclusive rewards. This, in turn, fuels creativity, as it is easier to collaborate and create interactive experiences.
- Platforms like Opensea[22] and Foundation[23] make it easier for beginner NFT creators to join with a low barrier to entry. Note, however, that Foundation joiners require an invitation code from someone who has sold at least one NFT. Experienced NFT creators can join SuperRare,[24] a curated platform for high-end digital art.

It is important to conduct extensive research into creating NFTs. For example, as an artist, you will need to choose which blockchain to mint your NFT on. It is the blockchain that affects fees, environment, impact and audience, and it is the blockchain that secures your ownership. You will also need to decide which platform to sell your NFT through, as this affects visibility and the features of your NFT.

Quantum Computing

Quantum computing is an advanced field that leverages principles of quantum mechanics to process information in ways that classical computers (the ones most of us use) cannot. Unlike classical computers, which use bits representing 0 or 1, quantum computers utilize quantum bits (qubits). Qubits can exist in a state of 0, 1, or both simultaneously—a phenomenon known as superposition.

Additionally, qubits can become entangled, meaning one qubit's state can instantaneously influence another's state, regardless of the distance between them. These unique properties enable quantum computers to perform complex calculations at unprecedented speeds.[25] But qubits are also unstable and prone to error, which have been bottlenecks for the development of the field.

In February 2025, Amazon unveiled its new quantum chip, Ocelot, which uses a scalable architecture that can reduce error correction tasks by 90%, making it more cost-efficient. In the same month, Microsoft announced that it had found a new type of matter that's not solid, liquid, or gas: Topoconductor. This material can produce more reliable and scalable qubits. Microsoft uses the topoconductor as the core of its new quantum chip, Majorana 1. These two developments follow the December 2024 news from Google about its new quantum computing chip, Willow. This chip can process complex problems in under five minutes—tasks that would take classical supercomputers an impractical amount of time, highlighting the potential of quantum computing to tackle challenges previously deemed unsolvable.

Quantum computing aids in areas such as:

- AI and machine learning: Enhancing data pattern recognition and processing capabilities, leading to more efficient and accurate AI models.
- Cryptography: Potentially breaking traditional encryption methods while paving the way for more secure communication protocols.
- Drug discovery and material science: Simulating molecular and atomic interactions to accelerate the development of new medications and materials.
- Financial services: Optimizing complex financial models and risk assessments, leading to better investment strategies.

However, qubits are highly sensitive to environmental disturbances, leading to calculation errors. Advancements like Google's Willow chip aim to address this by reducing error rates as the number of qubits increases.

How Quantum Computing can Enhance Creativity:

1. Revolutionizing artistic expression
   Generative art and music: Quantum algorithms can generate complex patterns and compositions, inspiring new artistic and musical expression forms. For instance, the QAC Toolkit integrates quantum computing into real-time creative practices, enabling innovative musical compositions.
   A concrete example is quantum artist Libby Heaney's installation "Ent-, most recently exhibited at the HEK in Basel (2024). Heaney used IBM's quantum computers and Unreal Engine for animation to create visual art that simultaneously explores quantum superposition—images that exist in multiple states. The resulting pieces challenge conventional perspectives about reality and perception, creating visual experiences impossible with classical computing.[26]

2. Enhancing design and innovation
   Complex problem-solving: Quantum computing's ability to process vast datasets and perform intricate calculations facilitates innovative solutions in design and architecture, leading to more efficient and creative outcomes.
   Material discovery: By simulating molecular interactions at an unprecedented scale, quantum computing aids in discovering new materials with unique properties, expanding the palette available to designers and artists.

3. Transforming creative industries
   Personalized marketing: Quantum computing enables real-time data processing, allowing highly customized marketing strategies that resonate more deeply with individual consumers. This capability fosters more engaging and creative advertising campaigns.
   Collaborative opportunities: Bringing quantum computing with art and design encourages interdisciplinary collaborations, leading to innovative projects that blend technology and creativity. Google's Quantum AI Lab, for example, integrates artistic expression to inspire advancements in computing.[27]

4. Educational and exploratory platforms
   Quantum art exhibitions: Institutions organize events exploring quantum computing through creative lenses, demonstrating the intersection of art and science. The "Exploring Quantum Through Art and Design" colloquium is one such initiative that fosters public engagement with quantum concepts.[28]
   Academic programs: Universities are developing curricula integrating quantum computing with the arts and humanities, preparing a new generation of thinkers to explore this interdisciplinary frontier.
   The University of Maryland's Arts for All initiative and the Mid-Atlantic Quantum Institute have collaborated to fund seven research projects that explore the intersection of quantum science and creative disciplines.[29]

Precision Medicine

Precision medicine, also known as personalized medicine, is an innovative approach to health care that tailors medical treatment to the individual characteristics of each patient. This customization is based on a person's unique genetic makeup, environment, and lifestyle, enabling more effective disease prevention, diagnosis, and treatment.

In recent years, personalized medicine has gained significant momentum, with advancements in genomics and biotechnology playing pivotal roles. For instance, developing CRISPR-based gene editing therapies has opened new avenues for treating genetic disorders. A notable example is the approval of a CRISPR-based treatment for sickle-cell disease, marking a significant milestone in genetic medicine.

Moreover, integrating AI into genomics has accelerated the discovery of new therapeutic targets and the development of personalized treatment plans. AI algorithms can analyze vast genomic datasets to identify patterns and predict individual responses to specific treatments, thereby enhancing the precision of medical interventions. The field continues to evolve, with ongoing research and clinical trials aimed at expanding the applications of personalized medicine across various diseases.

How Precision Medicine Sparked Creativity:

Researchers developed precision oncology that treats patients based on the genetic profiles of their tumors. The 3D printing of medical implants tailored to the individual reduces the risk of rejection and improves patient outcomes. Also, precision medicine has led to innovations in gene therapies, where altering cellular functions has made it possible to address conditions once seen as untreatable.

Johnson & Johnson's DePuy Synthes unit creates patient-specific, 3D-printed titanium facial implants that precisely match a patient's anatomy. For patients with severe facial trauma or congenital disabilities, these customized implants have transformed outcomes, reducing surgical complications compared to standard implants.[30]

Precision medicine has also led to innovations in gene therapies, where altering cellular functions has made it possible to address conditions once seen as untreatable. A striking example is Luxturna, the first FDA-approved gene therapy for a genetic disease. It treats a rare inherited blindness by delivering a functioning copy of the RPE65 gene directly to retinal cells. Patients who were previously going blind have experienced restored vision, with some able to see stars for the first time.

> " Emerging technologies expose us to possibilities we might have never before conceived. "

How Advances in Technology can Enhance Creativity

Today's technologies and further advances can transform creative processes in numerous ways:

1. Inspiration and imagination enhancement: Emerging technologies expose us to possibilities we might never have conceived, expanding our creative horizons. AI algorithms can analyze vast datasets to generate unique concepts, abstract patterns, or entirely new compositions that artists might never have conceived independently.[31]
2. New platforms for expression: Technologies provide novel mediums for creative expression. AR company Magic Leap collaborated with the Royal Shakespeare Company to create an immersive version of 'The Seven Ages of Man' speech from Shakespeare's 'As You Like It,' where digital elements interacted with live actors, reinventing theatrical experiences.[32]
3. Hyper-personalization: Advanced technologies enable unprecedented levels of customization. Spotify's use of advanced technologies to curate personalized playlists[33] for each user can inspire artists to explore new creative avenues, such as tracks that can change based on listener preferences and moods.[34]
4. Enhanced human-AI collaboration: Technologies facilitate new forms of creative partnership between humans and machines. Fashion designer Zac Posen used 3D-printed components to create a dress resembling giant rose petals, which British model Jourdan Dunn wore to the 2019 Met Gala.[35]
5. Immersive storytelling: Technologies enable more engaging and interactive narratives. Filmmaker Alejandro González Iñárritu's VR installation 'Carne y Arena' (Virtually present, Physically Invisible) places viewers inside the experience of refugees crossing the US-Mexico border, creating empathy through immersion in ways traditional film cannot achieve.[36]

Understanding these technologies offers several benefits for your creative practice:

- Expanded creative horizons: Exposure to cutting-edge technologies broadens your acceptance of ideas that might have seemed far-fetched previously.
- Cross-disciplinary inspiration: Technologies like quantum computing demonstrate the power of interdisciplinary thinking, reinforcing other creative approaches discussed throughout this book.
- Future-oriented thinking: Familiarity with emerging technologies helps you anticipate future trends so your creative work can stay ahead of the curve.

i Exercise

1. Choose a technology you use regularly but haven't explored creatively (smartphone, AI assistant, social media platform, and the like).

2. Ask yourself, 'What if this tool could help me create something that feels impossible?'
3. Within five minutes, rapidly list 10 ways this technology could push your creative boundaries. Be wildly imaginative and don't self-censor.
4. Circle the three ideas that excite you most.
5. For each circled idea, spend 3 minutes sketching a mini-project plan:
   - What would you create?
   - What specific features of the technology would you leverage?
   - What creative problem would this solve?
   - What's one small step you could take today to begin?

Select one idea and commit to a 7-day experiment: use the technology in this new way for at least 15 minutes daily, documenting your process and unexpected discoveries.

In Summary

1. Break physical boundaries with immersive technologies.
Virtual reality, augmented reality, and mixed reality transform how you create and experience art. Writers escape distractions in virtual workspaces. Artists sculpt digital masterpieces in three dimensions. Musicians perform with virtual instruments in impossible spaces. These technologies redefine what's possible in your creative practice.
What physical limitation in your creative work could you completely eliminate with immersive technology?

2. Step into new creative dimensions.
VR, AR, and MR break physical limitations. Writers find distraction-free spaces, artists sculpt in 3D, musicians play virtual instruments—all opening doors to expression impossible before.
Ask yourself: What creative challenge could you tackle in an entirely new way using immersive technologies?

3. You can build on blockchain's foundation.
NFTs and blockchain give you the power to create unique digital assets with verified ownership. This technology lets you connect directly with your audience, building new relationships and funding models.
Ask yourself: How could you use blockchain to create value from your creative work in ways that weren't possible before?

In Summary (contd.)

---

4. Think quantum for breakthrough ideas.

Quantum computing's ability to process multiple possibilities simultaneously mirrors creative thinking. Artists using quantum algorithms generate works that challenge conventional perspectives about reality.

What seemingly impossible creative problem might you solve by applying quantum-inspired thinking?

5. Personalize your creative output.

Precision medicine shows the power of personalization. Apply this mindset to your creative work by tailoring experiences to individual needs and preferences.

Ask yourself: How could you make your creative work respond and adapt to each person who experiences it?

6. Cross boundaries between disciplines.

The most exciting innovations happen at the intersection of different fields. Emerging technologies, the ones discussed here and many others, thrive when artists collaborate with scientists; designers work with engineers.

Ask yourself: What unexpected field or technology could you explore to bring fresh energy to your creative practice?

7. Follow new technologies.

Given the magnitude and speed of scientific and technological advances, you must be continuously on the lookout for these developments and their impact as tailwinds of headwinds.

Ask yourself: Do I have an early warning system to alert me to these new scientific and technological developments and their likely impact on my opportunities and threats?

While the illustrative technologies in this chapter will open new creative frontiers for you, your next challenge lies in weaving them and other scientific and technological advances together with the approaches in the next chapter to build your own personalized creativity toolkit.

Notes

[1] Margherita Pagani and Yoram Wind. "Unlocking Marketing Creativity Using Artificial Intelligence," *Journal of Interactive Marketing* 60, no. 1 (2025): 25–43, accessed March 8, 2025. https://www.skema.edu/en/faculty-and-research/publications/unlocking-marketing-creativity-using-artificial-intelligence

[2] Ibid.

[3] "Sougwen Chung," *AIArtists.org*, accessed March 8, 2025. https://aiartists.org/sougwen-chung.

[4] Katherine Mitchell. "The Algorithmic Gesture: Sougwen Chung's MEMORY," *Victoria and Albert Museum Blog*, December 14, 2022, accessed March 8, 2025. https://www.vam.ac.uk/blog/digital/the-algorithmic-gesture-sougwen-chungs-memory

[5] "Sougwen Chung | Relational Gestures," *HOFA (House of Fine Art)*, October 14–25, 2023, accessed March 8, 2025. https://thehouseoffineart.com/exhibitions/159/overview/

[6] Rachel Douglass. "Coach Steps into Roblox and Zepeto Metaverses." *FashionUnited*, July 19, 2024. https://fashionunited.com/news/fashion/coach-steps-into-roblox-and-zepeto-metaverses/2024071961029

[7] Forbes. "18 Transformative Ways Industries Are Leveraging AR and VR." *Forbes Technology Council*. Published May 17, 2024. https://www.forbes.com/councils/forbestechcouncil/2024/05/17/18-transformative-ways-industries-are-leveraging-ar-and-vr/

[8] Improbable. "Artists and Fans Collaborate in the Metaverse for a Collective Songwriting Session." https://www.improbable.io/news/artists-and-fans-collaborate-in-the-metaverse-for-a-collective-songwriting-session

[9] Jussi S. Jauhiainen. "The Metaverse: Innovations and Generative AI," *Science Direct, International Journal of Innovation Studies*, Vol. 8, Issue 3, September 2024, Pages 262–272, accessed May 9, 2025. https://www.sciencedirect.com/science/article/pii/S2096248724000183

[10] *Vogue Business*. "Gucci Retains Index Leadership, but Hugo Boss and Versace Surprise with Virtual Activations," accessed January 25, 2025. https://www.voguebusiness.com/story/technology/gucci-retains-index-leadership-but-hugo-boss-and-versace-surprise-with-virtual-activations

[11] VirtualSpeech. "VR Applications: 25+ Real-World Use Cases." *VirtualSpeech*, accessed January 25, 2025. https://virtualspeech.com/blog/vr-applications

[12] TDK. "AR, VR, MR: Past, Present, and Future of the Technology." *TDK Tech Mag*, accessed January 25, 2025. https://www.tdk.com/en/tech-mag/past-present-future-tech/ar-vr-mr

[13] Immersed. https://immersed.com/

[14] Microsoft Mesh. https://learn.microsoft.com/en-us/mesh/

[15] Sketchar. https://sketchar.io/

[16] Adobe Medium. https://www.adobe.com/uk/products/medium.html?msockid=1cc31249bd0f635914a506a2bc3e623b

[17] Virtuoso-VR. https://virtuoso-vr.com/

[18] Tolentino, Terry. "20+ NFT Stats in 2024: Market Size, Companies, Users, & More." *MarketingScoop*, March 17, 2024. https://www.marketingscoop.com/ai/nft-stats/

[19] Mohammad Shahid. "The Top 10 Most Expensive NFTs Ever Sold: A Closer Look." *CryptoManiaks*, last updated July 31, 2024. https://cryptomaniaks.com/top-ten-most-expensive-nfts-ever-sold

[20] LfDecentralizedTrust. "Walmart Case Study." *LfDecentralizedTrust*, accessed January 25, 2025. https://www.lfdecentralizedtrust.org/case-studies/walmart-case-study

[21] ICAEW. "Blockchain Case Studies." *ICAEW*, accessed January 25, 2025. https://www.icaew.com/technical/technology/blockchain-and-cryptoassets/blockchain-articles/blockchain-case-studies

[22] Opensea. https://opensea.io/

[23] Foundation. https://phemex.com/academy/what-is-foundation

[24] SuperRare. https://superrare.gallerynft.pro/en/?utm_source=bing_original_site=successfully&utm_source=bing&utm_medium=cpc&utm_term=trading_platforms

[25] Schneider, Josh, and Ian Smalley. "What Is Quantum Computing?" *IBM*, August 5, 2024. https://www.ibm.com/topics/quantum-computing

[26] "Libby Heaney 'Ent-'," *Google Arts & Culture*, accessed March 8, 2025. https://artsandculture.google.com/story/libby-heaney-39-ent-39-lightartspace/WgXBT2i_jZsa0g?hl=en

[27] James Dargan, "Google Quantum AI Lab: A Fusion of Art & Science to Inspire Next-Gen Computing," *The Quantum Insider*, January 23, 2024, accessed March 8, 2025. https://thequantuminsider.com/2024/01/23/google-quantum-ai-lab-a-fusion-of-art-science-to-inspire-next-gen-computing/

[28] "Exploring Quantum Through Art and Design," *Goethe-Institut*, accessed March 8, 2025. https://www.goethe.de/prj/lqs/en/eve/vir.html

[29] Kelly Blake, "Newly Funded Artistic Collaborations Seek to Explain Quantum Concepts," *University of Maryland College of Arts and Humanities*, July 25, 2024, accessed March 8, 2025. https://arhu.umd.edu/news/art-science-projects-explore-quantum-creativity

[30] Katie Armstrong, "DePuy Synthes Now Offering Titanium Facial Implants," *3D Printing Industry*, July 22, 2016, accessed March 8, 2025. https://3dprintingindustry.com/news/depuy-synthes-now-offering-titanium-facial-implants-87817/

[31] Andres Fortino, "Embracing Creativity: How AI Can Enhance the Creative Process," NYU School of Professional Studies Emerging Technologies Collaborative Blog, November 2, 2023, https://www.sps.nyu.edu/homepage/emerging-technologies-collaborative/blog/2023/embracing-creativity-how-ai-can-enhance-the-creative-process.html

[32] "Seven Ages of Man Speech," YouTube video, 1 minute, posted on October 22, 2019, accessed on March 8, 2025. https://www.youtube.com/watch?v=s_W9bOYsmCk&t=13s

[33] "Introducing Niche Mixes, Personalized Playlists for Almost Anything You Can Think Of," *Spotify Newsroom*, March 28, 2023, accessed March 8, 2025. https://newsroom.spotify.com/2023-03-28/introducing-niche-mixes-personalized-playlists-for-almost-anything-you-can-think-of/

[34] Ezra Sandzer-Bell, "Machine Learning is Changing Adaptive Music for Video Games," *AudioCipher*, October 11, 2023, accessed March 8, 2025. https://www.audiocipher.com/post/adaptive-music-machine-learning

[35] Erin Winick, "These Amazing Met Gala Looks Took More Than a Thousand Hours of 3D Printing," *MIT Technology Review*, May 7, 2019, accessed March 8, 2025. https://www.technologyreview.com/2019/05/07/239148/these-amazing-met-gala-looks-took-more-than-a-thousands-hours-of-3d-printing/

[36] Liliana Torpey, "CARNE y ARENA (Virtually Present, Physically Invisible)—Review," *NACLA*, March 17, 2023, accessed March 8, 2025. https://nacla.org/carne-y-arena-virtually-present-physically-invisible-review

Creating Your Customized Toolkit

APPROACHES TO ENHANCE CREATIVITY

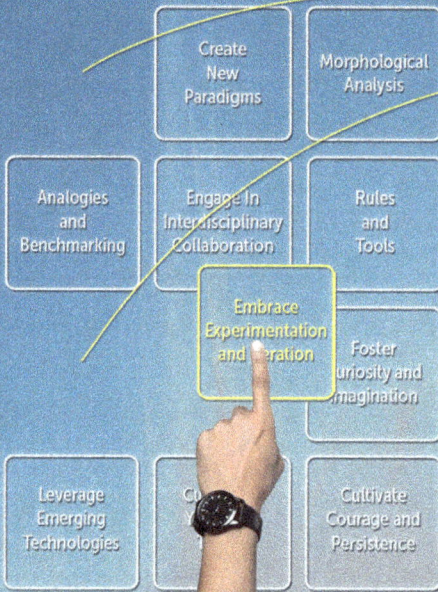

MY PERSONALIZED TOOLKIT

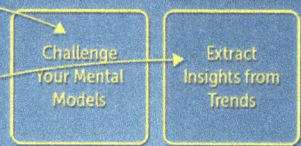

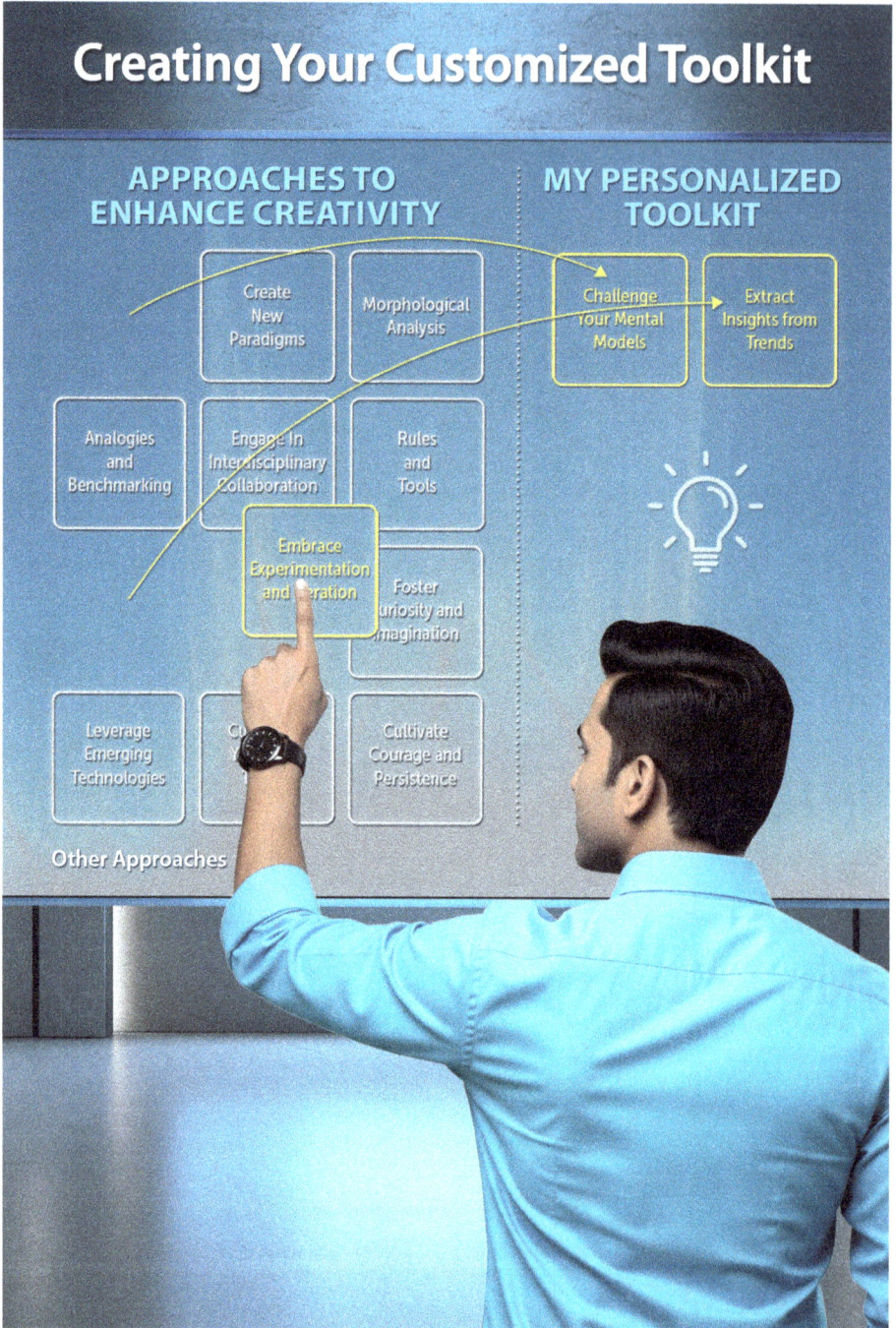

Create New Paradigms

Morphological Analysis

Challenge Your Mental Models

Extract Insights from Trends

Analogies and Benchmarking

Engage in Interdisciplinary Collaboration

Rules and Tools

Embrace Experimentation and Iteration

Foster Curiosity and Imagination

Leverage Emerging Technologies

Cultivate Courage and Persistence

Other Approaches

Chapter 15
Approach #11: Customize Your Own Toolkit

I will go where there is no path, and I will leave a trail.
—Muriel Strode, poet

By its very definition, unleashing creativity will never be a one-size-fits-all endeavor. And yet, established processes often treat the pursuit of innovation within set constraints. This chapter will help you create your customized portfolio of approaches based on the ten sets of approaches you have learned thus far.

You've learned about 10 sets of approaches to creativity. But how should you apply them? Which ones should you use to address your goal or challenge? Should you apply an approach as is, modify it, or create your own customized solution? The answer, of course, would depend on your idiosyncratic circumstances, needs, and preferences. We have a unique way of generating ideas, solving problems, and bringing our visions to life. And while only you can make these decisions, this chapter will showcase a few conceptually sound and empirically tested processes to get you thinking.

This chapter focuses on:
A. Following an established creative process
B. Identifying specific approaches to achieve particular objectives, such as growth strategies
C. Applying a portfolio of evaluative frameworks that fit your unique needs
   Add
D. Creating your customized portfolio of approaches

A. Following an Established Creative Process

IDEO's Design Thinking is a human-centered, creative, interdisciplinary approach to problem-solving that focuses on understanding users' needs, generating innovative ideas, and prototyping solutions. It combines empathy, ideation, experimentation, and practicality to create products, services, and experiences to meet users' needs. Notably, IDEO comes up with disruptive solutions rather than incremental ones and aligns with other parts of the organization to make them more feasible to implement.

IDEO's co-founder and Stanford professor, David Kelley, established the university's Hasso Plattner Institute of Design. Commonly known as the d.school, it has become a global hub for teaching design thinking.

One notable case study from IDEO revolves around global retailer H&M, whose goal was to eliminate its use of plastic packaging. IDEO helped it develop a new paper packaging system that has cut 2,000 tons of plastic from H&M's operations in the last two years. Rather than merely hiring a sustainability consultant, H&M rethought its packaging design process, and it continues to disrupt the supply chain and customer experience.[1]

Key stages of the IDEO process:

1. Empathize: Understand the users' experiences and needs through observation, interviews, and immersive research.
   Example: When IDEO redesigned the shopping cart, their team visited grocery stores to observe how people shopped, noting frustrations like stolen carts or hard-to-maneuver designs.[2]

2. Define: Synthesize findings from the empathy stage into a clear problem statement.
   Example: After observing health care challenges, IDEO framed the problem as "How might we improve patient experiences in emergency rooms?"[3]

3. Ideate: Generate creative solutions through brainstorming and collaborative workshops.
   Example: For Bank of America, IDEO brainstormed ways to help people save money, leading to 80 product concepts. The winning idea resulted in the "Keep the Change" program, where spare change from transactions automatically transfers to savings accounts.[4]

4. Prototype: Create low-fidelity prototypes to explore how ideas might work in practice.
   Example: IDEO built multiple rough prototypes using materials like ballpoint pen parts and soap bars while designing Apple's first computer mouse.[5]

5. Test: Test prototypes with real users, gather feedback, and refine the solution iteratively.
   Example: IDEO tested various hospital waiting room layouts to reduce patient anxiety, continually adjusting the design based on user feedback.[6]

IDEO's design thinking succeeds because it balances creativity with practicality, ensuring that solutions are innovative yet feasible. IDEO has transformed industries from healthcare and finance to consumer products and digital experiences by centering the process around people's real needs.

> **"** IDEO's design thinking succeeds because it balances creativity with practicality, ensuring that solutions are innovative yet feasible. **"**

Consider a challenge you're currently facing. How might you apply the five stages of IDEO's design thinking to address it? Start by identifying a specific user or stakeholder whose needs you want to understand better. Conduct at least three interviews or observations to gain insights into their experience. Based on these insights, define a clear problem statement and brainstorm at least 20 potential solutions.

The Front2Back Transformation operationalizes the idea of putting the customer first. The customer-centric approach can be visualized through three concentric circles:

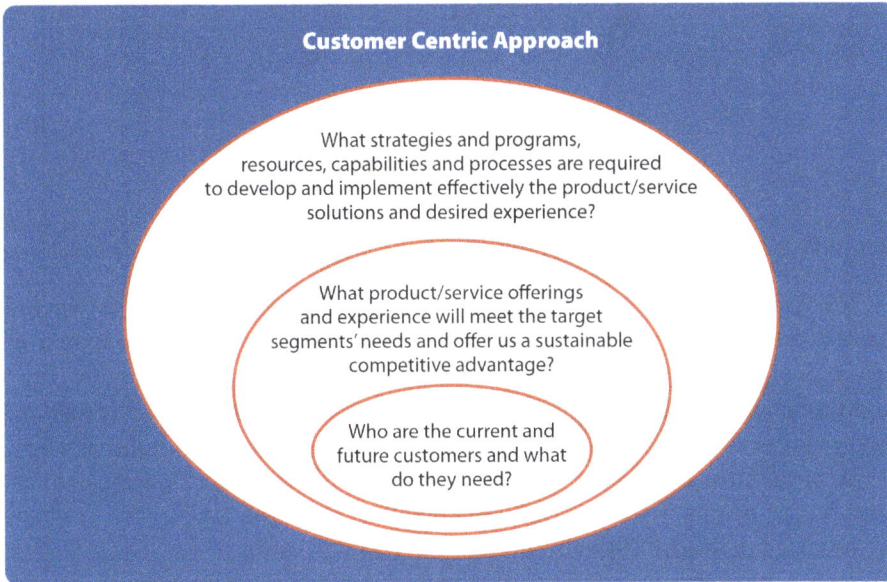

Figure 15.1. Customer Centric Approach (Coursera Creativity Course)

- At the core is the customer, whether current or future.
- The second circle represents the products, services, and experiences that will address their current and emerging needs.
- The outermost circle is everything the organization has to do to develop and deliver the products, services, and experiences the customer desires.

This conceptualization provides a valuable framework for any customer-centric approach. The Front2Back Transformation developed by Mphasis is a comprehensive methodology incorporating these principles into a structured process for digital transformation. The process is outlined on Figure 15.2 on next page.

Mphasis CEO Nitin Rakesh said the company's mission is to apply new technology to solve their clients' problems. Front2Back is their process for sparking clients' digital transformation. "We believe every enterprise, every business, should have a customer obsession and build their business from the customer backwards. Don't start in the back office. Start in front of the customer."

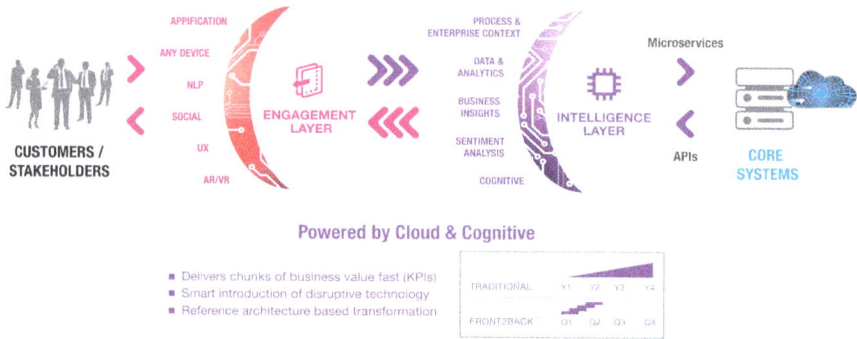

Figure 15.2. Front2Back Strategy (Mphasis)7

What makes Front2Back unique is the insertion of an 'intelligent layer' between the customer-facing front end and the back-end systems. This intelligent layer is the new core of operations, leveraging AI, analytics, and automation to create a more responsive and adaptive organization. The layer acts as a bridge that transforms legacy systems into modern, customer-centric operations without requiring a complete infrastructure overhaul. Organizations can rapidly innovate and respond to customer needs by implementing this intelligent layer while gradually modernizing their core systems.

Rakesh cited the insurance industry, which has functioned for over a century. Over the decades, many insurers' systems have been added to through acquisitions or expanded over the years. The result was a "spaghetti-mess of multiple systems," pervasive in the industry. These systems spanned underwriting, policy administration, claims, brokers, and a customer master list. Back then, insurers didn't deal directly with the public, but sold through brokers. So brokers were their clients.

But in the digital age, the game changed. Not only did every business become a digital business, but every business also became a consumer business.[8] Rakesh believes that every customer, whether an organization or individual, now expects the same level of customer service as they experience when using Netflix, Amazon, or Google. Pragmatically speaking, "there is no B2B company left in the world," Rakesh said. "This consumerization of the entire enterprise landscape has fundamentally unleashed this thinking of Front2Back Transformation."

This concept has profound implications for traditionally B2B companies like IBM, Salesforce, or industrial manufacturers. These organizations must now design their customer experiences with the same attention to user satisfaction, personalization, and seamless interaction that consumer brands prioritize. Companies that fail to recognize this shift risk becoming obsolete as competitors deliver more intuitive, responsive experiences.

This process entails starting by identifying the customers' needs and thinking of ways to meet them, instead of beginning at the back office and letting what's available and possible dictate what you offer customers. But it's not just adding an app on top of core legacy systems; rather it is a rethinking of the entire structure. Going back to the insurance industry example, this means insurers cannot wait until the weekend to batch-process insurance policies customers bought; they should be able to produce a digital record of the purchase right after it's made.

Rakesh recounted the experience of a life insurance company client. It approached Mphasis to help it simplify its multiple core systems. But upon further probing, Mphasis discovered that the real problem they were trying to address was that they didn't have a high customer Net Promoter Score (NPS), which gauges how likely they will recommend the company to others. They did not cross-sell their products very well.

"It was very clear to us that doing a core transformation will give them savings, but deploying this Front2Back mindset with this intelligence layer becoming the new core is really what they needed. And that's exactly what we did." The results? NPS rose by 30%, cross-selling rose four-fold, cost of operations fell by 34% and time-to-market plunged by 60%.

⚡ Exercise

Apply the customer centric approach to your organization:

1. Identify your current and future customers and their specific needs in detail.
2. List your current products and services in the second circle, then evaluate if they fully address the customer needs you identified.
3. If gaps exist, explore what new products or services should be added to your portfolio.
4. Once you've identified these new offerings, map out everything required to design and deliver them effectively.
5. Consider which of the creative approaches discussed in this book could help you at each stage of this process.

B. Identifying Specific Approaches for Particular Objectives: Growth-focused Strategies

Growth is one of the most common objectives of organizations. When focusing on the generation of creative growth strategies, you can draw from multiple frameworks tailored to specific strategic goals. Here are several frameworks to consider:

1. Product × Market

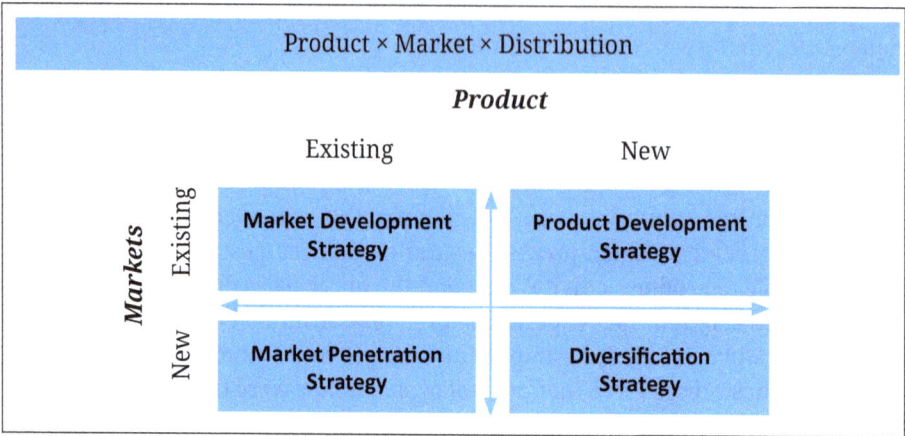

Product × Market × Distribution

Product

	Existing	New
Existing (Markets)	Market Development Strategy	Product Development Strategy
New (Markets)	Market Penetration Strategy	Diversification Strategy

2. Product × Market × Distribution

This tool simply adds distribution as an explicit layer, where (say) a Market Penetration or Product Development Strategy can be enacted via a new channel of distribution (row 2 of the matrix). Numerous research studies have shown that innovation on the "4th P" (Place) can create outsized wins for companies, e.g. Apply stores to existing distribution approaches.

Product × Market × Distribution				
	Product/Market			
Distribution	Current/Current	Current/New	New/Current	New/New
Current				
New				

3. Product Line Extensions

Line extensions are the lifeblood of new product developments that leverage existing brand equity, especially in consumer goods and software. Horizontal and vertical are the easiest to enact, e.g., adding flavors, or sizes, or different price-quantity combinations. New product lines can have dramatic effects, e.g. Porsche's introduction of SUVs to allow "all year selling" and move away from reliance on sports cars and convertibles.

> ### Product Line Extensions
>
> - Horizontal Product line extensions (strength, size, variety...)
> - Vertical product line extensions niche and/or lower price
> - New product line extensions (related and unrelated products)

4. International Expansion

International expansion comes in a variety of colors, with the core delineation being the degree of integration with the international partner, and with franchising and licensing being more arms-length, all the way to full mergers.

> ### International Expansion
>
> - Licensing/franchising
> - Joint Ventures
> - Direct foreign investment
> - Mergers & Acquisitions
> - Others

5. Speeding the Launch and Penetration

Product diffusion almost always follows an 'S-shaped' curve (shown on the right), which parallels the product life cycle stages of Introduction, Growth, Maturity, and Decline. An Expedited curve can be generated by tactics like penetration pricing, which encourages faster early adoption, heavy communication spending, early mass distribution, or some combination.

> ### Speeding the Launch and Penetration
>
>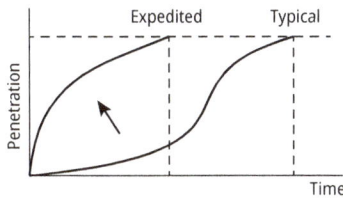

6. Leveraging SWOT

SWOT is a 'bread and butter' thought experiment central to growth in which the positive and negative aspects of external market dynamics are explicitly matched against the firm's ability to exploit (or be harmed by) these forces.

Leveraging SWOT			
		Internal	
		Strengths	Weaknesses
External	Opportunities		
	Threats		

7. Gap Analysis

The essence of gap analysis is a comparison of the status quo—what has been achieved to date in a number of core areas—against the potential in each of those areas. It also highlights the "levers" e.g., use per customer is maximized, but distribution is not fully exploited. The obvious implication is to explore additional channel intensity.

Gap Analysis

• *Product* line gap
  ◦ Fill out existing product lines
  ◦ Create new product line elements
• *Distribution* gap
  ◦ Expand distribution coverage
  ◦ Expand distribution intensity
  ◦ Expand distribution exposure
• *Usage* gap
  ◦ Stimulate non-users
  ◦ Stimulate light-users
  ◦ Increase amount used on each use occasion
• *Competitive* gap
  ◦ Penetrate substitute's positions
  ◦ Penetrate direct competitor's position(s)
• *Regulatory* gap
  ◦ Take advantage of regulatory opportunities
• *Technology* gap
  ◦ Capitalize on opportunities offered by the internet and other news information technology capabilities

8. Reformulating the Business (under alternative scenarios)

The Problem-Solution mindset forces the decision maker to address the fundamental customer or market problem that is being solved.

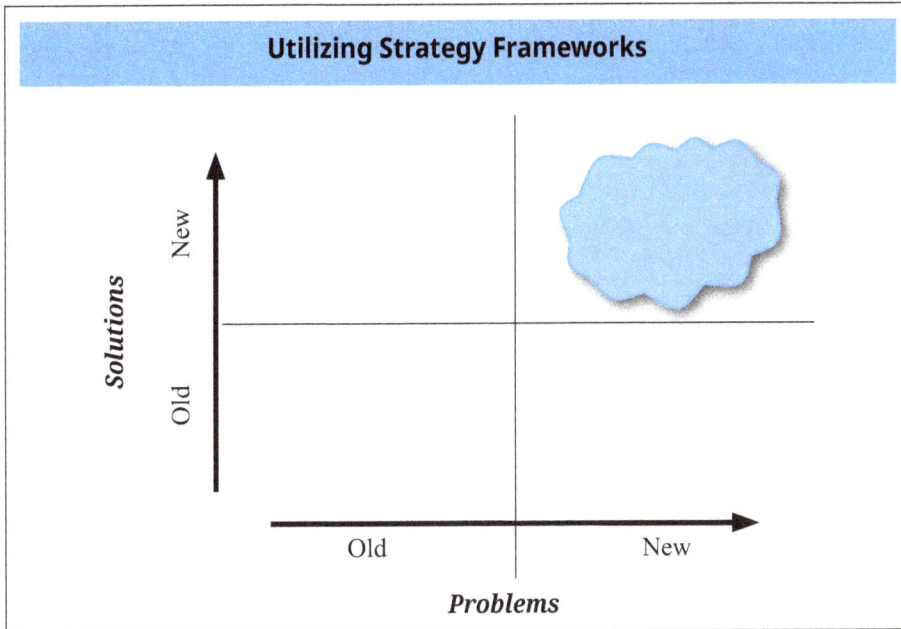

Utilizing Strategy Frameworks

Solutions — New / Old (vertical axis)

Problems — Old / New (horizontal axis)

9. Increasing the Efficiency and Effectiveness of Marketing Activities

This framework makes explicit the distinction between "optimizing resource allocation" (efficiency) against "allocating resources correctly" (effectiveness).

Increasing the Efficiency and Effectiveness		
Strategies	Increasing Efficiency	Increasing Effectiveness
• Advertising/P.R./ Communication		
• Pricing and Promotion		
• Positioning		
• Distributors and Logistics		
• Customer Service and Involvement		
• Cross Selling/Bundling		
• Loyalty Programs		
• Co-marketing		
• Others		

10. Mergers & Acquisitions

Mergers and acquisitions are a prominent growth driver in several sectors, but especially in software and technology, financial services, and healthcare, where it can be extremely costly to innovate internally and more attractive to "buy" rather than "make". Nevertheless, the strategy entails risk, with McKinsey and others finding that up to three-quarters of all M&A events fail to deliver the envisioned benefits.

M & A
• Consolidation
• Vertical Integration
• Horizontal Integration
• Other

In the preceding ten boxes, we have illustrated the growth framework.

One classic framework is Ansoff's Product-Market Growth Matrix, which identifies four key strategies:

1. Market penetration: Selling more existing products to existing markets
2. Market development: Introducing existing products to new markets
3. Product development: Creating new products for existing markets
4. Diversification: Developing new products for new markets

Morphological Analysis for Growth

A morphological analysis framework can be particularly effective for generating growth strategies. Table 15.1 is an illustrative partial framework integrating some of the approaches discussed in the previous chapters:

Table 15.1: Illustrative Morphological Analysis Framework

Market Segments	Product Categories	Geographic Reach	Distribution Channels	Revenue Models	Marketing Approaches
Current customers	Current products	Current regions	Direct sales	One-time purchases	Digital marketing
Competitors' customers	New product lines	Adjacent regions	Retail partners	Subscription	Referral programs
Adjacent segments	Premium versions	International	E-commerce	Freemium	Content marketing
Untapped demographics	Complementary versions	Global	Mobile	Licensing	Experiential marketing
New use cases	Value-priced options	Rural markets	Third-party market-place	Data monetization	Community building
Other	Other	Other	Other	Other	Other

This framework is meant to be a starting point. You should expand it by identifying additional categories and elements relevant to your business context. Use generative AI to help complete and enhance this structure with your industry-specific options.

To use this framework effectively:

1. Select one element from each category to create a potential growth strategy
2. Evaluate the feasibility and attractiveness of each combination
3. Prioritize the most promising options for further development

For example, a combination might be to develop premium versions of current products for competitors' customers in adjacent regions through e-commerce using a subscription model promoted via content marketing.

i Exercise

Build your morphological analysis for growth by doing the following:

- Adding at least three new categories relevant to your industry or challenge
- Expanding each category with at least three additional elements
- Creating at least five different strategic combinations
- Evaluating each combination using criteria such as feasibility, potential impact, and alignment with company strengths

C. Applying Evaluative Frameworks Like RAVES and BOSS

While developing growth strategies, it's essential to also apply frameworks for evaluating and refining your ideas for marketing communication and go-to-market approaches. Two powerful frameworks for doing just that are RAVES[9] and BOSS.

RAVES Framework

RAVES was co-developed by Jerry Wind and Cathrine Hays as a criteria for evaluating advertising, marketing, and promotional strategies. The acronym stands for

- **R**elevant and Respectful: Does the strategy resonate with target audiences and respect their values and preferences?
- **A**ctionable: Can the strategy be implemented effectively with available resources?
- **V**aluable (cognitive, emotional, and financial): Does it provide tangible and intangible benefits to customers and the organization?
- **E**xceptional experience: Does it create a memorable and distinctive experience with the brand?

- **S**hareable story: Will people naturally want to tell others about the brand story and their experiences?

The RAVES framework which was developed as part of Wharton's Future of Advertising project[10] helps ensure that your growth strategies will drive business results and create meaningful connections with customers.

BOSS Framework

Professor and venture capitalist David Bell created the BOSS Framework. It is a growth strategy focused on effective marketing and go-to-market in the digital age. Today's consumers have different expectations and behavior and are looking for a seamless online and offline experience. BOSS stands for[11]:

(B) Branding as Bonding, where branding is viewed through the lens of a "relationship based on shared experiences" underpinned by:

- Delivering functional, emotional and symbolic value, i.e., products that work, make customers feel good, and signal wise choices to others.
- Transparency and authenticity in communication.
- Compelling content and engaged community.

(O) Customers as Orators, where customers are viewed as conduits of the firm's value proposition via:

- A Compelling Story/Narrative, which is inherently "share-worthy" from existing to potential customers.
- "Special people" who when they speak, are aspirational for others.
- Incentives to motivate action, i.e., intrinsic and extrinsic motivators that encourage existing customers to propagate word-of-mouth.

(S) Stores as Showrooms, where physical spaces deliver transformative experiences such as:

- Experiential and experience-first manifestations of the brand.
- Inventory-efficient locations which fulfil products via e-commerce.
- Through appropriate and liberal use of technology in the showroom.

(S) Service as Science, where interactions feel highly personal, but are meticulously executed via:

- "Surfacing" not searching, where customers are alerted to relevant products and experiences without having to explicitly seek them out.
- Personalization and customization of product and content.

- Use of (seemingly) unrelated information, to deliver deep customer insights, e.g., a purchase history of economics and personal finance books on Amazon as indicators of creditworthiness.

BOSS has been successfully applied by companies like eyewear brand Warby Parker, which uses physical showrooms and home try-on programs to allow customers to experience the product assortment, while fulfilling orders online, and beverage brand Lemon Perfect which partnered with lemon-colored Rivian vehicles on a 2024 "Hydration Tour" to showcase the brand in cities throughout the US.

D. Creating Your Customized Portfolio of Approaches

Based on the processes and frameworks we've explored and others you are familiar with, it's time to consider how to assemble your creative toolkit. This involves selecting, adapting, and combining approaches to match your needs and context.

> **"** Consider how to assemble your creative toolkit... by adapting and combining approaches to match your needs. **"**

A good starting point is the 10 sets of approaches discussed in the last 10 chapters. You can use these approaches as is or modify them. In addition, you can add other approaches.

Here, for example, is an illustrative list of additional approaches you can consider for your customized portfolio:

Table 15.2: Additional Approaches

Approach	Description	Best Used For
TRIZ[12]	Systematic innovation method based on patterns of invention	Technical and engineering challenges
Lean Startup[13]	Build-measure-learn cycle for rapid iteration	New ventures and product development
Design Sprint[14]	Google Ventures' 5-day process for solving problems	Rapid prototyping and validation
Jobs-to-be-Done[15]	A framework focusing on customer needs rather than attributes	Product innovation and positioning
Appreciative Inquiry[16]	Focusing on strengths and possibilities rather than problems	Organizational development
Scenario Planning[17]	Developing multiple future scenarios to guide strategy	Long-term strategic planning
Business Model Canvas[18]	Visual tool for developing new business models	Business model innovation

The key to developing an effective customized portfolio is to select approaches that

1. Align with your organization's cultural values and capabilities
2. Address your specific innovation challenges
3. Complement each other to cover different aspects of the creative process
4. Balance structured and unstructured thinking
5. Accommodate both individual and collaborative creativity
6. Balance consumer and expert based approaches.

		Unstructured Approaches	Structured Approaches
Source	**Consumer Focused**	• Motivation research • Focused group interviews • Consumption system analysis • Consumer complaints	• Need/benefit segmentation • Problem detection studies • Market structure analysis/Gap analysis • Product deficiency
	Expert Focused	• Brainstorming • "Synectics" • Individual writing • "Suggestion box" • Independent inventors	• "Problem/opportunity" analysis • Morphological analysis • Growth opportunity analysis • Environmental trends analysis • Analysis of competitive products • Search of patents and other sources of new ideas • Scenario planning/contingency plans

The R&D Process

Figure 15.3. Illustrative Approaches for Generating New Ideas

Putting It All Together: Creating Your Customized Portfolio

To build your personalized creativity toolkit, consider these steps:

1. Assess your current creativity approaches: What methods do you use, and how effective are they?
2. Identify your creative strengths and weaknesses: Are you better at generating or refining ideas? Do you excel in structured or free-form environments?
3. Match approaches to challenges: Select different approaches for different types of challenges you face.
4. Experiment and iterate: Try different approaches and combinations, noting what works best in various situations.
5. Refine your portfolio over time: As you gain experience, continually update your toolkit with new approaches and modifications.
6. Include items you experimented with, enjoyed, or had a good experience with.

7. Be sure to continuously look for approaches used by others that you can learn from. The resulting customized toolkit will be a dynamic and relevant set of approaches.

In Summary

1. **Build your personal creativity approach** by combining proven approaches like IDEO Design Thinking and Front2Back Transformation with your unique strengths.

What specific combination of creative approaches would work best for your thinking style and the challenges you face?

2. **Put customers at the core of your strategy.**
Start with their needs, then design products and services, rather than starting with what's possible in your back office.

How might you restructure your approach to innovation by starting with customer needs instead of internal capabilities?

3. **Apply different growth strategies based on your specific goals**—market penetration, product development, diversification, or line extensions all serve different purposes.

Which growth strategy aligns most closely with your current business challenges?

4. **Evaluate your ideas using frameworks** like RAVES (Relevant, Actionable, Valuable, Exceptional, Shareable) or BOSS (Bonding not branding, Orator not customer, Showroom with online fulfillment, Science not service).

How would your current projects score against these evaluation criteria?

5. **Remember, there is no perfect, one-size-fits-all creative process.**
The most successful innovators adapt their approaches to the specific context and challenge. Continuously experiment, refine, and adapt your personalized toolkit based on what works for you in different situations.

What creative approaches have you tried recently, and which ones might you add, delete or modify from your toolkit?

As you contemplate customizing and applying your toolkit for your unique circumstances, you must face the future with courage and persistence, as you will face inevitable risks and challenges. This is the focus of the next chapter.

Notes

[1]   IDEO. https://www.ideo.com/

[2]   Tom Kelley and Jonathan Littman. *The Art of Innovation* (New York: Currency/Doubleday, 2001).

[3]   Tim Brown. *Change by Design* (New York: Harper Business, 2009).

[4]   IDEO Case Study: *Keep the Change*. IDEO.com. https://thisisdesignthinking.net/2018/09/feeling-in-control-bank-of-america-helps-customers-to-keep-the-change/

[5]   Tom Kelley and Jonathan Littman. *The Art of Innovation* (New York: Currency/Doubleday, 2001); Tim Brown, *Change by Design* (New York: Harper Business, 2009).

[6]   Tom Kelley, and Jonathan Littman. *The Art of Innovation* (New York: Currency/Doubleday, 2001).

[7]   Nitin Rakesh and Yoram Wind. *Transformation in Times of Crisis: Eight Principles for Creating Opportunities and Value in the Post-Pandemic World* (Notion Press, 2020).

[8]   Mphasis's official description of the Front2Back™ approach, emphasizing customer-centric digital transformation and hyper-personalization. https://www.mphasis.com/home/our-approach-new.html

[9]   Yoram (Jerry) Wind, Catharine Findiesen Hays. *Beyond Advertising: Creating Value Through All Customer Touchpoints* (Wiley, 2016).

[10]   Yoram Wind. Catharine Findiesen Hays, and The Wharton Future of Advertising Innovation Network. *Beyond Advertising: Creating Value Through All Customer Touchpoints* (Wiley, 2016).

[11]   This formulation of the BOSS model is based on the recent discussion with David Bell. The original BOSS model developed over a decade ago, was: (B) Bonding, not branding: Focus on creating emotional connections rather than just building brand awareness. (O) Orator, not customer: Recognize that consumers share their experiences, making them storytellers for your brand. (S) Showrooms, not stores with online fulfillment: Use physical spaces for experience and digital channels for convenience. (S) Science, not service: Use data and analytics to drive personalization and improvement.

[12]   WikipediaTRIZ. https://en.wikipedia.org/wiki/TRIZ

[13]   University Lab Partners. "What is the Lean Startup Methodology?" https://www.universitylabpartners.org/blog/what-is-lean-startup-methodology

[14]   Sprint. https://www.thesprintbook.com/the-design-sprint

[15]   Christensen Institute. "Jobs to Be Done Theory." https://www.christenseninstitute.org/theory/jobs-to-be-done/

[16]   Wikipedia, Appreciative Enquiry. https://en.wikipedia.org/wiki/Appreciative_inquiry

[17]   MIT Sloane. "Scenario Planning." https://sloanreview.mit.edu/article/scenario-planning-a-tool-for-strategic-thinking/

[18]   Strategyzer. "The Business Model Canvas." https://www.strategyzer.com/library/the-business-model-canvas

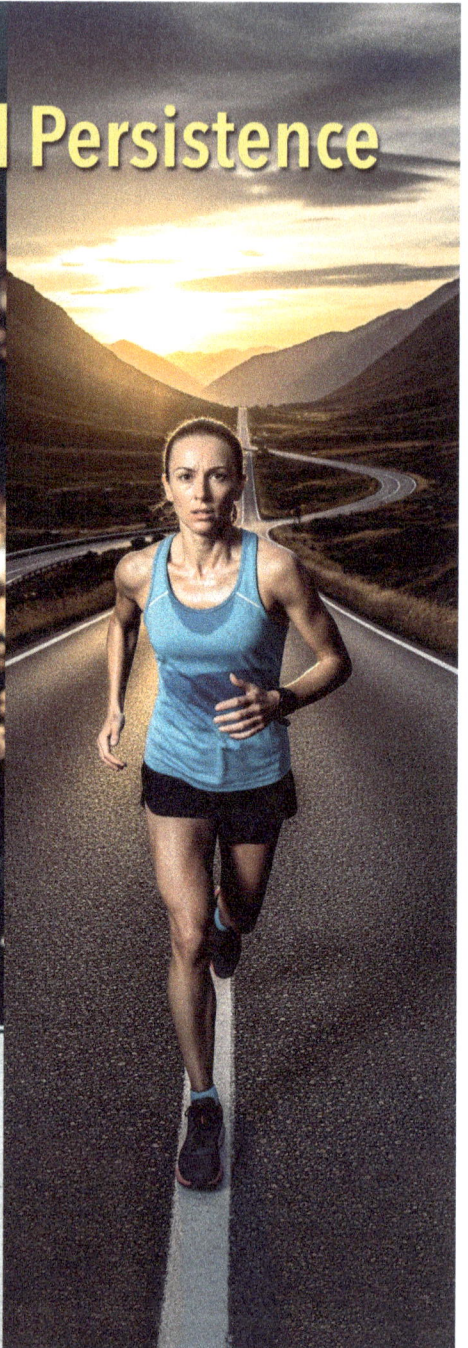

Chapter 16
Approach #12: Cultivate Courage and Persistence

I learned that courage was not the absence of fear, but the triumph over it. The brave man is not he who does not feel afraid, but he who conquers that fear.
—Nelson Mandela

We have followed the previous 11 toolkits with a call to courage and persistence. Why? Change is hard, and courage allows you to face uncertainty, experiment with new ideas, and risk failure. Persistence keeps you moving forward when progress feels slow or obstacles seem insurmountable. Creativity must be coupled with courage and persistence for inspirational and practical change that lasts.

Identifying the right approach for you or your organization will be moot without the courage to experiment and implement it, along with the persistence to see it through your project's inevitable ups and downs. The Merriam-Webster dictionary appropriately defines courage as "having the mental or moral strength to venture, persevere, and withstand danger, fear, and difficulty."

> **Courage is having the mental or moral strength to venture, persevere, and withstand danger, fear, and difficulty.**

To be an innovator often requires a blend of creativity and courage. It demands a willingness to step beyond the familiar, to challenge the status quo, and to embrace uncertainty. Persistence, the steadfast companion to courage, is equally vital. It fuels the determination to overcome obstacles, learn from failures, and refine ideas. Most of us live with constraints, whether our budget, office politics, family conflicts, and the like. It is far too easy to go with the flow and takes courage to upend the cart.

Courage in Action Across Disciplines

Art and Design

Claude Monet displayed remarkable courage when he broke from traditional painting techniques to pioneer Impressionism in the late 19th century. Despite harsh criticism from the established art world and financial struggles (he often could not pay for necessities), Monet persisted with his unique style of capturing light and color. The Paris Salon repeatedly rejected his works, with critics dismissing them as "mere impressions" rather than proper paintings—a criticism Monet and his colleagues eventually embraced in naming their movement. Today, his water lily paintings are among the world's most beloved and valuable artworks.

Monet is not alone in this regard; consider the many other pioneers of art movements such as Duchamp with his readymade (works of art made from manufactured objects), Picasso with Cubism, Jackson Pollock with his abstract drip paintings, and many others.

Zaha Hadid, known as the 'Queen of the Curve,' faced discrimination as both a woman and an Arab in the male-dominated field of architecture. Her boldly futuristic designs were initially dismissed as unbuildable fantasies. She taught and created theoretical projects for years, with her first central building not realized until she was 44. Despite being told her designs were impossible to construct, Hadid persisted, eventually transforming architecture with her revolutionary fluid forms and becoming the first woman to win the prestigious Pritzker Architecture Prize.

Consider as well other renowned architects such as Frank Gehry, mentioned at the outset of this book, with his distinct, bold, deconstructivist and sculptural style, or Frank Lloyd Wright with his organic, harmonious, and connected-to-nature style, and the many other architects who dared to break from the dominant style of their time.

The journey of courage and persistence in creative work often differs from heroic narratives of unwavering determination. After working as a publicist, Filmmaker Ava DuVernay didn't begin her directorial career until age 32. Her path wasn't a straight line of immediate successes but included multiple career pivots, self-funded projects, and gradual building of her craft before achieving recognition with films like 'Selma' and 'When They See Us.'

Similarly, biochemist Katalin Karikó faced decades of setbacks while researching mRNA technology. Universities demoted her, rejected grant applications, and colleagues dismissed her work as impractical. Yet she continued refining her research through incremental progress rather than dramatic breakthroughs, ultimately developing, with her collaborator Dr. Drew Weissman, the COVID-19 vaccines.

These stories reveal persistence often involves adaptation, recalibration, and managing doubt, not just pushing forward through sheer force of will. They demonstrate that creative courage includes the willingness to take calculated risks, to pivot when necessary, and to continue despite uncertainty about the outcome."

While we often imagine courage as bold, dramatic action, creative courage frequently manifests in quieter, more vulnerable moments: sharing an unfinished draft, presenting work before you feel it's ready, acknowledging when you don't know the next step, or expressing an idea that might sound naive.

These acts require facing the deep-seated fear of judgment that inhibits many creative endeavors. Research from Harvard Business School professor Amy Edmondson suggests that 'psychological safety'—the belief that one won't be punished for mistakes or speaking up—is crucial for innovation precisely because it enables these seemingly small acts of courage to flourish.

Rather than just rewarding dramatic successes, organizations that celebrate these quiet moments of vulnerability cultivate environments where continuous creative risk-taking becomes possible. Consider how you might recognize and appreciate these less visible forms of courage in yourself and others.

Business and Technology

Elon Musk demonstrated extraordinary courage in founding SpaceX in 2002, when conventional wisdom held that space exploration was exclusively the domain of governments. Musk invested $100 million of his fortune from PayPal's sale, facing skepticism from the aerospace industry and enduring three failed rocket launches that nearly bankrupted the company. The fourth launch succeeded with just days of remaining funds. Today, SpaceX has revolutionized space transportation with reusable rockets, dramatically reducing costs and making Musk's seemingly impossible vision a practical reality. (Musk is also the CEO of Tesla, xAI, Neuralink, and Boring Company).

When returning to a struggling Apple in 1997, Steve Jobs showed courage and persistence. Against conventional business wisdom, he dramatically streamlined Apple's product line by 70% and pursued radical design innovations with the translucent iMac G3. His most courageous move came with the iPhone's development, which required Apple to cannibalize its successful iPod business. When engineers said his demands were impossible, Jobs refused to compromise his vision. Despite initial skepticism from industry leaders (with Microsoft's CEO famously dismissing it), the iPhone transformed multiple industries and changed how we interact with technology.

Consider the many brave inventors who created new industries and breakthrough products, services, and experiences that changed how we work, live, and play.

Music and Performing Arts

Lin-Manuel Miranda displayed creative courage by reimagining American founding father Alexander Hamilton's life as a hip-hop musical with a predominantly non-white cast. This radical approach to historical storytelling broke conventions about musical theater and how American history is portrayed. When he first performed material from 'Hamilton' at the White House in 2009, many laughed at the concept. Miranda spent six years developing the show despite uncertainty about its reception. The result was a revolutionary cultural phenomenon that won 11 Tony Awards, a Grammy, and a Pulitzer Prize while transforming musical theater.

Lady Gaga demonstrated remarkable courage early in her career by creating a provocative artistic persona when record executives wanted her to be more conventional. She faced rejection from numerous labels before finding success, then continued to take creative risks with each album rather than settling into a comfortable formula. Her album "Artpop" was commercially less successful and critically divisive, but she persisted through this setback. She later showed courage by revealing her struggles with fibromyalgia and PTSD, using her platform to destigmatize mental health issues. Her willingness to reinvent herself led to success in new realms, including acting in and winning an Oscar for 'A Star Is Born.'

Who are the musicians and performers who showed unusual courage you admire, and what can you learn from them?

Political and Social Movements

Malala Yousafzai showed extraordinary courage as a young activist for female education in Pakistan, continuing to speak out despite death threats from the Taliban. After surviving an assassination attempt at age 15, she recovered and amplified her advocacy on the global stage rather than retreating from public life. Her persistence turned personal tragedy into a powerful platform for change, leading to the Malala Fund, which ensures girls' education worldwide. At 17, she became the youngest Nobel Peace Prize laureate in history.

Nelson Mandela personified persistence through 27 years of imprisonment for fighting against South Africa's apartheid system. Despite harsh conditions and isolation, he refused multiple conditional offers of release that would have required him to renounce his principles. After his release, he showed tremendous courage by pursuing reconciliation rather than retribution, working with former enemies to dismantle apartheid and establish a peaceful transition to democracy. His persistence in pursuing equality despite decades of setbacks transformed a nation and inspired movements for justice worldwide.

Who are the courageous leaders of political and social movements you admire, and what can you learn from them?

Science and Innovation

Marie Curie displayed remarkable courage by pursuing a scientific career in the late 1800s when women were largely excluded from higher education and scientific research. Facing gender discrimination throughout her career, she persisted through difficult working conditions, conducting her radioactivity research in an unheated shed. Her determination led to discovering two elements and pioneering work on radioactivity, making her the first to win Nobel Prizes in two different scientific fields (Physics and Chemistry). During World War I, she further demonstrated courage by developing mobile X-ray units and driving them to the front lines herself to help wounded soldiers.

George Washington Carver, born into slavery, showed incredible perseverance in pursuing education despite systemic racism. Walking miles to attend school and working multiple jobs to support himself, he eventually became the first Black student at Iowa State Agricultural College. When Southern farmers faced economic ruin from soil depleted by cotton, Carver courageously advocated for crop rotation with peanuts—a radical idea at the time that was initially rejected. His persistence in developing hundreds of applications for peanuts created new markets that revitalized Southern agriculture and improved nutrition for millions of people.

For a fascinating refresher course on scientific innovations, review the stories of the Franklin Institute laureates. What can you learn from their amazing discovery journeys?

Advertising and Marketing

The Dove Real Beauty campaign launched in 2004 represented a courageous departure from beauty industry conventions. At a time when digitally altered images of flawless models dominated advertising, Dove featured women of diverse ages, body types, and ethnicities in their natural state. Many industry experts warned that showing "real bodies" would alienate consumers accustomed to aspirational imagery. Despite initial skepticism and criticism, the campaign's persistence over nearly two decades has helped shift cultural conversations about beauty standards while driving significant business growth. Dove's parent company, Unilever, demonstrated courage by maintaining the campaign's core message even as competitors attempted similar but less committed approaches.

Nike's Colin Kaepernick campaign in 2018 showed remarkable courage by embracing the controversial NFL quarterback's protest against racial injustice at a time when it divided the nation. The company faced immediate backlash, including boycotts, burning of Nike products, and a brief stock dip. Market research indicated potential alienation of core customer segments, but Nike persisted with the campaign centered on the tagline "Believe in something. Even if it means sacrificing everything." This bold stance on a divisive social issue ultimately strengthened Nike's brand among younger consumers, with the company's value increasing by $6 billion following the campaign.

While established companies like Nike have long excelled at trend-based innovation, newer entrants often demonstrate even more agility in translating emerging trends into creative offerings. Consider how Oatly transformed plant-based milk from a niche alternative to a cultural phenomenon by identifying converging trends in sustainability concerns, food transparency, and irreverent brand authenticity. Their rapid iteration between product formulation, packaging design, and marketing messaging created a virtuous feedback loop that accelerated their growth.

Similarly, Glossier built a billion-dollar beauty brand by identifying the shift from expert-driven to community-driven beauty advice, creating products directly responding to their online community's expressed needs and preferences. Their 'minimum viable product' approach allowed them to test and refine concepts quickly, with each iteration incorporating customer feedback in visible ways that strengthened community connection.

For further inspiration from and insights into the most effective and creative advertising initiatives, explore the rich archives of the Effie Awards, Cannes Lions awards, and other global competitions for the most creative and effective advertising.

Culinary Innovations

Ferran Adrià, as head chef of the restaurant El Bulli, courageously reimagined fine dining through molecular gastronomy, introducing unconventional techniques like spherification, foams, and liquid nitrogen cooking when traditional cuisine dominated high-end restaurants. Many critics initially dismissed these methods as gimmicks or science experiments rather than serious cuisine. Adrià persisted despite skepticism, closing El Bulli for six months each year to experiment with new techniques and flavors. His persistence paid off as El Bulli became widely regarded as the world's best restaurant, and his innovative approaches fundamentally changed global culinary practices.

After years working as a pastry chef at high-end restaurants, Dominique Ansel faced numerous rejections when trying to open his bakery. When he finally opened a small bakery in 2011, he courageously experimented with hybrid pastries despite warnings from colleagues about deviating from traditional French techniques. His creation of the Cronut (croissant-donut hybrid) in 2013 was initially met with skepticism from the culinary establishment but quickly generated block-long lines and international attention. Despite numerous imitators and the risk of being defined by a single creation, Ansel has innovated, creating new viral desserts like the Cookie Shot and Frozen S'more, demonstrating that his success wasn't just a one-time phenomenon.

Explore innovative culinary experiences in 3-Michelin star restaurants or new cutting-edge eateries, enjoy the experience, speak with the chefs, and reflect on what you can learn about creativity.

Space and Exploration

Katherine Johnson, a Black female mathematician at NASA in the 1950s and 1960s, showed remarkable courage by asserting her capabilities in the male-dominated, segregated environment of the early space program computing. Despite facing both racial and gender discrimination, she persisted in demanding to attend meetings previously closed to women and insisted that her calculations be taken seriously. Her extraordinary accuracy in computing orbital trajectories was so trusted that astronaut John Glenn requested she verify the electronic computer's calculations before his historic orbital flight. Johnson's courage and persistence helped enable the success of the Mercury and Apollo programs, though her contributions remained largely unrecognized until decades later.

Jane Goodall courageously challenged scientific consensus about chimpanzees and research methodology when she began her work in Tanzania in 1960. She employed unconventional research methods without formal scientific training, including naming the chimps she observed rather than assigning them numbers (standard practice). Goodall persisted despite criticism from the scientific establishment about her methodology and her findings that chimps used tools, displayed distinct personalities, and had complex social relationships–all ideas contradicting prevailing views. Over more than 60 years of research and advocacy, her persistence has transformed our understanding of primates and animal cognition while establishing new standards for conservation efforts worldwide.

Look for other space pioneers, explorers, and innovative scientists and engineers in all domains. The rich library of the Franklin Institute's laureates is a great source of inspiration. Understand their journeys of discovery and reflecting on what you can learn from these experiences, can help guide your creativity journey.

Business literature is full of examples of product and business failures. Ask any AI chatbot for examples and lessons from these failures. Select the ones you can relate to and ask yourself what they could have done to get the courage and persistence to avoid failure.

When Courage and Persistence Falter

While the examples above inspire us, it's equally instructive to examine cases where promising ideas failed due to a lack of courage or persistence:

> **What can be done to get the courage and persistence to avoid failure?**

Kodak engineers invented the first digital camera in 1975, but failed to pursue this innovation with courage. Fearing they would cannibalize their profitable film business, executives ignored the technology as a niche invention and shelved its development rather than embracing the digital future they had glimpsed. This lack of courage to disrupt their business model eventually led to Kodak's bankruptcy in 2012, as competitors without legacy investments in film eagerly advanced digital photography.

Xerox PARC developed revolutionary computing innovations in the 1970s, including the graphical user interface, mouse, Ethernet networking, and one of the first personal computers, Xerox Alto. However, leadership lacked the courage to pivot from their copier business to commercialize these breakthroughs. This strategic myopia allowed Apple and Microsoft to adapt these ideas and build the personal computing industry, while Xerox missed perhaps the most significant business opportunity of the 20th century.

The Risk of Not Experimenting

Beyond the courage to implement new ideas, there's a significant risk in not experimenting. Organizations that fail to cultivate a culture of experimentation often find themselves vulnerable to disruption and irrelevance.

Blockbuster had the opportunity to purchase Netflix for $50 million in 2000 but lacked the courage to experiment with the streaming model, instead clinging to their traditional retail approach. This failure to experiment cost them their business, as they filed for bankruptcy in 2010 while Netflix became a $100+ billion company.

Traditional taxi companies resisted technological innovation and experimentation, maintaining their radio dispatch systems and refusing to improve customer experience. This lack of courage to experiment left them vulnerable to Uber and Lyft, which used mobile technology to transform the transportation industry, decimating traditional taxi businesses in many markets.

Strategies for Individuals to Build Courage and Persistence

1. Start small: Test ideas with minimal viable experiments before fully committing resources
2. Build resilience: Develop emotional and mental fortitude by gradually increasing risk exposure
3. Create a support network: Surround yourself with people who believe in your vision and provide constructive feedback
4. Study success stories: Learn from others who persevered through similar challenges
5. Embrace failure as learning: Reframe setbacks as valuable data rather than personal defeats
6. Visualize success: Maintain a clear image of your goal to stay motivated during difficult periods
7. Break down significant challenges: Divide intimidating goals into smaller, achievable milestones
8. Recognize progress: Celebrate small wins to maintain momentum and build confidence
9. Develop contingency plans: Map out potential obstacles and prepare alternative approaches
10. Practice self-care: Maintain physical and mental well-being to sustain long-term effort

Strategies for Organizations Building Courage and Persistence

1. Start small: Encourage experimentation through low-risk, minimal viable projects to build confidence before scaling up. Amazon has created "two-

pizza" teams (on the concept that no team should be big enough that it would take more than two pizzas to feed them) to enable teams to innovate quickly, unhampered by complications often found in large teams.[1]

2. Build resilience gradually: Help individuals and teams develop mental and emotional strength by exposing them to greater challenges and uncertainties.
3. Create a supportive network: Foster a culture of trust and collaboration where team members encourage one another and offer constructive feedback.
4. Learn from success stories: Share examples of individuals or teams who overcame adversity, highlighting their persistence strategies.
5. Reframe failure as learning: Normalize setbacks by treating them as opportunities to gather insights and improve, rather than signs of inadequacy.
6. Visualize success: Encourage clear goal-setting and visualization practices to help maintain focus and motivation during tough periods.
7. Break down big goals: Make large objectives more manageable by dividing them into smaller, actionable steps that build momentum. Agile methodologies help companies like Atlassian tackle large projects through sprints and smaller, iterative steps. This builds progress and persistence incrementally.[2]
8. Celebrate small wins: Recognize incremental progress to boost morale and reinforce the value of persistent effort.
9. Develop contingency plans: Anticipate challenges and prepare flexible strategies so obstacles become navigable rather than discouraging.
10. Prioritize Self-Care: Promote mental, emotional, and physical wellness to ensure sustained performance and resilience over time.

Keith Grossman, former president of Time magazine, has had to make tough decisions. During his tenure, which coincided with the COVID-19 lockdown, he was charged with turning around an iconic American brand that had fallen on hard times. Time had been around for a century, and he needed to modernize the magazine for the future while retaining the features that made it great.

Grossman said he realized he couldn't make a hard break from Time's past since, for many American families, it captured living history—from man's landing on the moon to the JFK assassination and, most recently, global singer and songwriter Taylor Swift as its 2023 Person of the Year. So, he kept Time's core readership and simultaneously developed a Web 3.0[3] presence to nurture new readers. He launched Time's first NFT collections and accepted cryptocurrency as payment, among other innovations. Grossman bravely steered the magazine toward these radically different directions, even though he resigned to join a startup after three years.

Other examples of courage and persistence were ones we discussed in prior chapters, including the 20-year research efforts of Dr. Drew Weissman, who won a Nobel Prize, along with Kariko, for their work in the development of the COVID-19 vaccine, and Uriel Reichman, who overcame incredible odds to found Israel's first not-for-profit international and interdisciplinary university.

Now that we have shared with you our 12 approaches, it is up to you to use them to unlock your own creativity. Importantly, it's through the courage to experiment, fail, and learn that true creativity flourishes. By cultivating a mindset of curiosity and openness, and not being afraid to change the status quo, you can foster a dynamic and inspiring creative environment. Dare to deviate from the norm, trust your intuition, and let your creative spirit soar.

i Exercise

Creating your own approach
Review the 12 approaches covered in the book and choose three that address your weak spots. Identify how you can modify each to better suit your needs. Then apply each customized approach to your challenge or situation.

Overcoming Fear

1. Identify a creative idea or project you've been hesitant to pursue. Write it on a piece of paper.
2. Draw a vertical line down the middle of your page, creating two columns.
3. In the left column, list all your fears or concerns about pursuing this idea. Be specific and honest.
4. In the right column, beside each fear, write
   – A small, low-risk first step you could take to test the validity of your concerns
   – A potential learning opportunity if this aspect fails
   – A contingency plan or alternative approach
5. Identify one person who could support you in this endeavor, and what specific help you might ask for.
6. Circle the smallest, least intimidating action from your right column and commit to completing it within the next 48 hours.

> **"** Where have you been playing it safe creatively? **"**

Reconnecting with Abandoned Creativity

What project or creative direction have you set aside that deserves reconsideration? Perhaps it was an initiative that encountered obstacles, an idea that seemed too ambitious, or a passion that life circumstances forced you to postpone. What wisdom or resources do you have now that you didn't have then? How might you approach it differently based on your current experience?

Alternatively, consider: Where have you been playing it safe creatively? What conservative choices have you been making that limit your potential impact? Identify one area where you could take a calculated risk toward a more ambitious vision, and outline one small, concrete step you could take in that direction within the next week.

This exercise helps you confront fear strategically, transforming vague anxieties into concrete steps and contingencies. By mapping your courageous journey, you'll build confidence through small wins and calculated risks rather than waiting for fear to disappear.

In Summary

- **Courage manifests in quiet moments of vulnerability.**
  Sharing unfinished work, presenting before you feel ready, and expressing ideas that might sound naive all require facing judgment fears.

  What small act of creative vulnerability could you practice this week to build your courage muscle?

- **Persistence involves adaptation and recalibration.**
  Stories like Katalin Karikó's mRNA research and Ava DuVernay's filmmaking journey show that creative persistence means adjusting course while maintaining direction.

  Where in your current projects might you need to pivot rather than push harder?

- **Organizations that lack the courage to experiment face extinction.**
  Kodak, Blockbuster, and traditional taxi companies demonstrate that playing it safe becomes the riskiest strategy.

  How can your organization demonstrate it has the courage to experiment? What can your team or organization launch this month to test a bold new direction?

- **Building courage starts with small, manageable risks that gradually expand your comfort zone.**
  Success stories across all fields show pioneers taking calculated steps before making revolutionary leaps.

  What minimal viable experiment could you launch today to test your most exciting creative idea?

- **Support networks and psychological safety enable continuous creative risk-taking.**
  Research shows that environments celebrating small acts of vulnerability foster the biggest breakthroughs.

  Who in your network could you ask to support your next creative risk, and how might you reciprocate for others?

The approaches in this book only work when paired with the courage to try them and the persistence to see them through. Our concluding chapter discusses how you can get the most from this book to propel you forward with your future goals.

Notes

[1] AWS. "Powering Innovation and Speed with Amazon's Two-Pizza Teams." https://aws.amazon.com/executive-insights/content/amazon-two-pizza-team/

[2] Atlassian. "The Agile Coach." https://www.atlassian.com/agile

[3] Web 3.0 is the next evolution of the internet, built on blockchain technology incorporating AI and machine learning. Web 3.0 aims to be decentralized, moving away from the centralized control of the current Web 2.0, allowing users to have greater control over their data and interactions. The blockchain technology, which is also responsible for cryptocurrency, is a key component to Web 3.0, theoretically enabling secure transactions and data storage.

And now it is your time to use the approaches to enhance your creativity

Just Do It.
Nike ®

Be What's Next.
Microsoft ®

Think different.
 ®

Creativity for All.
Adobe ®

Impossible Is Nothing.
adidas®

Never Stop Exploring
THE NORTH FACE ®

The Power of Dreams
HONDA ®

Where Dreams Come True
Disney ®

And reap the benefit of enhanced creativity

open happiness
Coca-Cola ®

i'm lovin' it
M ®

imagination at work
GE ®

Real Beauty
Dove ®

Solutions for a Small Planet
IBM ®

Belong Anywhere
airbnb ®

Happiest Place on Earth
Disneyland ®

Conclusion
Ignite Your Creative Future: Experiment, Evolve, Excel

The best way to predict the future is to create it.
— Peter Drucker

You've just completed a journey through the expansive landscape of human creativity, amplified by cutting-edge AI tools. The 12 sets of approaches you've discovered are proven pathways to unlock the creative potential that already exists within you.

But here's the real question: What will you do with this knowledge?

Creativity is a dynamic force that grows stronger when you nurture it, challenge it, and continuously refine it. In this age of AI, creativity is being redefined, offering unprecedented opportunities for you to generate breakthrough solutions, reimagine your industry, and shape the future in ways that matter to you.

The difference between reading about creativity and becoming genuinely creative lies in one simple choice: Will you act on what you've learned?

Your Creative Foundation

Let's revisit the essential groundwork we laid in Part 1:

Chapter 1 revealed that creativity demands both imagination and impact. Your ideas must matter to others, not just impress yourself. You learned that four forces drive creative success: deep expertise in your field, fresh thinking methods, genuine internal drive, and supportive surroundings. Most importantly, you discovered that you don't wait for inspiration, you build daily habits that generate ideas consistently.

Chapter 2 took you inside your brain to understand the science of creative thinking. You learned about three neural networks that generate, evaluate, and select creative ideas. You discovered how to design spaces that match your creative phase and why stepping away from repetitive work activates breakthrough thinking.

Chapter 3 showed you how AI can be your most valuable creative partner, amplifying it in ways that seemed impossible just years ago. AI sparks imagination by combining unrelated concepts, streamlines routine tasks to free your strategic thinking, and serves as an objective sounding board for your boldest ideas.

Chapter 4 equipped you to overcome the barriers that block creative breakthroughs. You learned to recognize when fear paralyzes innovation, how resource constraints can actually spark creative solutions, and why short-term thinking destroys long-term creative value.

Your Creative Arsenal: The 12 Approaches

These are your personal approaches for transforming how you think, work, and innovate:

1. **Challenge Your Mental Models: Question the status quo that keeps you trapped in conventional thinking**
2. **Create New Paradigms**: Break free from industry assumptions to build entirely new frameworks
3. **Apply Morphological Analysis**: Systematically break problems into components and recombine them in revolutionary ways
4. **Use Analogies and Benchmarking**: Connect seemingly unrelated fields to unlock breakthrough insights
5. **Engage in Interdisciplinary Collaboration**: Harness the power of diverse perspectives and open innovation
6. **Follow Creativity Rules and Tools**: Use structured approaches like SCAMPER and Six Thinking Hats to amplify your output
7. **Extract Insights from Trends**: Identify shifts before others catch on to unlock transformative opportunities
8. **Embrace Experimentation and Iteration**: Test boldly with minimal resources rather than planning endlessly
9. **Foster Curiosity and Imagination**: Ask better questions and expand your horizons beyond conventional limits
10. **Leverage Emerging Technologies**: Understand the capabilities and creative opportunities offered by AI, blockchain, AR/VR, and other advances in science and technology.
11. **Customize Your Toolkit**: Build your personalized toolkit combining proven methods with your unique strengths and preferences.
12. **Cultivate Courage and Persistence: Develop the emotional resilience and courage to push boundaries and navigate uncertainty.**

You've drawn inspiration from Nobel Prize winners, breakthrough entrepreneurs, transformational artists, and visionary leaders who prove that remarkable creativity comes from applying these approaches with intention and persistence.

Your Personal Roadmap to Creative Breakthrough

The true power of this book lies not in what you've read, but in what it will empower you to do. These are your pathways to unlocking the creativity that's already within you.

1. Claim Your Creative Identity

Right now, complete this sentence: "I am someone who…" Don't say "wants to be creative" or "hopes to innovate." Say "I am someone who sees possibilities others miss" or "I am someone who turns problems into opportunities."

Take 20 minutes to reflect on which stories in this book resonated most deeply with you. Was it Uriel Reichman building a university from nothing? Tesla reimagining transportation? The NASA crowdsourcing breakthrough? Your reaction reveals your creative DNA. Write it down. This is who you are becoming.

Your AI Partner: Ask ChatGPT, Claude, or Gemini: "Based on [describe your biggest challenge or goal], which creative approaches would help me think differently about this?" Use their insights to mirror your own creative potential back to you.

2. Build Your Personal Creative Arsenal

Look at your most pressing challenge right now, the one that matters most to your life, work, or dreams. Which three to four approaches from this book feel like they could unlock it? Trust your instincts here.

Don't just pick approaches, make them yours. If you choose "Challenge Mental Models," define exactly which of YOUR mental models need challenging. If you select "Interdisciplinary Collaboration," identify the specific outside perspectives you need.

Create a simple document titled "My Creative Toolkit" that includes:

- Your chosen approaches (and why they matter to YOU)
- Specific AI tools you'll use with each approach
- One real challenge you'll test them on first
- How you'll know when it's working

Update this monthly. Your creativity will evolve as you do.

3. Start Your First Creative Experiment Today

Not tomorrow. Not next week. Today.

Pick the smallest, lowest-risk version of your biggest challenge. Apply one approach from your toolkit. Give yourself permission to experiment poorly rather than plan perfectly.

Maybe it's spending 15 minutes using morphological analysis on a work problem. Perhaps it's asking three people from different fields about your challenge. Or using AI to generate 20 wild analogies for your situation.

The goal is momentum. Document what happens, what surprises you, what you learn about your own creative process.

Remember: Every expert was once a beginner. Every breakthrough started with someone willing to try something new.

4. Create Your Creative Future, One Project at a Time

Start a "Creative Projects" list that excites you. Not a boring to-do list, but a collection of possibilities that make you lean forward with interest.

Include wild dreams alongside practical goals. Mix personal passions with professional challenges. Add ideas that scare you a little. Those are often the most important ones.

Examples:

- "Redesign how my team approaches problem-solving"
- "Create a solution for [specific problem I've always noticed]"
- "Build something that combines my love of [X] with my expertise in [Y]"
- "Start the project I've been talking about for years"

Review this list weekly. Let it evolve. Use AI to help you break big dreams into actionable steps, generate new possibilities, or see connections you might miss.

The key: Choose projects that matter to YOU, not what you think you "should" be creative about.

5. Create a Creative Organization

Whether you are a business startup or a multinational firm, a nonprofit or government organization, you can enhance the creativity of your organization by following the 10 guidelines for creativity, which are based on concepts and approaches we discussed in this book.

These guidelines, organized around the framework **C-R-E-A-T-I-V-I-T-Y**, provide a comprehensive roadmap for building and sustaining organizational creativity:

C—Culture: The Key to Success

Establish a culture that values and rewards creative thinking at all levels. Create psychological safety where team members feel empowered to share bold ideas without fear of judgment or retribution. Make innovation a core organizational value.

R—Reexamine Your Mental Models

Regularly challenge existing assumptions, beliefs, and ways of doing business. Encourage teams to question "the way we've always done things" and create structured processes for identifying and breaking through limiting mental models that hamper innovative thinking.

E—Empower All Involved

Give every team member and business unit the authority and resources to contribute creatively. This goes beyond traditional suggestion boxes. It is crucial to create genuine opportunities for participation in innovation processes. Encourage team members to experiment with the approaches discussed in this book and develop their own toolkit of creativity-enhancing methods, each turbocharged with AI tools.

A—Align Rewards with Objectives

Design compensation and recognition systems that explicitly reward creative efforts and risk-taking, not just successful outcomes. Celebrate intelligent failures that generate valuable learning. Ensure that performance metrics include creativity indicators alongside traditional business measures.

T—Tools: To Generate Creative Options

Provide access to diverse creativity tools and methodologies. This includes both traditional brainstorming techniques and cutting-edge AI-powered platforms. Train team members in the systematic use of morphological analysis, analogical thinking, design thinking, and other structured approaches to creative problem-solving covered throughout this book. Encourage them to be on the alert for new approaches that they could add to their customized toolkits

I—Iterative (Adaptive) Experimentation

Build experimentation into your organizational DNA. Create rapid prototyping capabilities, establish learning laboratories, and implement "fail fast, learn faster" principles. Use data and feedback loops to continuously refine creative initiatives and scale successful innovations.

V—Virtual and Networked Organization

Leverage technology and networks to expand creative capacity beyond traditional organizational boundaries. Connect with external partners, open talent platforms, customers, and even competitors to source fresh perspectives and collaborative innovation opportunities.

I—Interdisciplinary and International Focus

Adopt a global mindset that seeks diverse perspectives from different cultures, markets, and contexts. International and interdisciplinary diversity in teams and partnerships often sparks breakthrough innovations by combining different ways of thinking and solving problems.

T—Talent: Finding, Developing, Retaining

Redefine talent acquisition and development for the AI age. Beyond traditional skills, focus on finding, developing, and retaining individuals and groups who can effectively integrate AI tools into their creative work and coordinate seamlessly with both robotic systems and open talent networks.

Y—Yield: The Payoff of Creativity

Recognize that creativity yields multiple forms of value—not just innovative products and services, but also enhanced employee engagement, improved problem-solving capabilities, and increased organizational agility. Celebrate both the inventive outcomes and their benefits to all stakeholders, including the enjoyment of the creative process itself and the resulting workplace happiness.

By implementing these ten guidelines, organizations can systematically build their creative capacity while leveraging the powerful amplification effects of artificial intelligence. The key is not to apply these guidelines mechanistically, but to adapt them thoughtfully to your unique organizational context and challenges.

Remember, every individual and organization has untapped creative potential. These guidelines provide a structured path to unlock that potential and channel it toward meaningful innovation and positive impact.

6. Deepen Your Journey with 60 Creative Visionaries

Ready to go deeper? Our companion Coursera course features in-depth conversations with 60 remarkable innovators, from Nobel laureates to breakthrough artists, from startup founders to transformation leaders. These aren't just interviews; they're masterclasses in creative thinking from people who've changed the world.

The following figure lists the creators and their topics. These videos are presented as part of Jerry Wind's Coursera course, *Creativity in Business and Other Disciplines* (https://www.coursera.org/learn/creativity-in-business/).

The Wind Coursera Creativity Course

Lesson I

Inspirational Examples for the Coursera Creativity Course (Intro)	
Discovering the COVID-19 Vaccine	*Dr. Drew Weissman*, Nobel laureate, professor in vaccine research and medicine, Perlman School of Medicine, University of Pennsylvania) *Dr. Mindy Schuster* (professor of medicine and attending physician, Hospital of the University of Pennsylvania)
Magic	*David Morey* (chairman and CEO, DMG Global; vice chairman of Core Strategy Group; author and founder of Washington Magic)
Creative Breakthroughs and Psychological Paradigms	*Thom Collins* (Neubauer Family executive director and president, Barnes Foundation)
Creativity Lessons from Neuroscience	*Michael Platt* (professor of neuroscience, University of Pennsylvania, director of Wharton Neuroscience)
What is Beauty and Why Does it Matter	*Anjan Chatterjee* (professor of neurology, Perelman School of Medicine, professor, Center for Functional Neuroimaging)

Lesson II

The First 6 Sets of Approaches to Enhance Your Creativity	
Creating Minerva, the Most Innovative University in the World	*Ben Nelson* (founder and chancellor, Minerva University)
Art to Address Major Social Challenges	*Jane Golden* (founder and executive director, Mural Arts Philadelphia)
Creating a University	*Uriel Reichman* (founder, president and chairman of the board, Reichman University)
Follow Your Passion to Create the Best Pizza	*Joe Beddia* (owner, Pizzeria Beddia)
Creativity from the Crowd for NASA's Challenges	*Steve Rader* (program manager, NASA Tournament Lab, Center of Excellence for Collaborative Innovation)
Creating Business Schools Around the World	*Pedro Nueno* (emeritus professor of entrepreneurship, IESE Business School, Univeristy of Navarra, founder and honorary president, CEIBS)

Lesson III

The second set of Approaches to Enhance Your Creativity	
Mixmaster of Ideas—Creativity for the World	*Howard Moskowitz* (co-founder and scientific director, World Institute of Competitive Excellence, LLC)
Creating a Movement—From the Girls' Lounge to the World Economic Forum	*Shelley Zalis* (founding CEO, The Female Quotient)
Creativity and AI	*Margherita Pagani* (professor of digital marketing, SKEMA Business School)
AI for Human Creativity	*Arik Shamir* (professor, Efi Arazi School of Computer Science, Reichman University)
AI for Customer Engagement in the Intelligent Metaverse	*Arif Khan* (CEO and founder, Alethea AI)
Front to Back Transformation	*Nitin Rakesh* (CEO, Mphasis)
Analytic Hierarchy Process	*John Saaty* (CEO and co-founder, Decision Lens) and *Kevin Conner* (chief product officer, Decision Lens)
New Lessons for New Solutions	*David Yager* (former president and CEO, University of the Arts)
The Transformation of TIME	*Keith Grossman* (former president of Time, Enterprise, MoonPay)

Lesson IV

Creativity Lessons From Art, Music, Opera, Poetry and Dance	
Creating the American Glass Art	*Dale Chihuly* (artist, Dale Chihuly Studio)
Art	*Derek Gilman* (distinguished teaching professor; executive director, University Collections and Exhibitions, Westphal College, Drexel University)
Digital Art, NFTs and Reinventing the Metaverse	*Refik Anadol* (artist, Refik Anadol Studio)
Immerse the Body, Create with Others, Become One	*Takashi Kudo* (global brand director, teamLab)

Creativity Lessons From Art, Music, Opera, Poetry and Dance	
The Power of Art and Culture	*Thom Krens* (chairman and CEO, Global Cultural Asset Management, former director of the Gugenheim Museum)
Music Composition: Lessons in Creativity	*David Ludwig* (dean and director of the Music division, Julliard School)
Creative Insights with Music and Words	*David Devan* (general director and president, Opera Philadelphia)
Everything Depends Upon a Poem	*Al Filreis* (Kelly Family professor of English; director, Center for Programs in Contemporary Writing; faculty director, Kelly Writers House, University of Pennsylvania)
BalletX	*Christine Cox* (artistic and executive director, co-founder, BalletX)

Lesson V

Creativity Lessons from Architecture and Design—Moderator: Barbara Eberlein	
Introduction to Lesson V and Design	*Barbara Eberlein* (president and creative director, Eberlein Design Consultants)
Landscape Architecture	*Janice Parker* (owner and landscape architect, Janice Parker Landscape Architecture)
Utopia and Oblivion	*Carlo Ratti* (director of MIT Senseable City Lab, founding partner at Carlo Ratti Associati design and innovation office)
Architectural Awakening	*David Rau* (partner, Hart Howerton Architects)
Urban Planning	*Eric Osth* (chairman, Urban Design Associates)
Space Planning for Problem Solving	*Barbara Eberlein* (president, Eberlein Design Consultants)
Architecture and Neuroscience	*Don Ruggles* (CEO emeritus, Don Ruggles Mabe Studio)

Lesson VI

Creativity Lessons from Science, Medicine and Engineering—Moderator: Eric Burnstein	
Intro to Lesson VI	*Eric Burnstein* (director, Main Line Center for Laser Surgery)
Creativity Lessons from The Franklin Institute, 125 Years of Award Winners	*Don Morel* (chairman of the Board, Franklin Institute)
Nuclear Waste Plant Inspection Leads to a Steerable Needle	*Mark Yim* (director, GRASP Lab, Penn Engineering, University of Pennsylvania)
Goats as Bioreactors and an incubator for biotech companies	*Scott Parazynski* (physician and veteran NASA Astronaut, Everest climber)
Using figure skating to protect the Hubble telescope	*Story Musgrave* (physician and former NASA Astronaut)
Tackling extreme challenges and achieving unprecedented heights on earth and beyond	*Dr. Yann Echelard* (operating partner, Flagship Pioneering)

Lesson VII

Creativity Lessons from Games Advertising and Marketing	
Case Studies on Duolingo, Axie Infinity and Sky Manis	*Kevin Werbach* (Liem Sioe Liong First Pacific Company professor of legal studies and business ethics)
Game Thinking for Replika.ai	*Amy Jo Kim* (CEO, Game Thinking Academy)
Creativity As a Force for Good and Growth: Lessons from the ANA's Global CMO Growth Council	Nick Primola (executive vice president, Association of National Advertisers)
Creativity Lessons from Cult Brands	*Chris Kneeland* (CEO, Cult Collective)
Creating an Iconic Brand	*Tommy Hilfiger* (fashion designer and founder, Tommy Hilfiger Corporation)
Creativity Lessons from the Cannes Lions Award Winners	*Fiorenza Plinio* (global head, Creative Excellence Development, Cannes Lions)
Creativity Lessons from the Effie Award Winners	*Traci Alford* (president and CEO, Effie Worldwide) and *Jae Goodman* (board chair, Effie Worldwide)

Lesson VIII

Creativity Lessons from Business and Entrepreneurship and Lessons from The Start up Nation	
The Future of Work	*John Winsor* (founder and CEO, Open Assembly)
Fin Pay	*Arthur Spector* (founder, FinPay, LLC) and *Christopher Wolfington* (founder, FinPay, LLC)
The Transformation of a Family Business	*Victor Fung* (group chairman, Li & Fung Group) and *Sabrina Fung* (group managing director of Fung Retailing Group)
Getting to The Moon and Your Backyard on a Shoestring Budget	*Yariv Bash* (co-founder and CEO, Flytrex)
The Creation of Wireless Mobile Computing—The Intel Centrino Chip	*Dadi Perlmutter* (technology and social entrepreneur/investor; former executive vice president, general manager, The Intel Architecture Group (IAG) and chief product officer, Intel Corporation)
Getting to Every Pocket in the World: the USB Flash Drive	*Dov Moran* (managing partner, Grove Ventures)
The Secret Sauce of Israel's Innovation	*Yossi Vardi* (chairman, International Technologies Tel Aviv)
Country Branding Through Innovation: The Case of No Camel	*Noam Latar* (founder and dean, Head of Innovation Center, Reichman University)

AI as Your Creative Partner

Throughout history, creativity has driven progress. Each new wave of technology has reshaped how we think and create, from the Renaissance to the Industrial Revolution to the digital age. Today, we stand at the dawn of the AI revolution.

The future of creativity is neither entirely human nor entirely artificial; it's a fusion of both. The most significant breakthroughs will come from those who can seamlessly integrate AI's capabilities with human ingenuity, emotion, vision, and ethical values.

AI will amplify your unique perspective, but it cannot replace what makes you human: your lived experiences, your values, your ability to care about outcomes that matter. The magic happens when you combine AI's processing power with your human insight and purpose.

You're living through a unique moment in human history. Never before have individuals had access to such powerful creative tools. Never before has the gap between having an idea and testing it been so small. Never before has the world needed your unique perspective more.

But tools alone don't create breakthroughs. Vision does. Courage does. The willingness to start before you feel ready does. Your creativity is about seeing what others miss, connecting what seems unconnected, and having the audacity to believe you can make things better.

The approaches in this book are proven pathways used by Nobel laureates, breakthrough entrepreneurs, and transformational leaders. They work. But only if you make them work for you.

Your Creative Legacy Starts Now

The mark you leave on how you live, work, and play is limited only by your imagination and your willingness to act. Your next creative breakthrough is within reach.

Your creativity journey doesn't end with the last page of this book. It begins with the choice you make right now, in this moment, to see yourself as someone who creates rather than just consumes, who experiments rather than just plans, who contributes rather than just observes.

The page may be ending, but your story is just beginning. What will you create in the next hour? Next week? Next year? The world is waiting for your unique contribution.

We invite you to share your creative journey with us. Tag *#CreativityInTheAge OfAI* in your social media posts to connect with fellow innovators applying these approaches. Your story might inspire someone else's breakthrough.

Now close this book, open your mind, and create something extraordinary. The future you want to live in? You have the tools to build it.

What will you create?

Index

About the Author

Yoram (Jerry) Wind is the Lauder Professor Emeritus and Professor of Marketing at the Wharton School. A renowned innovation expert, he taught the popular Wharton MBA creativity course that forms the foundation of this book. He has founded numerous initiatives including the Wharton Executive MBA and the Lauder Institute, published over 300 articles, authored or edited 30 books, and received all four major marketing awards. His work spans academia, business consulting, and nonprofit leadership.

www.ingramcontent.com/pod-product-compliance
Lightning Source LLC
Chambersburg PA
CBHW051115200326
41518CB00016B/2512